COMPUTER
BOOK SERIES
FROM IDG

dBASE 5 For Windows
For Dummies

Cheat Sheet

C0-AVF-641

Basic Survival Skills

Start dBASE	Double-click on the dBASE icon in the Windows Program Manager.
Open a catalog	Click on the Catalogs icon in the left side of the Navigator window. Then, in the right side of the window, double-click on the icon for the catalog you want to open.
Create a table	Click on the Tables icon in the left side of the Catalog window. Then, in the right side of the window, double-click on the Untitled icon. The Table Designer window appears. For each field in the table, specify the name, type, width, and say if it should be indexed. To save the table definition, open the File menu and select Save. Give the table a DOS-compatible filename (up to eight characters, including letters, numerals, and underscores, but no spaces) and close the Table Designer window.
Open a table, form, and so on	Double-click on its icon in the Catalog window.
Add some data to a table	Right-click on the table's icon in the Catalog window. From the SpeedMenu, select Add Records. After entering each field in a record, press Enter. At the end of each record, press Enter again, and dBASE displays a blank record.
Quit dBASE	Press Alt+F4 or select Exit from the File menu.
Get an acting job in New York	Work at Zabar's Deli to meet producers; drive a cab; go back to school and finish B.A. in history; wait tables; get M.A. in history; drive a cab; get Ph.D. in history; work at Zabar's; get acting job as a talking potato in off-Broadway show; move back to Cleveland; drive a cab.

Creating Your Database

To create a database, first *plan* the database. Then, start dBASE. Follow these steps:

1. In the Navigator window, create the catalog that will hold the parts of the database. You can do this by clicking on the Catalogs icon at the left, then double-clicking on the Untitled icon at the right. Then, simply enter the name of your new catalog.

2. With the catalog open, create the tables for your database. To create a table, first click on the Tables icon at the left side of the Catalog window. Then, double-click on the Untitled icon in the right side of the window. If you need to link the tables in your database, make sure they have a common field (such as account number) and that the field is indexed.

3. Create the other elements of your database, such as forms, reports, and queries. You can create each by clicking on the appropriate icon in the left side of the Catalog window, then double-clicking on the *Untitled* icon in the right side of the window.

4. Congratulate yourself on a job well done.

IDG
BOOKS

... For Dummies: #1 Computer Book Series for Beginners

dBASE 5 For Windows For Dummies

Cheat Sheet

Planning Your Database

The basic principles of database design are:

1. A catalog is a wrapper that goes around tables, forms, reports, and so on. Always create and open a catalog before you do anything else.

2. Each table should contain only one kind of data. For example, you should not mix customer and sales data in the same table.

3. When you need to combine data from different tables, they must have a common field, such as an account number. The common field should be indexed.

4. Each piece of data should appear only *once* in the database. For example, you shouldn't have one copy of a sales record in a Sales table and another copy in a Customer table. That wastes disk space and may corrupt your data.

5. Do *not* wear a red-and-white polka-dot shirt when designing a database. This will not corrupt your data, but it exhibits a complete lack of fashion sense.

Creating a Table

To create a table, first create the catalog it goes into. Then follow these steps:

1. Click on the Tables icon in the left side of the Catalog window. Then, double-click on the Untitled icon in the right side of the window.

2. For each field in the table (name, address, and so on), type the field name, pick the data type, specify the width, and say how (or if) it should be indexed. An *ascending* index puts the records in A to Z order, while a *descending* index puts them in Z to A order.

3. When you're finished creating fields, save your work by opening the File menu and selecting Save.

dBASE Terms You Need to Know

Catalog: A wrapper that goes around all the tables, forms, reports, queries, and other things that work together.

Browse window: A way of displaying table data in a row-and-column format on the PC's screen.

Data type: The kind of thing a data item is. A data item can be text, a number, a time or date, a memo, and so on.

Field: A slot in a record that holds an individual data item. Each table is made up of records, and each record is made up of one or more fields.

Form: A way of displaying table data on the PC's screen so that it looks like a paper form, with explanatory text and blanks for each data item.

Fun: What you should be having with dBASE. If you're not having fun, you're missing the point.

Query: A question you ask about your database. You construct a query in the dBASE Query Designer window.

Record: All the data items (fields) about a particular thing, such as a person, a sales transaction, or an inventory item. Each record is made up of fields, and each table is made up of records.

Relation: A link between two or more tables that lets you draw information from the tables just as if they were a single table.

Report: A custom-designed printout of your database data. dBASE lets you create reports in a variety of formats; you can include graphics and calculations if needed.

Table: The basic building block of a dBASE database. A table is made up of one or more records. Each record has information about an individual thing, such as a person or a sales transaction.

References for the Rest of Us

TM

COMPUTER BOOK SERIES FROM IDG

Are you intimidated and confused by computers? Do you find that traditional manuals are overloaded with technical details you'll never use? Do your friends and family always call you to fix simple problems on their PCs? Then the . . . *For Dummies™* computer book series from IDG is for you.

. . . *For Dummies* books are written for those frustrated computer users who know they aren't really dumb but find that PC hardware, software, and indeed the unique vocabulary of computing make them feel helpless. . . . *For Dummies* books use a lighthearted approach, a down-to-earth style, and even cartoons and humorous icons to diffuse computer novices' fears and build their confidence. Lighthearted but not lightweight, these books are a perfect survival guide to anyone forced to use a computer.

> *"I like my copy so much I told friends; now they bought copies."*
>
> **Irene C., Orwell, Ohio**

> *"Quick, concise, nontechnical, and humorous."*
>
> **Jay A., Elburn, IL**

> *"Thanks, I needed this book. Now I can sleep at night."*
>
> **Robin F., British Columbia, Canada**

Already, hundreds of thousands of satisfied readers agree. They have made . . . *For Dummies* books the #1 introductory level computer book series and have written asking for more. So if you're looking for the most fun and easy way to learn about computers, look to . . . *For Dummies* books to give you a helping hand.

IDG BOOKS

dBASE
FOR WINDOWS
FOR
DUMMIES™

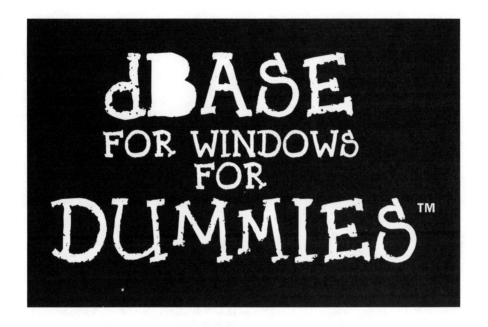

by Scott Palmer

Foreword by Larry Mollin
Supervising Producer, *Beverly Hills, 90210*

IDG BOOKS

IDG Books Worldwide, Inc.
An International Data Group Company

San Mateo, California ◆ Indianapolis, Indiana ◆ Boston, Massachusetts

dBASE For Windows For Dummies

Published by
IDG Books Worldwide, Inc.
An International Data Group Company
155 Bovet Road, Suite 310
San Mateo, CA 94402

Library of Congress Catalog Card No.: 94-76888

ISBN 1-56884-179-5

Printed in the United States of America

10 9 8 7 6 5 4 3 2 1

1B/QX/QR/ZU

Distributed in the United States by IDG Books Worldwide, Inc.

Distributed in Canada by Macmillan of Canada, a Division of Canada Publishing Corporation; by Computer and Technical Books in Miami, Florida, for South America and the Caribbean; by Longman Singapore in Singapore, Malaysia, Thailand, and Korea; by Toppan Co. Ltd. in Japan; by Asia Computerworld in Hong Kong; by Woodslane Pty. Ltd. in Australia and New Zealand; and by Transword Publishers Ltd. in the U.K. and Europe.

For general information on IDG Books in the U.S., including information on discounts and premiums, contact IDG Books at 800-762-2974 pr 415-312-0650.

For information on where to purchase IDG Books outside the U.S., contact Christina Turner at 415-312-0633.

For information on translations, contact Marc Jeffrey Mikulich, Foreign Rights Manager, at IDG Books Worldwide; FAX NUMBER 415-358-1260.

For sales inquiries and special prices for bulk quantities, write to the address above or call IDG Books Worldwide at 415-312-0650.

About the Author

Scott Palmer has over ten years of experience with database systems, including dBASE, Paradox, Access, XDB, and several others.

In addition to writing, he works as a consultant on database management and computer security. During his copious free time, he writes popular music and PC game programs.

Welcome to the world of IDG Books Worldwide.

IDG Books Worldwide, Inc., is a subsidiary of International Data Group, the world's largest publisher of business and computer-related information and the leading global provider of information services on information technology. IDG was founded more than 25 years ago and now employs more than 5,700 people worldwide. IDG publishes more than 200 computer publications in 63 countries (see listing below). Forty million people read one or more IDG publications each month.

Launched in 1990, IDG Books is today the fastest-growing publisher of computer and business books in the United States. We are proud to have received 3 awards from the Computer Press Association in recognition of editorial excellence, and our best-selling *...For Dummies* series has more than 7 million copies in print with translations in more than 20 languages. IDG Books, through a recent joint venture with IDG's Hi-Tech Beijing, became the first U.S. publisher to publish a computer book in the People's Republic of China. In record time, IDG Books has become the first choice for millions of readers around the world who want to learn how to better manage their businesses.

Our mission is simple: Every IDG book is designed to bring extra value and skill-building instructions to the reader. Our books are written by experts who understand and care about our readers. The knowledge base of our editorial staff comes from years of experience in publishing, education, and journalism — experience which we use to produce books for the '90s. In short, we care about books, so we attract the best people. We devote special attention to details such as audience, interior design, use of icons, and illustrations. And because we use an efficient process of authoring, editing, and desktop publishing our books electronically, we can spend more time ensuring superior content and spend less time on the technicalities of making books.

You can count on our commitment to deliver high-quality books at competitive prices on topics customers want to read about. At IDG, we value quality, and we have been delivering quality for more than 25 years. You'll find no better book on a subject than an IDG book.

John J. Kilcullen

John Kilcullen
President and CEO
IDG Books Worldwide, Inc.

Dedication

Dedicated to Mort and Roberta Goren, two of the finest people I've ever known.

Acknowledgments

Though my name is on the cover, this book was not a solo effort. Several other people helped make it the best book for beginning users of dBASE for Windows.

Most involved on a day-to-day basis was Mary Corder, my project editor at IDG Books, who guided the project at every step with encouragement, constructive criticisms, and an endless supply of good ideas. The book's technical editor, Stuart Stuple was also a joy to work with and made many helpful suggestions. Thanks also go to Michael Simsic, my copy editor, and all the hard-working folks in IDG's production department.

The book originated with Janna Custer and Megg Bonar in the acquisitions department at IDG, who took a still-inexperienced author (me) and provided him with another enjoyable and challenging experience. David Solomon, publisher at IDG, and John Kilcullen, IDG's president, also helped to launch the project, and I owe them both my sincere thanks.

Larry Mollin, supervising producer of the hit TV series *Beverly Hills, 90210,* took time from his busy work schedule and Little League duties to write the foreword. What can I say except that he's a heck of a guy and it's a heck of a show? (Wednesday nights on FOX, if there's still anyone in the world who can't tell the difference between Dylan and Brandon or between Donna and Kelly.)

My agent, Connie Clausen of Connie Clausen Associates in New York, handled the business end of the project and continues to give me good advice on just about everything. My family put up with me all the way and continues to give me good advice (some of which I even take!) on just about everything.

(The publisher would like to give special thanks to Patrick J. McGovern, without whom this book would not have been possible.)

Credits

Publisher
David Solomon

Managing Editor
Mary Bednarek

Acquisitions Editor
Janna Custer

Production Director
Beth Jenkins

Senior Editors
Tracy L. Barr
Sandra Blackthorn
Diane Graves Steele

Production Coordinator
Cindy L. Phipps

Associate Acquisitions Editor
Megg Bonar

Project Editor
Mary C. Corder

Editor
Michael Simsic
Kristin A. Cocks
Barbara L. Potter

Technical Reviewer
Stuart Stuple

Production Quality Control
Steve Peake

Production Staff
Tony Augsburger
J. Tyler Connor
Sherry Gomoll
Adam P. Harrison
Angie Hunckler
Tricia Reynolds
Gina Scott
Robert Simon

Proofreader
Michelle Worthington

Indexer
Ann Leach

Cover Design
University Graphics

Book Design
Kavish + Kavish

Contents at a Glance

Foreword xxiii

Introduction 1

Part I: All the Databasics You Have to Know 7
Chapter 1: What the Heck Is dBASE Anyway? 9

Chapter 2: Setting Up a Database: Rule #1 Is Think Ahead 21

Chapter 3: How to Use the dBASE Screens 33

Chapter 4: Using Catalogs and Tables 43

Chapter 5: Putting Data in Your Table 57

Chapter 6: Looking at Your Data 73

Chapter 7: Get Help Whenever You Need It 83

Chapter 8: Redesigning Your Table 95

Part II: Finding and Playing with Your Data 107
Chapter 9: Adding and Using Memo Fields 109

Chapter 10: Creating Your Own Forms 115

Chapter 11: Finding Stuff Fast in Your Database 125

Chapter 12: Queries Have More Power to Find Stuff 137

Chapter 13: Using Logical Operators and Replacing Data 153

Chapter 14: Hot Stuff! Customizing Your Forms 165

Part III: Organizing and Printing Your Data 179
Chapter 15: Sorting and Indexing Even When You're Out of Sorts 181

Chapter 16: Quick and Easy Ways to Print Database Stuff 195

Chapter 17: Creating Simple Reports with dBASE 205

Chapter 18: Divvy Up Your Database and Put It Back Together 215

Part IV: Really Advanced Stuff to Impress Your Friends *223*

Chapter 19: Hot Stuff! Creating Sophisticated Reports 225

Chapter 20: Creating and Printing Form Letters 239

Chapter 21: Designing and Printing Mailing Labels 251

Chapter 22: Secret Power Tricks with dBASE 263

Part V: The Part of Tens *271*

Chapter 23: Ten Things to Do When You're Really in Trouble 273

Chapter 24: Ten Awful Database Terms
(And Suggested Penalties for Using Them) 283

Chapter 25: Ten Things to Know if You've Used dBASE II, III, or IV 287

Chapter 26: Ten Fun Facts about dBASE 293

Part VI: Appendixes *295*

Appendix A: Database Data for This Book 297

Appendix B: Installing dBASE 301

Index *303*
Reader Response Card .... *Back of Book*

Cartoons at a Glance

By Rich Tennant

page 107

page 7

page 271

page 136

page 179

page 267

page 94

page 295

page 194

page 223

Table of Contents

· ·

Foreword ....*xxiii*

Introduction *1*
   About This Book 1
   How to Use This Book 2
   What You're Like (According to Your Mother) 2
   How This Book Is Organized 3
      Part I: All the Databasics You Have to Know 3
      Part II: Finding and Playing with Your Data 3
      Part III: Organizing and Printing Your Data 3
      Part IV: Really Advanced Stuff to Impress Your Friends 4
      Part V: The Part of Tens 4
      Part VI: The Appendixes 4
   Icons Used in This Book 4
      Technical Stuff 4
      Note 5
      Tip 5
      Remember 5
      Warning 5
   Where to Go from Here 5

Part 1: All the Databasics You Have to Know *7*

Chapter 1: What the Heck Is dBASE, Anyway? **9**
   What Is dBASE? 9
      Ready, set . . . computerize! 11
      Create a database to organize your data 12
   Get the Data You Need — Easily! 13
      Print reports about your data 14
      Annoy people with form letters and mailing labels 14
      Exchange data with other programs 16
   Starting dBASE 16
      Reading the dBASE Screen 17
      Opening a Menu 18
      Getting Help (Not Including Psychiatric Help) 19
      Quitting dBASE 20

Chapter 2: Setting Up a Database: Rule #1 Is Think Ahead! 21

The Parts of a dBASE Database 22
    Use catalogs to keep database stuff together 22
    After you've created a catalog 23
Use Tables to Hold Your Data 23
Rows and Columns and Bears (Oh, My!) 24
    Use queries to find your data 25
    Use forms to enter your data 26
    Use reports to print your data 27
Planning Your Database 27
Creating A Database Catalog 29
    Basic steps for creating a catalog 29
    Basic steps for changing the current directory 30
    Hands on: creating a sample catalog 31

Chapter 3: How to Use the dBASE Screens 33

Parts of the dBASE Screen 34
Using the Menus 36
    Using shortcut keys 36
    Using submenus 37
    What the different menus do 38
Using the SpeedBar 39
Using Icons 40
Permanently Changing the Current Directory 41

Chapter 4: Using Catalogs and Tables 43

Planning the Structure of Your Table 44
Remember to Open a Catalog 46
    Creating a new catalog 46
    Opening or closing a catalog 47
    Adding something to a catalog 47
    Deleting something from a catalog 48
Basic Steps for Creating a Table 48
Rules for dBASE Field Names 49
What the Heck Is a Data Type? 50
Hands-On: Creating the Custdata Table 51
    Creating the table's fields 52
Saving the Table Design 54

Chapter 5: Putting Data in Your Table 57

Preparing to Add Data to a Table 58
    Using the dBASE SpeedMenus 59
    Form, Browse, and Columnar Layouts 60

Using the Browse Layout 61
Entering Customer Data 62
Basic steps for entering data 63
Hands on: entering data in the Customer table 63
Moving around in the Browse Layout 68
Editing Data and Fixing Mistakes 69
Replacing text completely 69
Editing text without replacing it 70
Editing keys in dBASE 70
Closing the Customer Table 71

Chapter 6: Looking at Your Data **73**

Changing the Look of Your Browse Window 73
Changing column headings 75
Hands on: changing Bookcust table column headings 75
Changing Column Widths 77
Changing column widths using the mouse 77
Changing column widths with more precision 78
Widening a column 79
Moving Columns 79
Saving Your Changes 81

Chapter 7: Get Help Whenever You Need It **83**

Getting Help in dBASE 84
What the other Help menu choices mean 84
Using hypertext links 86
Using the Help buttons 87
Using the Help menus 88
Searching for a Topic 91
Using Interactive Tutors 92

Chapter 8: Redesigning Your Table **95**

What Changes Can You Make? 96
Adding Fields 96
Adding a field at the end of the table 98
Inserting a field in the middle of the table 98
Moving Fields 99
Deleting Fields 101
Changing Fields (Or Fooling with Field Properties) 102
Turning on automatic uppercase 103
Setting field properties 104
Using templates to insert formatting characters 105
Filling in Phone Numbers 106

Part II: Finding and Playing with Your Data 107

Chapter 9: Adding and Using Memo Fields 109

Adding a Memo Field 110
Entering a Memo 111
Viewing and Editing a Memo 113

Chapter 10: Creating Your Own Forms 115

What Are Forms Good For? 116
Calling Up a Form Expert 116
Hands on: Creating a Form 121
    Selecting and arranging fields 122
    Previewing your form 122
Moving Around in the Table 123
Entering Data with a Form 124

Chapter 11: Finding Stuff Fast in Your Database 125

Finding Stuff the Easy Way 127
    Options in the Find Records dialog box 128
    Hunting down the hidden options 129
Hands on: Finding a Customer Record 131
Finding Something Buried in a Field 133
Finding and Replacing Stuff 134
Do You Have to Index? 135

Chapter 12: Queries Have More Power to Find Stuff 137

Three Steps for Perfect Queries 138
How to Create a Query in dBASE 139
    Editing data in the query answer 142
    Changing the order of fields in the answer 142
How to Search for Stuff 143
    Using the query operators 144
    Using wildcards 144
Important Points to Remember 145
Drudge Work Alert! Setting Up a Sales Table 146
Creating a Simple Query 147
    Running the query 150
    Saving the query 151
    Rerunning a query 151

Chapter 13: Using Logical Operators and Replacing Data 153

Creating Multiple-Condition Queries 154
    Using AND and OR: the basics 154

Combining conditions with AND 155
Hands on: querying the Sales table 157
Looking for Mr. Range of Values 158
Combining conditions with OR 159
Putting OR conditions in different fields 159
Doing Calculations in a Query 160
Replacing Data in a Table 162

Chapter 14: Hot Stuff! Customizing Your Forms 165

Moving Fields and Captions 166
Moving stuff in the Custform 168
Dragging things around 168
Changing a Control's Properties 170
Understanding object properties 172
Changing text and fonts 172
Resizing a control 174
Changing a Form's Colors 175
Adding Text to a Form 176
Saving a Form Design 178

Part III: Organizing and Printing Your Data 179

Chapter 15: Sorting and Indexing, Even When You're Out of Sorts 181

Doing Simple Sorts 182
The basic steps for sorting records 183
Sorting on more than one field 184
Basic steps for a multifield sort 186
Sorting character fields that contain numbers 186
Indexing: Usually Better Than Sorting 187
The basic things you have to know 189
Making sure that the correct fields are indexed 190
Displaying your records in indexed order 190
Indexing on multiple fields 192

Chapter 16: Quick and Easy Ways to Print Database Stuff 195

Different Kinds of Reports 196
Printing from a Browse Window 197
But it doesn't all fit on one page! 197
Hiding columns in the Browse window 199
Making hidden columns visible again 201
Hands on: hiding columns in the Customer table 201
Printing a Browse window in Landscape mode 202
Printing from a Form 203

Chapter 17: Creating Simple Reports with dBASE 205

Creating a Simple Report 206
Parts of the Crystal Reports window 207
Understanding a report layout 208
Laying out the report 208
Previewing the report 210
Changing report column width 211
Using the Ribbon to change text appearance 212
Saving and Printing the Report 213

Chapter 18: Divvy Up Your Database and Then Put It Back Together 215

The Basic Idea: Divide and Conquer 216
Dividing your data into different tables 217
Linking tables with a query 217
Different types of relations between tables 218
To be related, tables must share a field 219
The Practical Part: Here's How You Do It 219
Checking the Sales table 219
Setting up the relation 220
Deleting a relation 222

Part IV: Really Advanced Stuff to Impress Your Friends 223

Chapter 19: Hot Stuff! Creating Sophisticated Reports 225

The Basic Ideas 226
The Basic Steps 227
Creating a Grouped Report 227
Setting up the basic report 228
Adding the group sections 230
Parts of the grouped report design 232
Saving the report 232
Doing Calculations in a Report 232
Changing the height of a report band 233
Inserting a summary field 233
Jazzing it up a little 234
Basing a Report on a Query 236
Creating a Multitable Report 236

Chapter 20: Creating and Printing Form Letters 239

The Basic Ideas 240
In dBASE, a form letter is a report ... sort of 241
Using formulas to fix things 242
How to Do It: Setting Up a Form Letter 243

Inserting the recipient's name 244
Adding the address lines 247
Entering the letter's text 248
Previewing and saving the form letter 249
Printing the form letter 250

Chapter 21: Designing and Printing Mailing Labels 251

The Basic Ideas 252
The Basic Steps 252
In dBASE, a label is a report … sort of................................255
Using formulas to fix things 256
Hands on: Labels for a Bookstore Mailing 256
Adding the name line 257
Adding the address lines 260

Chapter 22: Secret Power Tricks with dBASE 263

Selecting Which Records to Print 263
Quick-and-dirty with the Print dialog box 264
Using the For option 265
Being more sophisticated with a formal report 268
Printing Stuff Sideways 268
Putting a Graphic in a Report 269

Part V: The Part of Tens *271*

Chapter 23: Ten Things to Do When You're Really in Trouble 273

Before Disaster Hits: Back Up, Back Up, Back Up! 274
When dBASE Locks Up 275
The simplest solution: reboot 276
Common reasons for lockups 276
When dBASE Is Really Slow 277
When You Make a Terrible Mistake
in Data Entry 278
When You Make a Terrible Mistake
in Design 278
When You Accidentally Delete a Table 279
When dBASE Can't Load a Database File 279
When Something Won't Print at All 280
When Something Won't Print Right 280
When You Finish Your Work And There's Nothing Good on TV 281

Chapter 24: Ten Awful Database Terms
(And Suggested Penalties for Using Them) 283

Chapter 25: Ten Things to Know if You've
Used dBASE II, III, or IV 287

  Unlike Tom and Roseanne, dBASE for Windows Is Very Compatible 287
  But There's No Control Center 288
  The Dot Prompt Is Now the Command Window 288
  You Pretty Much Have to Use the Mouse 288
  Some Files You Need, Some Files You Don't 289
  You May Need to Update Catalog Paths 289
  On-Screen Help Is Much Better 289
  The SpeedBar Is a Big Improvement 290
  It's Easier to Customize Than It Used to Be 290
  Basic Tasks Remain the Same 291

Chapter 26: Ten Fun Facts About dBASE 293

Part VI: Appendixes *295*

Appendix A: Database Data for This Book 297

  The Customer Records Table 297
  The Sales Table 299

Appendix B: Installing dBASE 301

  What You Need to Install and Run dBASE 301
  Installing dBASE on Your PC 302

Index *303*

Reader Response Card .... *Back of Book*

Foreword

*W*hat do I know about dBASE?

Until last week — nothing. I don't have it, and I'm okay. Hell, I'm better than okay. I'm writing and producing a hit television show. All without dBASE.

But here's where fate intrudes.

What I do do is log onto Compuserve to check out the "ZIP code forum" there. It's pretty cool. Sharp commentary. Bright people. Quick electronic feedback. And one guy, Scott Palmer (the author of this very book), who — I swear — maybe minutes after each *BH, 90210* broadcast, would post an electronic synopsis of the show — complete with praise, criticism, and speculation— all with a sense of fun. I was impressed. He seemed like a very together guy. So when he asked if I'd do the foreword for *dBASE For Windows For Dummies,* I agreed. Why? I guess because I liked Scott, I'm a writer, and maybe I'd get some free software. Solid.

Then I panicked. I had not the slightest idea what a database was. What if I didn't even have the right stuff to be a dummy? I mean, I may be pretty damned hip around my office with my little old laptop, but it's just a facade. I only know what I know about computing. Not a lot more. I'm no cyberpunk conversant in binary. I *am* a dummy. What if I don't get it? No problem! I realize that I can always tell Scott I suddenly got busy with the show. He'll understand. Whew!

Now the book arrives at my house (with no software) and I figure I'll read a chapter or two and then just make something up. It's only four to six paragraphs he wants.

But then it happened. I got hooked! I mean I was right with it. Chapters were melting away. The style caught me up. It seemed like Scott was talking to me. In my world. It was fun, but all the time I was learning about dBASE, my new cyber-secretary. Something I definitely didn't want to be without. I read it cover to cover and it was time well spent. I grokked it. I felt like a master. And I didn't even have the software!

Now I guess they'll be a little embarrassed and send me the software, and I'll install it and get cracking with all I know. Start "tabling" up, "cataloging," and doing the dBASE dance. I'm no dummy anymore. You?

Larry Mollin
Supervising Producer, *Beverly Hills, 90210*

Introduction

Do you just *love* computers? When you wake up in the morning, is your first thought about how to frimmitz the programming subroutine to the relational zignab so you can print out reports that nobody but *you* will understand?

If so, then you've got the wrong book.

This book is for people who *have a life* outside of sitting at the computer, and want to get their work done as easily, enjoyably, and *quickly* as possible. If you need the answer to a specific question, want to learn how to do something, and *don't* want to waste a lot of time with computer mumbo jumbo, then this is the book for you.

About This Book

You can read this book in two ways. If you wish, you can read it from front to back, just like a novel. When you read it this way, you'll find that each chapter gives you new dBASE skills, which you can immediately put to use. Unfortunately, it has much less sex and violence than a novel, but it *does* have lots of nice pictures and cartoons.

If you prefer, you can just dip into it whenever you need help on a particular topic. Though each chapter builds on the ideas that came before it, the chapters are also self-contained. You can pick and choose what you want to read about. Each chapter begins with a summary of what you need to know to get the most out of the chapter. If you want to pursue things in more depth, there are also cross-references to other parts of the book. For example, by going to a particular chapter, in a few minutes you could learn how to

- Design a database in dBASE.
- Create and print simple reports that are ready in a matter of seconds.
- Find any data you need, no matter how big your database.
- Include graphics and photographs on a printed report.
- Create and print form letters and mailing labels.
- Frimmitz the programming subroutine to the relational zignab — no, wait, that's *one* thing you *won't* find in this book!

How to Use This Book

This book is a little different from some other ... *For Dummies* books. That's because using a database package like dBASE requires both *knowledge* and *skill.* Knowledge you can get by reading, but skill you can get only by *doing.*

To give you both knowledge and skill, each chapter gives you both *instruction* and *hands-on steps.* The instructional parts cover basic ideas that you need to understand as well as the basic moves involved in database tasks. To read these sections, all you need is a brain: some sections are so easy that you don't even need that! You can read these parts on the subway, while doing your laundry, or (depending on your job) while sitting in a getaway car outside the bank.

The hands-on steps assume that you're sitting at your PC and working with dBASE. These steps show you the specific things you do to set up databases, print reports, and so on. You can use the same steps either with the example database in the book or with your own real-life database.

If you're already stuck with a problem in dBASE, then you can jump directly to the chapter you need. Just check out the Table of Contents or the Index. At the beginning of each chapter, you'll see a list of things you can learn in that chapter. If you don't need help on a specific problem, then just browse through the book and read whatever interests you. Or check out the cartoons.

What You're Like (According to Your Mother)

This book assumes that you're a *regular person.* That has nothing to do with a daily serving of bran flakes. It means that you're not a computer expert and, frankly, don't want to be *bothered* with a lot of technical hocus-pocus. You want the facts, plus a little encouragement, and maybe a stupid joke now and then. No 25-syllable words. Just useful information and skills.

This book also assumes that you have dBASE for Windows on your PC. The book is geared for use with version 5 of dBASE for Windows, the exciting first release of a package that's been over five years in the making.

How This Book Is Organized

This book has five main parts. Each part focuses on giving you specific knowledge and skills. Within each part, the chapters are deliberately kept short so that they're easy to finish without a big time commitment on your part. Inside each chapter, the sections are clearly marked so that you can pick and choose the parts you want to read.

Here's the big picture of what's in each part:

Part I: All the Databasics You Have to Know

If you just want to *get to it* in as short a time as possible, this is the place to go. This part gives you all the basic knowledge and skills you need to get started with dBASE *right now*. You'll learn how to plan a database, put information in the database, look at the information when you need it, and get help when you're confused. ("Tell me about ze relationship with your muzzer, mein Kind. Vere you confused, even as a child?")

Part II: Finding and Playing with Your Data

Although Part I shows you how to view your data, this part shows you several more powerful ways to view and find your data, even if your database is really huge. You'll learn how to create on-screen forms that catch errors and explain what's in your database, how to do simple searches for information, and how to use logical operators for *really powerful searches*. It's not necessary for you to work out at a gym before doing really powerful searches, but it helps.

Part III: Organizing and Printing Your Data

Your data is even easier to find if you know how to organize it in a way that's most useful to you. This part shows you how to sort the information in your database so that it's in alphabetical or numerical order — for example, by last name, account number, or date. You also learn how to design and print simple reports about your data. Finally, you learn how to divide up your database so that it's totally and completely (timid souls might even say *frighteningly*) efficient.

Part IV: Really Advanced Stuff to Impress Your Friends

This part shows you how to do things that other people only dream about. You learn how to create reports that group your data and do calculations, design and print form letters and mailing labels, and use graphics or artwork to spruce up your work.

Part V: The Part of Tens

This last part tells you things that you probably never wanted to know, but should. If you really get in trouble on your PC — whether it's with dBASE or not — this part offers tips on how to fix whatever's gone wrong. It also explains database words that only a computer nerd could love.

Part VI: The Appendixes

In humans, the appendix is a vestigial organ, similar to the coccyx, a vestigial tail we inherited from our ancestors, who were all headbangers, in the 1800s. It doesn't do much of anything. In this book, however, the appendixes provide useful information that doesn't quite fit in any of the chapters. Appendix A gives you some customer and sales data to play with in the book's example database. Appendix B tells you how to install dBASE on your PC. And Appendix C gives you a 100 percent foolproof method to guess winning lottery numbers — oops, sorry, they had to cut that appendix.

Icons Used in This Book

Technical Stuff

This icon says that something is technical. Not that you absolutely don't *want* to know this stuff — some of it is pretty interesting, in a "nerds go berserk" sort of way — but you don't really *need* to know it to work with dBASE.

Note

Pay attention. Something interesting is on its way.

Tip

This icon marks a useful tip, "inside information," or a shortcut that helps you work with dBASE more easily.

Remember

This icon marks something you should remember, not only because you'll find it useful, but because there'll be a quiz next period.

Warning

This icon marks things that can get you into trouble if you aren't careful. Even dBASE, easy and friendly as it is, has a few time bombs hidden here and there. If you pay attention to the Warnings, you shouldn't have any trouble.

Where to Go from Here

At this point, you've spent enough time reading the introduction. It's time to get to it! If you have a specific problem to solve, go ahead and jump to that chapter of the book. If not, start in Part I and learn the basics—just enough to be dangerous. Then get ready to have some fun with dBASE!

If your screens don't exactly match the screens in the book, *don't panic*. Like all good software products, dBASE for Windows is constantly being improved. If a dialog box looks or works differently from the way it does here, that just means you have a later — and probably even *better* — version of dBASE than the one I used to write the book. Nothing big is likely to change, so you can handle any minor discrepancies with no trouble.

Part I
All the Databasics You Have to Know

YES, MASTER?

In this part . . .

1 n the early years of database management, people were ignorant. So ignorant, in fact, that many so-called experts mistakenly bought automobile-repair shops on the theory that they'd be able to use the same tools for both transmissions and databases. A tool is a tool, right?

This part shows you how to use the most basic tools for managing information with dBASE. It shows you how to plan a database, set up a table, and put in the data. Then it shows you how to look at your data and, if you need it, how to get on-screen help in dBASE.

Sadly, this part does *not* show you how to manage an auto-repair shop or fix a transmission. Even the embarrassed database experts from the early days don't know stuff like that.

Chapter 1

What the Heck *Is* dBASE, Anyway?

In This Chapter

▶ What is dBASE for Windows?

▶ How dBASE organizes your data

▶ How dBASE makes it easy to get data you need

▶ Starting dBASE

▶ Reading the dBASE screen

▶ Getting Help

▶ Quitting dBASE

*T*o get the most out of this chapter, you need to have

✔ Installed dBASE for Windows on your PC.

✔ Paid for the book.

✔ Put on clean underwear — just in case.

This chapter gives you an overview of dBASE for Windows (dBASE for short) and how it can make your life easier. *Relax* — I'm not going to talk about a lot of abstruse technical stuff that only someone with a pocket protector and a Ph.D. can understand. This chapter explains *just what you need to know* to start dBASE and have some idea of what you're doing. You'll learn about specific skills (creating a database, printing a report, monster truck driving) in later chapters. Here, you're just getting your feet wet.

What Is dBASE?

The answer is simple: It's a *database management system* (DBMS). If you don't know what *that* is, don't worry. You've used database management systems all your life. You just haven't *called* them that.

I'll begin with what dBASE is supposed to manage: data. Data is a bunch of disconnected, disorganized information — just like the receipts you shove into your desk drawer or the contents of the latest trashy novel. And if you've ever tried to find a receipt in that desk drawer — or the "good parts" of a trashy novel — you know that data by itself often doesn't do you much good. After all, how does it help you to have a receipt for that life-saving operation you bought your mother if you can't find it at tax time? We all love our mothers, but let's be serious: a deduction is a deduction.

To make data useful, you need a way to *manage* it — a database management system. You need to organize all the scattered receipts (data) into an orderly form so that you can find what you need when you need it. An organized collection of data is called a *database*.

For your receipts, your database management system might be a set of file folders with a label on each one: "Car expenses," "House payments," "Medical expenses," and so on. Instead of shoving all your receipts into a drawer, you put each receipt into the appropriate file folder. When you need to find a receipt, you no longer have to muddle through a drawer full of wadded-up paper. You just go to the correct file folder, look inside, and presto! There's the receipt you wanted. In the secret language of computer geeks, each receipt is called a *record*. This database is illustrated in Figure 1-1.

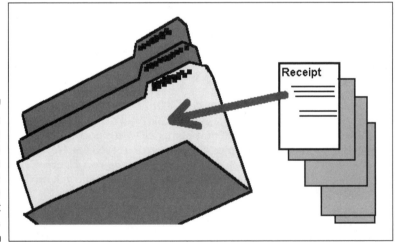

Figure 1-1:
Organizing
receipts
with a
simple
database
management
system.

You can see now that there's nothing at all mysterious about the idea of a database. A database is simply an organized collection of data, and a database management system is what organizes it for you. Some databases are computerized and some aren't.

Where did dBASE come from?

dBASE for Windows is the Windows version of dBASE, one of the most popular PC database management systems in history. Based on work done during the late 1970s by Wayne Ratliff at the Jet Propulsion Laboratory in Palo Alto, California, dBASE was the dominant — and by some lights, the *only* — PC database management system of the 1980s. There were versions of dBASE for most small computers, including PCs, and many big computers.

Originally, you did everything in dBASE by typing commands at what many users came to hate and fear as the infamous dBASE *dot prompt.* The dBASE dot prompt just sat there, waiting for you to type a command — meaning that you were *totally* on your own.

Eventually, Ashton-Tate (which sold dBASE before the company was acquired by Borland International) added some simple drop-down menus, but they didn't really do much, which caused some users to give up data management entirely and join the Roller Derby.

Since Borland acquired dBASE, it's added both power and ease of use to the venerable data manager. And dBASE for Windows goes even further by using the Windows *graphical user interface* (GUI, pronounced *gooey)* to let you use a mouse for most tasks.

Ready, set . . . computerize!

Because you bought this book, it's a safe bet that you're interested in computerized database management. The big advantage of computerized databases is that all the data is at your fingertips, so you don't need to get up out of your chair (groan!) and make that long trek to the filing cabinet (huff, puff). (Did you ever think of getting more exercise?) And computerized databases offer other advantages as well:

- A computerized database is *fast.* Even if you only have a few hundred file folders, it can take a lot of time to find the file you want. With dBASE, you can go right to the data you need in a matter of seconds.

- A computerized database is *flexible.* If you need to present your data in a variety of ways, dBASE does most of the work for you. Need a row-and-column report? Done. Need a summary of sales totals, grouped by region? Done. Need mailing labels? Done.

- A computerized database is *powerful.* Even a jumbo, heavy-duty file folder can't hold a million employee or sales records. But dBASE can hold as many records as you need — one, a hundred, a million — all on your PC's hard disk.

Don't worry about the word *relational*

Sooner or later, you'll hear someone refer to dBASE as a *relational database management system* (RDBMS, for a longer-than-usual acronym). People get into lots of arguments about what that term really means. For practical purposes, it means that you can divide your computerized data into different "file folders" for efficiency, but easily combine the data from different file folders when you need to get data from your database. Beyond that, it's just a bunch of pointy-headed computer scientists jabbering at each other. Don't worry about it.

✔ A computerized database is *deductible.* Yes, if you use it in your business, dBASE is fully tax-deductible, so you can use it to offset all those profits you made from offshore oil drilling.

dBASE gives you a fast, flexible, powerful, deductible, and easy way to make sense out of any data you throw at it.

Create a database to organize your data

One drawback of computerized databases is that they've often been hard to work with — until now. With the new dBASE, you don't need to remember a lot of commands. You don't need to be a database expert. You don't even need to be good-looking, although you are, of course. All you need to do is open menus, click on buttons, and follow the instructions that appear on the screen.

When you create the basic building block of a database — in dBASE, it's called a *table* — the first thing you need to decide is what kind of data should go into it. A customer table, for example, may have each customer's account number, first and last names, address, city, state, zip code, and telephone number. Each of these items goes into its own separate column in the table, as shown in Figure 1-2. dBASE guides you as you create each column. (I take you step by step through the whole process in Chapter 4.)

In older versions of dBASE, a table was called a *database file*. The only reason that the name was changed to "table" was to make dBASE terminology easier to understand. There is no difference between a database file and a table.

Smile when you data entry, pardner!

Data entry is when you sit down at the PC's keyboard and start putting information into a database. When you do that, dBASE helps save you from unnecessary typing and also prevents some common kinds of mistakes.

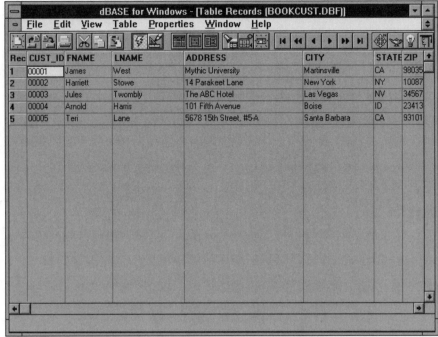

Figure 1-2:
A row-and-column table of customer data.

If you're worried about accidentally putting in the *wrong* data — say, a salary of $100,000 for your most junior clerical employee — you can tell dBASE to refuse any data that looks suspicious. And if someone else is entering the data for you, dBASE can help prevent mix-ups by displaying an on-screen explanation of what each data item is supposed to be.

Get the Data You Need — Easily!

Of course, putting your data into a database is only the beginning. You also have to get the data *out* of the database when you need it. dBASE not only lets you see multiple records in a row-and-column screen, as in Figure 1-2, but also lets you see one record at a time, as in Figure 1-3.

Speeding Around the dBASE SpeedBar

On the third line down from the top of your screen is the dBASE *SpeedBar*. You can click on the buttons on the SpeedBar with your mouse to bypass the menus and perform a specific database task quickly and with minimum hassle.

dBASE displays different SpeedBar buttons, depending on what type of work you're doing at the moment. In this book, the buttons are identified whenever they're relevant to what you're doing at the moment.

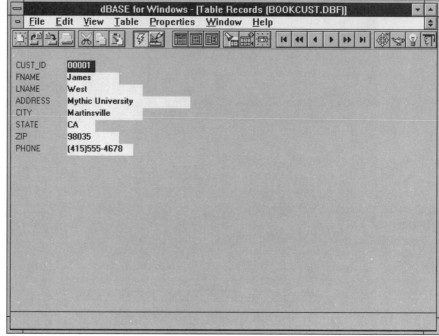

Figure 1-3:
dBASE lets
you see all
the details
of a single
record on
the screen.

Print reports about your data

dBASE does more than just display your data on-screen. You can print out reports in any format you choose: row and column, one record on a page, summaries only, totals and calculations — you name it. If you're ambitious, you can lay out the report yourself. If you're in a hurry, you can let the dBASE Report Expert do most of the work for you. Figure 1-4 shows a sample of dBASE's snazzy report capabilities.

Annoy people with form letters and mailing labels

In addition to using your data in reports, you also can use it to create form letters ("Dear Mr. McMahon: *You may already be a winner . . . !*") and mailing labels. One thing dBASE *cannot* do is write the letters and stamp the envelopes for you. But there's always next year. . . . Figure 1-5 illustrates a form letter and some mailing labels created in dBASE.

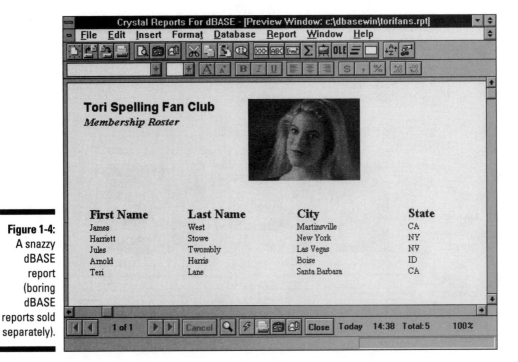

Figure 1-4:
A snazzy
dBASE
report
(boring
dBASE
reports sold
separately).

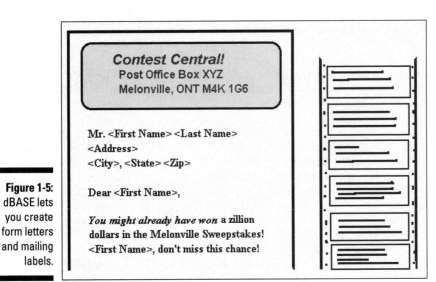

Figure 1-5:
dBASE lets
you create
form letters
and mailing
labels.

Exchange data with other programs

If you work in an office in which different people use different programs, dBASE makes it easy to exchange data with your coworkers. Whether they're using Lotus 1-2-3, Access, Paradox, FoxPro, or even a simple word processor, dBASE can import data from and export data to their programs, as shown in Figure 1-6.

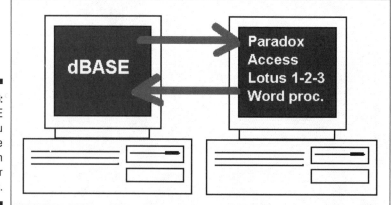

Figure 1-6: dBASE lets you exchange data with other programs.

Starting dBASE

Starting dBASE is easy — *if* the program is installed on your PC. If it's not installed, follow the instructions in Appendix B to put dBASE on your hard disk. Don't just copy the dBASE disks to your hard disk, because the program won't work if you do.

Before you can start dBASE, of course, you have to *find* it. When you installed dBASE on your PC, you automatically created a dBASE *group* in your Windows Program Manager. Open the window for the dBASE group and double-click on the dBASE program icon, which is a picture of a sword in a stone with "dBASE for Windows" under it

Go ahead and do it now; the next few sections of this chapter take you on a brief tour of the program, and it is more meaningful if you actually see what happens on-screen when you perform the steps I describe. (If you need help with Windows, a good way to learn is *Windows For Dummies* by Andy Rathbone, published by IDG Books Worldwide.)

If you don't use a mouse . . . you're crazy!

This book assumes that you're using a mouse or at least some kind of pointing device, such as a trackball. Yes, you can use Windows without a mouse. If you *want* to, you can also drop a hundred-pound rock on your foot. But why on earth would you want to do either?

My advice is simple: If you don't have a mouse, get one. If you have one, use it. And if you went out and dropped a hundred-pound rock on your foot, don't watch *Beavis and Butt-Head*. You're *much* too suggestible.

Reading the dBASE Screen

When dBASE first starts, you'll see the opening screen shown in Figure 1-7. Across the top line of the screen, as always with Windows programs, is the name of the program — dBASE for Windows. Underneath that is the dBASE Menu Bar. This is where you can click with the mouse to use the dBASE menus.

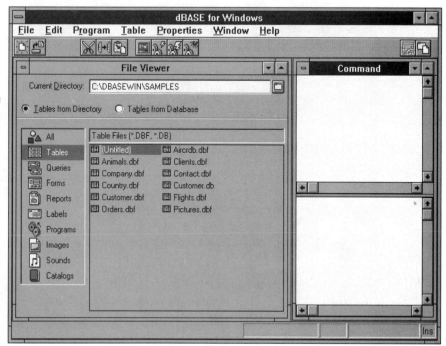

Figure 1-7: The dBASE opening screen. On the left is the dBASE Navigator. On the right, you can open two Command windows for typing dBASE commands.

Just under the Menu Bar is the SpeedBar, mentioned earlier. Different buttons appear on the SpeedBar, depending on where you are in the program.

At the left is the Navigator window. This lets you see what files are available in the current DOS directory. You'll learn how to use the Navigator later on, so don't worry about it right now.

At the bottom of the screen is the status line, which displays helpful information while you're working with dBASE. It tells you what different menu choices mean, what your next step should be, and so on.

Opening a Menu

Now that you've started up dBASE and learned a little bit about the dBASE screen, I want you to do a few simple things in dBASE before wrapping up this chapter. One way to create a database is to use the File menu. Try that now. Click on the word *File* in the Menu Bar. The File menu should appear, as shown in Figure 1-8.

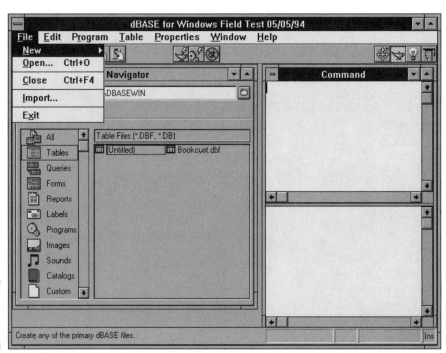

Figure 1-8:
Opening the
File menu.

As you can see, dBASE gives you menu choices to create new databases, open existing databases, and do other things that you'll learn about as you read later chapters. You'll use the File menu to create a new database in the next chapter; for now, just close the menu by clicking again on File in the Menu Bar.

Getting Help (Not Including Psychiatric Help)

dBASE is simple to use, but anytime you *do* have a problem, you can get help easily. Just click on the Help menu and select Contents. A help screen appears, as shown in Figure 1-9.

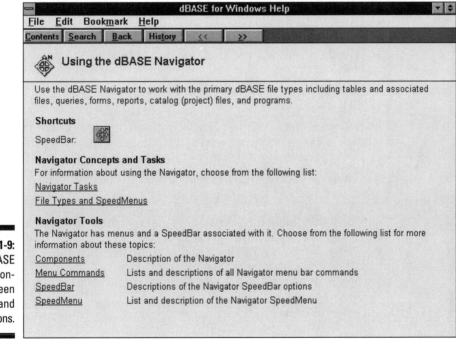

Figure 1-9: dBASE provides on-screen help and explanations.

Another easy way to get help is simply to press the F1 function key on your PC's keyboard. This calls up a "context sensitive" help screen: dBASE will display different information, depending on what you're doing at the moment.

Use the buttons at the top of the Help window to find your way around. If you click on Search, you can get help on a specific problem by typing in a name for what you're doing, such as "report." Clicking on the Back button takes you back to the help screen before the current one. And if you're in another help screen, you can return to the Contents screen by clicking on the Contents button.

The dBASE Help System is covered completely in Chapter 7.

Quitting dBASE

You've done enough for now, so go ahead and quit dBASE. Quitting is as easy as starting up. You can do it in four ways:

- ✔ With the dBASE window displayed, hold down the Alt key and press the F4 function key.

- ✔ Double-click on the Window Control button at the top left corner of the dBASE window.

- ✔ Click once on the Window Control button to open the Control menu. Then click on Close.

- ✔ Open the File menu and select Exit. You can do it with the mouse or, if you're a keyboard whiz, by pressing Alt+F to open the menu and then *X* to select *Exit.*

That's it for this chapter! You've learned the basic ideas of a database management system, as well as the main parts of dBASE. Congratulate yourself and take a break. Have a cappuccino. Learn a foreign language. Buy a cat. Sell the cat and buy a dog. Then, when you're rested, go on to Chapter 2, where you learn how to design and create a database without getting cat hair on your PC.

Chapter 2

Setting Up a Database:
Rule #1 Is Think Ahead!

● ●

In This Chapter

▶ Parts of a dBASE database

▶ What are data types?

▶ How to plan your database

▶ Changing the current directory

▶ Creating a database catalog

● ●

Many things in life don't require you to think ahead. Surprise parties, for example. Bad movies. Unexpected visits from your in-laws. Turning 30. Turning 40. All you need to do is keep breathing, and these things happen automatically.

But when it comes to setting up a database, thinking ahead is an absolute requirement. If you don't do it, you'll end up with a jumbled mess of data that isn't any good to anyone except the computer consultant you hire to fix it at a rate of $100 an hour. Plus tips.

This chapter shows you how to think ahead and plan your database — from analyzing your needs (the first step) to setting up the dBASE database you'll use. You'll also learn about the basic components of a database and what you can do with each.

To get the most out of this chapter, you need to have

✔ Learned what a database manager can do for you (Chapter 1).

✔ Some idea of the data you want to manage.

✔ Installed dBASE for Windows on your PC.

✔ Resolved any hidden psychological conflicts that make you giggle uncontrollably whenever you sit down at the computer.

The Parts of a dBASE Database

dBASE, like many PC database managers, creates a separate disk file for each different thing in the database. For example, if you want to keep a table of customer data, that's one file; if you want to sort the data by each customer's last name, that's another file; and if you want to link the customer data to sales records, that's another file.

The problem is that unless your database is *really* simple, it gets hard to remember which files go with which database. If you have the files from three different databases all mixed together in the same disk directory, it can be Nightmare on PC Street, just without the scary bad guy.

Use catalogs to keep database stuff together

dBASE gives you an easier way to manage your database. In dBASE, a database is a single big thing called a *catalog* that keeps all your little things together for you. With a click of the mouse, you can see a list of all of a catalog's tables, reports, and so on, as shown in Figure 2-1. The catalog itself is just kind of a wrapper that holds them all together. You can create as many different catalogs as you like: one could hold database stuff for your bookstore, one could hold personal data, and so on.

Before you create anything else in your database, you need to create a catalog and give it a name, such as *Fred.* After that, while you are working in dBASE and until you change to a different catalog or quit dBASE, everything you create is put into the Fred catalog. Moreover, when you look at the dBASE screen, the *only* database files you'll see are those in the Fred catalog. That way, you don't have to remember which file goes with which database. In essence, the catalog *is* the database. Even if it's called Fred.

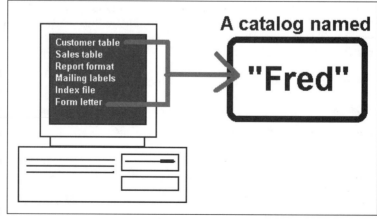

Figure 2-1:
dBASE
keeps all
your
database
stuff
together in a
catalog.

In the old days — *waaaay* back in the 1980s — dBASE did not have catalogs to hold your database files together. Then, you had to create a separate disk directory for each separate database. Today, dBASE catalogs make your database life much easier. If you'd prefer not to use catalogs (the Sharper Image and J.C. Penney catalogs notwithstanding), you can still use the older approach of creating a separate directory for each group of database files.

The information on your PC's hard disk is divided into *disk files,* which are like paper file folders in a filing cabinet. Every disk file has a name. The name begins with up to eight letters or digits, followed by a period and an *extension* of up to three letters or digits. Every disk file is kept in a disk *directory,* which is like one of the drawers in a filing cabinet. Each directory also has a name. If you're not sure that you understand disk files and directories, check out *DOS For Dummies* by Dan Gookin (IDG Books Worldwide) because it explains all that stuff.

After you've created a catalog ...

The catalog is only the wrapper. Before you do anything else on the computer, think about what kinds of data you need to manage. Then you can decide how to divide it between the different database tools that dBASE provides — tables, forms, reports, and so on.

To make those decisions, of course, you need to know what database tools can go into a catalog in dBASE. You use each tool to design a particular part of your database.

Use Tables to Hold Your Data

Inside the catalog "wrapper," the starting point of a dBASE database is called a *table.* A table holds all the data of a particular type. For example, a table may hold all your customer records, all your inventory records, or all your sales records. A table shouldn't hold more than one type of record. If you try to keep all your customer and sales data in a single table, you can plan on spending at least two or three fun weekends trying to figure out what's wrong with your database. Then it'll be time to visit the bank machine and get that $100 an hour for the guy in the pin-striped suit.

All records in a table should hold basically the same type and amount of data. If some records need to hold a lot more data than others, you need to redesign your database.

Each record in a table contains all the information about a single thing. A customer record, for example, may hold a customer's account number, name, address, phone number, and date of first purchase. A sales record may hold the account number of the customer who bought the item (more on that later!) and the item's inventory number, description, and price.

After you've created a catalog, the first step in designing a dBASE database is deciding which tables you should have. You shouldn't — and don't need to — put all your data in one table, because dBASE lets you put different kinds of data in separate tables. Any time you need to combine data from separate tables, you can do so easily. You don't need to cram all your customer, sales, and inventory data into a single table.

Rows and Columns and Bears (Oh, My!)

The easiest way to think of table data is, well, as a table. Figure 2-2 shows a row-and-column table of data in dBASE. There are no bears. I was only kidding about the bears. Honest.

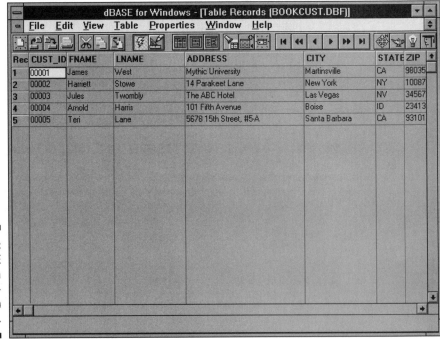

Figure 2-2:
How dBASE stores data in a row-and-column table.

Notice how the table is set up. When a table is displayed in this way — as a row-and-column table — you're looking at it in *Browse Mode,* or a browse table.

The names of the columns appear at the top of the browse table. Columns, in database jargon, are called *fields.* In a record, each field holds a single piece of information, such as a person's first name, a part number, or the number of commercials during a single evening of TV.

The rows are called *records.* Just as each field holds a single piece of information, a record holds *all* the pieces of information that pertain to a specific thing. For example, if there is information about *you* in a table, all of it goes into one record. Inside the record, there would be one field each for your first name, last name, street address, number of felony convictions, and favorite ice cream flavor. (Yes, you can use dBASE even if you have a criminal record or prefer raspberry-pistachio ice cream.)

In a single table, every record has the same fields, and the fields are the same size in each record. Thus, a First Name field that is 15 letters long in one record won't be 35 letters long in another.

The flip side of a browse table is a *form,* which you learn about in a minute. In the meantime, bear with me. (No, that's *not* a bear with me. There are no bears. Just be patient.)

One thing you can't see in Figure 2-2 is that different columns in a dBASE table often contain different *data types.* Just as it's more efficient for people to divide the world into solid objects, liquids, gases, and cream pies, database managers divide up *data* into different data types. Data types help dBASE zip through your data more quickly and accurately to get the information you need. Typically, database managers have data types for text, number, date, and yes/no fields. dBASE for Windows also has types for free-form memos, pictures, and other things — even financial worksheets or word processing documents! You learn the basics of how to use data types in Chapter 4.

Use queries to find your data

After you put data into a database, you sometimes need to search for specific pieces of data. Suppose that you're staffing the phones one Sunday night (you *do* work on Sunday nights, don't you?), and a customer calls to make sure that you sent an order to the right address.

You can handle the situation in three ways. The first, and easiest, is to put the customer on hold until he or she hangs up in disgust. If you ever called a business on Sunday night, you know how popular this method has become.

The second method is to scan down the customer data table, row by row, until you get to the customer record you want. If you have more than a few dozen records in your table, this option, too, will cause customers to hang up in disgust unless their lives are really boring.

The best choice, however, is to use a simple query to find the record you need. A *query* is a question that you ask dBASE, such as, "What records have the zip code 90210?" or "How many customers bought books on bungee-jumping?" or "Wouldn't you really rather be a toaster?"

When you create a query, you tell dBASE which field you want to look at — say, the field for last name — and what you want to search for — say, the name "Wilds." Then you just use the mouse to click on a little screen picture , and dBASE immediately shows you the record you need. (Unfortunately, the caller's name was "West," so he hung up anyway.)

Use forms to enter your data

Forms are another important dBASE tool. When you fill out a paper form, you write the data in blanks on a page. When you fill out a dBASE form, you type the data in blanks on the screen, as shown in Figure 2-3.

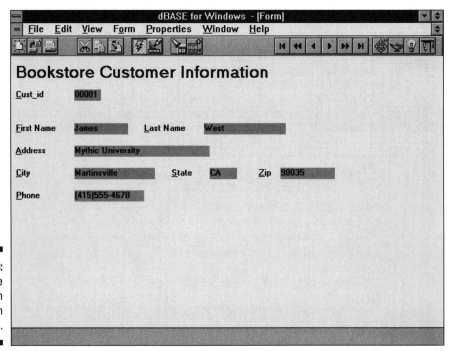

Figure 2-3:
Filling in the
blanks of an
on-screen
form.

When you enter data into your own database, it's easy to remember what data should go where. But if other people will be entering data for you, forms can be a big help.

When designing a form, always assume that it will be used by someone who knows nothing about your data and your database. In dBASE, you can include statements in your form that explain what type of data is supposed to go into a particular blank; be sure to take advantage of this feature. That way, if a data-entry person doesn't know, for example, what kind of data to put into the "MrMs" blank, help is available right on the form.

dBASE forms offer a lot of other terrific features that make data entry easier and more accurate. You can put radio buttons and check boxes on a form, for example. You can learn how to use many of these features as you work your way around this book.

Use reports to print your data

You can print reports in a variety of formats in dBASE. With Crystal Reports, dBASE's hot new tool for creating reports, you can design complete reports that include all the data in your database, summary reports that give you totals and calculations, or specialized reports that contain only one or two fields.

As far as layout goes, you can create a row-and-column report, a one-record-at-a-time report, form letters, or mailing labels. For the complete details, see Chapters 16 and 17.

Planning Your Database

Now that you know what tools dBASE has to offer, it's time to plan your database. You need to ask yourself two main questions:

- What data do you need to manage?
- What do you need to do with the data?

Let's look at an example. Suppose that you're the PC and database guru at a fictitious used-book store called *Caveat Emptor,* Latin for "Let the buyer beware." Your boss, a mysterious individual named Honest Janis, is the owner of the store.

Caveat Emptor has a large number of regular customers, many of whom have accounts at the store. In addition, the store has a vast inventory of used and rare books — including, of course, several copies of the book you're now reading. That adds up to three main groups of data:

- ✔ Customer names, addresses, and phone numbers
- ✔ Current books in stock
- ✔ Sales transactions

In dBASE, each of these groups of data will get its own table. Whenever necessary, you can combine the data from different tables to create consolidated forms or reports.

Janis needs to do several things with the data in his database, as shown in Figure 2-4. First, he needs to be able to locate the data for an individual customer by searching for the customer's account number or last name. Second, he needs to print form letters and mailing labels to keep customers up to date on the latest used-book acquisitions. Third, he needs to have dBASE update the inventory database and print reports.

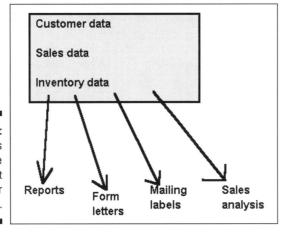

Figure 2-4:
Requirements
for the
Caveat
Emptor
database.

These requirements dictate how you need to set up each table in the database, as well as most of the forms and reports. The details of setting up a table are covered in Chapter 4.

Creating A Database Catalog

Now that you know what data you need to manage and what you want to do with it, you can get to the first big step at the PC: creating a dBASE catalog, which, as I noted earlier, is really the database itself. After all that buildup, the actual process of creating a catalog may be an anticlimax.

Basic steps for creating a catalog

The basic steps are very simple. To create a catalog, you:

1. **Start dBASE by clicking on its icon in the Windows Program Manager.**

   The dBASE icon is the one that shows a sword in a stone. Be careful not to grab the sword by its blade: you might cut yourself.

2. **Make sure that the Current Directory shown at the top of the Navigator window is the one you want.**

   If it isn't, follow the steps outlined in the section titled, "Basic steps for changing the current directory." (And relax: if you mess it up, the worst thing that can happen is you'll start over again. At a lower salary. In another job. At another company. In another city that's probably awful. On second thought, try *not* to mess it up.)

3. **Double-click on the icon marked Catalogs at the lower left corner of the Navigator window.**

   Be sure to double-click with the *left* mouse button. As soon as you do it, the Create Catalog dialog box appears.

   A dialog box provides an easy way for you to communicate with dBASE. Buttons that are labeled with words like "OK" are called *push buttons.* They tell dBASE to do something. If you need more help understanding dialog boxes, check out *Windows For Dummies* by Andy Rathbone (IDG Books Worldwide).

4. **Type the name for your new catalog in the File Name blank at the left corner of the dialog box.**

   The catalog name cannot be more than eight letters long. It can include letters, digits, and underscores, but no spaces or other characters. (It's an MS-DOS file name.)

5. Click on the OK button.

dBASE creates the new catalog. A Catalog window appears on your screen. In the Catalog window, the only files shown are the ones in the current catalog. Because you haven't created any yet, the window is empty except for an icon marked Untitled.

When the Create Catalog dialog box appears, the highlight should be in the File Name blank, so anything you type will go into that blank. If the highlight isn't in the blank, you can move it there by clicking in the blank with the mouse.

Basic steps for changing the current directory

To change the current directory, do the following:

1. In the Navigator window, click on the button at the right end of the Current Directory blank.

The Directory dialog box appears. Notice that on the left side of the dialog box is a list of directories on your hard disk. The current directory is highlighted.

2. If needed, use the scroll bar at the right side of the directory list to move up or down in the list.

You need to use the scroll bar only if the directory you want is above or below the part of the directory list that's visible in the window. If you need help understanding disk directories, see IDG's *DOS For Dummies;* if you need help with scroll bars, see *Windows For Dummies.* If you don't need help, give yourself a gold star.

3. With the left mouse button, double-click on the directory you want.

This selects the directory you want. It also exercises your mouse finger, and experts say that computer users need more exercise.

4. Click on the OK button in the dialog box.

dBASE returns you to the Navigator window. In the Current Directory blank, you now see the directory you just selected.

For more details on how to select directories and use the other parts of the dBASE screen, see Chapter 3.

Hands on: creating a sample catalog

Now try creating a catalog for the Caveat Emptor bookstore database. If you aren't already running dBASE, start it up by double-clicking on the dBASE icon in the Windows Program Manager. dBASE will usually have its own program *group* — a window or icon labeled *dBASE for Windows* — and that's where you're most likely to find the icon.

Changing to the main dBASE directory

When the dBASE screen appears, the current directory shown in the Navigator window will probably be the dBASE Samples directory. Change to the main dBASE directory by following these steps:

1. **Click on the button at the right end of the Current Directory blank.**

2. **In the Directories list of the dialog box, double-click on the main dBASE directory.**

   The main dBASE directory is probably called DBASEWIN.

3. **Click on the OK button.**

   The Navigator window should reappear, with the main dBASE directory shown in the Current Directory blank.

Creating the Caveat catalog

Now create the catalog for the book's example database. Because it's for the Caveat Emptor bookstore, you'll call it simply CAVEAT. Follow these steps:

1. **In the Navigator window, double-click on the icon labeled Catalogs.**

   The Create Catalog dialog box appears.

2. **In the File Name blank, type** caveat. **(Don't type the period.)**

3. **Click on the OK button.**

   A dialog box appears, asking for a description of the new catalog.

4. **For the description, type** Bookstore Database; **then click on OK.**

   dBASE creates a new catalog named Caveat. Anything you create now is included in the new catalog. If you want, you can close the catalog simply by double-clicking on the Window Control button at the top left corner of the Catalog window. Or you can use the dBASE menus to switch to a different catalog. These skills are explained in detail in Chapter 3.

For now, that's it! dBASE automatically saved your catalog to your PC's hard disk, so shut down dBASE and take a break. Whenever you set up a database, remember to analyze the data you need to manage, figure out what you need to do with the data, and use dBASE to create the database. And please, don't feed the bear. Bears are just like cats: give them a bowl of milk (or a side of beef) and you'll *never* get rid of them.

Chapter 3
How to Use the dBASE Screens

In This Chapter

▶ Parts of the dBASE screen

▶ Using the menus

▶ Using the SpeedBar

▶ Using icons

▶ Using the Navigator and Catalog windows

▶ Permanently changing the current directory

*F*ew things are as scary as looking at the PC's screen and having no idea what to do. Getting mugged in a dark alley comes close; meeting your prospective in-laws for the first time comes even closer.

In this chapter, you learn about the different parts of the dBASE screen and how to use each of them. That way, the only thing to be scared of when you use dBASE will be whether or not you remembered to put out the parakeet and feed the cat, or put out the cat and feed the parakeet, or feed the parakeet to the cat.

To get the most out of this chapter, you need to have

✔ Installed dBASE for Windows.

✔ Had a little practice using the mouse.

✔ Learned about the basic parts of a dBASE database, such as catalogs and tables (Chapter 2).

✔ Arranged for a sighted person to look at the screen for you (a seeing-eye dog will do, as long as the dog is very, *very* smart).

Parts of the dBASE Screen

When you first start up dBASE, you see the main dBASE window, as shown in Figure 3-1. (The Command windows at the right may or may not appear on your screen. Don't worry: you can open them if you ever want to.) This window has all the standard features of any window. So that what you see more or less matches what's in the book, make the window fill up the whole screen by clicking on the Maximize button at the top right corner of the window. That button has a little upward-pointing triangle.

In the top line of your screen, the title bar shows the name of the window — in this case, *dBASE for Windows*. At the top left corner is the Window Control button, which lets you close the window (thereby quitting dBASE), minimize the window, or switch to another program in Microsoft Windows. At the top right corner are the Minimize button (marked with a down-pointing triangle) and either the Maximize button (an up-pointing triangle) or the Resize button (a double triangle).

By the way, don't maximize all the windows on your screen. In fact, you don't have to maximize *any* windows. Sometimes, it's just easier to see what's going on if the Catalog window is taking up the whole screen.

Every window in dBASE has a Window Control button, a Maximize button, a Minimize button, and can be resized or dragged around the screen with the mouse. To move a window, position the mouse pointer over the solid border at the top of the window. Hold down the left mouse button and roll the mouse in the direction you want: that's called *dragging* the mouse. (You can't move a window that's maximized, because it already takes up the whole screen.) To resize a window, drag its right or bottom border in the direction you want.

None of these features is unique to dBASE. If you're hazy about how to use any of them, a good resource is IDG's *Windows For Dummies* by Andy Rathbone.

Like any good software package, dBASE is constantly being improved. If your screens don't *exactly* match those shown in this chapter, don't panic: nothing is wrong. You could either have a slightly upgraded version of dBASE for Windows, or it might just look different on your PC. Any differences are likely to be minor, so the instructions that I give here will still work.

The dBASE main window is divided into several parts. The following lists the different parts and what they're good for:

> ✔ The *Menu Bar* is the second line from the top and has menus that let you do things in dBASE, such as opening your database, creating new database items (such as tables and reports), and changing how dBASE is set up.

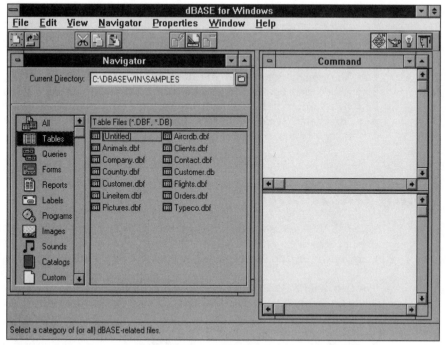

✔ *Icons* are the little on-screen pictures you see in the Navigator window and elsewhere in dBASE. Double-clicking on an icon with the mouse is often a faster way to do things than using the menus. However, there are some things you can do through the menus that you can't do by clicking on icons.

✔ The *SpeedBar* is the third line from the top and has buttons that you can click with the mouse. Like icons, SpeedBar buttons are often a faster way of doing things than using the menus. However, also like icons, the buttons don't let you do as many different things as the menus.

✔ The *Navigator window* is the big window on the left in Figure 3-1. A file is something that holds your database information, such as customer records. The Navigator window shows you all the files of a particular kind that are in the current disk directory.

✔ The *Catalog window* isn't visible in the figure, but you'll see plenty of it later on. It's visible only when you've opened a catalog. It shows all the files of a particular kind in the current catalog.

✔ The *Command windows* are the two big windows on the right of Figure 3-1. You don't need to use them unless you want to type dBASE commands, and you won't have to do that most of the time. Ignore them: they might not even appear on your PC when dBASE first starts up. If you ever need them, you can open them later.

✔ The *Status bar* often shows an explanation of what would happen if you clicked or double-clicked the mouse at its current screen location. For example, if you move the mouse over a SpeedBar button, the status line explains what that button does.

✔ The *window controls* are the standard window controls you find in every Windows program. They include the Maximize and Minimize buttons (top right corner of the window), the Window Control button (top left corner), "draggable" window borders, and, when appropriate, vertical and horizontal scroll bars.

Using the Menus

Using dBASE menus will be pretty standard stuff for you if you have more than five minutes of experience with a PC. There are a few special tricks you can learn, however, and it never hurts to rehearse the fundamentals.

The two main ways to open and close menus are with the mouse or with the keyboard. Most people use the mouse, but if you're a keyboard whiz, that's probably more efficient for you.

✔ With the mouse, you open a menu by clicking on its name in the Menu Bar. For example, to open the File menu, you click on the word *File* in the Menu Bar. To close the menu, you make a menu choice or click on the menu name again.

✔ With the mouse, you make a menu choice by clicking on the choice you want.

✔ With the keyboard, you open a menu by holding down the Alt key and pressing the key that matches the underlined letter in the menu name. For example, to open the Edit menu, press Alt+E; to open the View menu, press Alt+V. To close the menu, press Escape.

✔ With the keyboard, you make a menu choice by pressing the key for the underlined letter in the menu choice you want.

Using shortcut keys

One thing you'll notice as you use the menus is that many menu choices have key combinations next to them, as shown in Figure 3-2. These are *shortcut keys*.

Figure 3-2:
Most dBASE
menus show
shortcut
keys for
bypassing
the menus.

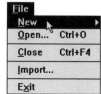

In the File menu, shown in the figure, the shortcut key for opening a file is Ctrl+O, and the shortcut key for closing a file is Ctrl+F4. You can close a file in any one of three ways:

✔ Open the File menu and select Close.

✔ Press Ctrl+F4 (hold down the Ctrl key on your keyboard and press the F4 function key simultaneously).

✔ Use the Window control button at the top left corner of the file's window. You can either double-click on the button (which immediately closes the window), or single-click on it, which opens the Window Control menu. From there, you select Close.

Using submenus

Some menus also have submenus that appear if you make a particular menu choice. If you look at the File menu shown in Figure 3-2, you can see that the menu choice to create a New file has a triangle to its right. Whenever you see that kind of triangle next to a menu choice, it means that there's a submenu. Figure 3-3 shows the submenu that appears when you select New.

Figure 3-3:
A triangle
to the right
of a menu
choice
means
selecting
that menu
choice
opens a
submenu.

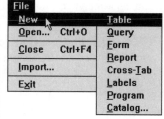

You open a submenu simply by selecting the menu choice. You can close a submenu in one of two ways:

- ✔ Using the mouse, click on the menu choice again. For example, to close the submenu you opened when you clicked on <u>N</u>ew in the <u>F</u>ile menu, just click again on <u>N</u>ew.
- ✔ Using the keyboard, press Escape.

What the different menus do

Most of the things that the menus do are concerned with creating and modifying stuff in dBASE. If you're reading this book from front to back, you might not yet understand some of the choices on the menus; here's an overview.

The <u>F</u>ile menu

The <u>F</u>ile menu lets you create new database items in dBASE, such as new tables, reports, and so on. It also lets you open things you've already created. For example, if you've previously created a table and stored it on your PC's hard disk, the <u>F</u>ile menu lets you retrieve it by choosing the <u>O</u>pen menu choice.

The <u>F</u>ile menu also lets you <u>C</u>lose a file (by closing its window on the screen) and lets you E<u>x</u>it from dBASE back to the Windows Program Manager.

The <u>E</u>dit menu

You can use the <u>E</u>dit menu to undo the last thing you did if you realize that the last thing you did was a *BIG* mistake. The <u>E</u>dit menu also lets you cut, copy, paste, and delete things you've selected. These menu choices work as follows:

- ✔ <u>U</u>ndo helps you if you make a change in a table and then decide you made a mistake. Selecting <u>U</u>ndo lets you change the table back to the way it was.
- ✔ Cu<u>t</u> deletes text (images, and so on) that you've selected with the mouse from the text's current location. What you delete is stored in a place called the *Windows Clipboard.* You can then copy the item from the Clipboard to a new location in dBASE. You can do this as long as you haven't Cu<u>t</u> or <u>C</u>opied something else, or quit Windows.
- ✔ <u>C</u>opy works like Cu<u>t</u>, except the item isn't deleted from its current location — it's only copied to the Clipboard, and from there, you can copy the item to other places.
- ✔ <u>P</u>aste is the menu choice that lets you insert items that you've cut or copied from the Clipboard to the current screen position — that's the *cursor location,* where text would go if you started typing.
- ✔ <u>D</u>elete deletes whatever you have currently selected.

The View menu

The View menu lets you control what is displayed in the Navigator and Catalog windows. You can put things in alphabetical order, change the size of icons, and tell dBASE to display only certain kinds of things, such as tables or reports.

The Navigator menu

What the Navigator menu does depends on what kind of file you have selected with the mouse. If you've clicked on the icon for a table, for example, the menu lets you make changes in the table's data, such as in customer records. The Navigator menu also lets you add new records to a table, redefine how a table is put together (change its structure), or delete the table. If another type of file is selected, the menu lets you do similar things depending on the file type.

The Catalog menu

This menu is just like the Navigator menu. It's displayed on the Menu Bar only when you have a Catalog window open on the screen.

The Properties menu

This menu lets you change how dBASE and the Navigator window work. You'll see an example of using this menu at the end of the chapter, when you see how to change the Current Directory used by dBASE.

The Window menu

This menu lets you switch from one screen window to another, as well as arrange the windows on your screen.

The Help menu

This menu gets you into the dBASE Help System where you can find information and advice on how to do almost anything in dBASE.

Using the SpeedBar

The SpeedBar, on the third line from the top of the screen, is the row of push buttons right underneath the Menu Bar. Often, the SpeedBar provides a faster way of doing things than by going through the menus. You activate a button in the SpeedBar by clicking on it once with the mouse.

If you're looking for a particular button on the SpeedBar but you don't see it, have no fear. Which buttons are displayed on the SpeedBar depends on what you're doing in dBASE at the moment. If you're in the middle of designing a table, different buttons are shown than if you've just started up dBASE.

When you move the mouse over a particular button, the dBASE status bar always displays an explanation of what that button does.

Using Icons

dBASE has loads of icons — those little screen pictures that usually have some text beside them. If you look at the Navigator window, you'll see quite a few.

The icons at the left side of the Navigator window control the kind of files displayed in the right side of the window. If you click once on the icon marked All, then an icon will be visible on the right side of the window for each file in dBASE's current directory on your hard disk. If you click on the icon marked Tables in the left side of the window, then only table files will be listed in the right side of the window, and so on. The basic things you can do with icons are

✔ *Select an item* by clicking once on the item with the left mouse button.

✔ *Create a new item* by clicking once on the icon in the left side of the Navigator window for the type of item you want to create and then double-clicking on the Untitled icon in the right side of the window. For example, if you want to create a new table, you click once on the left-side icon marked Tables and then double-click on the right-side icon marked Untitled.

✔ *Open an item you previously created.* Remember that the icons in the right side of the Navigator window represent files on your hard disk. You can open one of the files — display it on your screen — by double-clicking on its icon with the mouse. Each icon is next to the name of the file it represents.

✔ *Open a SpeedMenu for an item* by clicking on a file's icon with the *right* mouse button. This offers the most common things you might do with the file. A SpeedMenu for a table is shown in Figure 3-4.

Figure 3-4:
One of the
SpeedMenus
you can get
by right-
clicking on
an icon.

Table **P**roperties...	Alt+Enter
Delete	Del
Edit Records	F2
Add Records	
Design **T**able Structure	Shift+F2

Permanently Changing the Current Directory

When dBASE starts up, it most likely uses the DBASEWIN\SAMPLES directory as its current disk directory. If you change to a different directory by using the Navigator window (as explained in Chapter 2), dBASE will use only that directory until you exit from the program. The next time you start up dBASE, it goes back to using the same directory it used before.

You can permanently change the current directory used by dBASE to a different directory. This is what you do, for example, if you created a special directory to hold your dBASE database files. To change the current directory permanently (that is, until you permanently change it again, till death do you part), follow these steps:

1. In the Menu Bar, open the Properties menu and select Desktop.

The Desktop Properties dialog box appears, as shown in Figure 3-5. If what's on your screen doesn't look like the figure, you probably need to click on the Files tab at the bottom of the dialog box. At the left side of the box is a blank labeled Current Directory. At the right end of the blank is a button labeled with a little picture of a wrench.

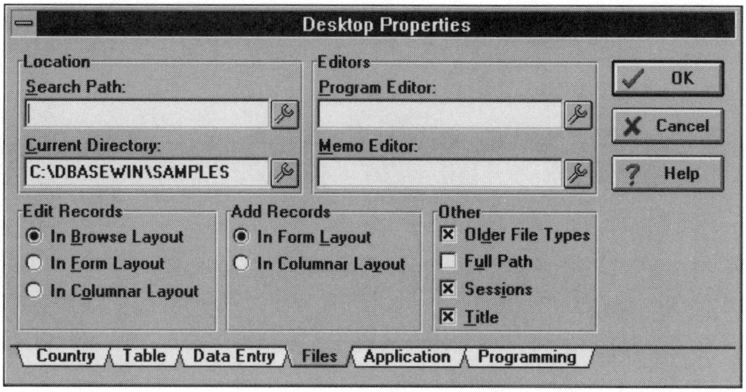

Figure 3-5: The Desktop dialog box. Notice that the Current Directory is shown at the left.

2. Click on the wrench button next to the Current Directory blank.

dBASE lists the directories on your disk.

3. In the list, click on the directory you want.

4. Click on OK.

dBASE returns you to the Desktop Properties dialog box. Notice that the Current Directory blank now shows the directory you selected.

5. Click on OK.

The deed is done! dBASE will use the directory you selected until you go through this same procedure to change the directory again.

Chapter 4

Using Catalogs and Tables

• •

In This Chapter

▶ Planning the structure of a table

▶ Working with database catalogs

▶ Creating a table

▶ Understanding fields

▶ Understanding data types

▶ Saving a table

• •

*T*o get the most out of this chapter, you need to have:

✔ An understanding of basic dBASE and database concepts (Chapters 1 and 2).

✔ An understanding of what catalogs are and how to create them (Chapter 2).

To create a table, you should have

✔ Created a catalog to keep the table together with other parts of the same database.

✔ An understanding of your subconscious motivations, and their origin in what was probably a traumatic childhood. Did you hate your muzzer? Ve alvays look to ze muzzer. Und your dog, Shpot? Did he hate hiz muzzer, too? Hmmm?

In Chapter 2, you created a sample dBASE *catalog*— a kind of wrapper that holds all your different data management tools together. Now it's time to create your first *table,* which is the basic building block of your database.

Each table holds data about a particular kind of thing. In this chapter, you'll learn how to create a table. The book's example table is called *Customers,* and it will hold all the customer data collected by Honest Janis, the bookstore owner whom I introduced in Chapter 2.

When you design a table, you should be guided by one consideration: What do you need to accomplish with your database? Because dBASE is so simple to use, it's a lot easier to focus on *what* you're doing than *how* you're doing it.

Planning the Structure of Your Table

When database people talk about the *structure* of a table, it sounds mysterious, but all *structure* really means is what fields the table contains. When you create a table, the first step is to figure out what fields you need, what kinds of fields they should be, and how big they should be. And those decisions, of course, are determined by what you need to do with the table.

A field just contains an item of information about something or someone in the database, such as a first name, street address, part number, or list price.

Suppose that you're designing the book's sample *Custdata* table for the Caveat Emptor bookstore, and that you have three main goals. You want to be able to do the following:

✔ Keep track of customer names and addresses

✔ Print reports of customer data

✔ Print form letters and mailing labels

To keep track of customer names and addresses, you might establish the following fields:

> Account Number
>
> Name
>
> Address
>
> City, State, ZIP

If you were keeping track of your customer information on paper, this four-field setup would be fine. (Actually, if you were writing the information on paper, you wouldn't even *worry* about things like fields. You'd only worry about whether people could read your handwriting!)

But dBASE has a lot of power that you can't use if you limit yourself to these four fields. Suppose that you wanted to put customer records in order by ZIP code or print the first and last names in a different order than they appear in the Name field. You'd be out of luck! With a computer database, you can do all those things as long as you separate the different items of information into different fields. If you don't, you might as well stick with paper.

If you want to take full advantage of dBASE, you need to put separate parts of the name and address data in separate fields, as follows:

Account Number

First Name

Last Name

Address

City

State

ZIP

That's a lot better. Indeed, this setup does a terrific job of taking care of the first two goals of the sample table: keeping track of customer names and addresses, and printing reports. As before, the table also contains an Account Number field in case two customers have the same first and last names. (This field will also be helpful later on when you create a sample Sales table and want to combine its data with the data from your Customers table.)

But what about the third goal of the sample table: to print form letters and mailing labels? In a form letter, you need to print *Mr., Ms.,* or something like it before the person's name in the address. And, in the case of Honest Janis, the owner of the Caveat Emptor bookstore, many of the customers are personal friends. He'd never address his pal Jim West as "Mr. West," even in a form letter, so you also need a field that indicates what name to use where the letter says, "Dear so-and-so."

After adding the Mr/Ms and Salutation fields to the mix, the final field list looks like this:

Account Number

First Name

Last Name

MrMs

Salutation

Address

City

State

Zip

These fields do everything necessary. Notice that nothing you've done so far is the least bit technical. It's all common sense and thinking ahead. If you have common sense and can think ahead, you can be a database expert with dBASE! If you don't have these qualities, maybe you can be a very successful politician.

Remember to Open a Catalog

Before you create a table, it's wise to open a database *catalog* to keep the table together with other files in the same database. There are two ways to open a catalog: use one way if you need to create the catalog, and use the other if you've already created the catalog and just need to retrieve it from your PC's hard disk.

Creating a new catalog

To *create a new catalog* and open it, follow these steps:

1. **Make sure that you're in the disk directory you want.**

   The current directory is shown at the top of the Navigator window.

2. **Double-click on the Catalogs icon at the bottom left corner of the Navigator window.**

   The Create Catalog dialog box appears on your screen.

3. **In the File Name blank, type the name you want for the new catalog.**

   The catalog name can have up to eight characters (letters, digits, dashes, and underscores, but no spaces, commas, or periods).

4. **Click on the OK button.**

   The Catalog Description dialog box appears on your screen.

5. **In the dialog box, type a brief explanation of what the catalog is all about.**

6. **Click on the OK button.**

   The dBASE Catalog window opens, with the catalog you just created as the current catalog.

Rules for naming files

The reason that catalog names can't be longer than eight characters (letters, digits, and underscores) has nothing to do with dBASE. The eight-character limitation is because MS-DOS, the PC's operating system, keeps track of disk files and limits their names to eight characters, a period, and a three-character extension. dBASE puts a period plus the extension CAT on catalogs and DBF on the disk file for each table, so that leaves only eight characters for you to play with.

If you're confused by MS-DOS, congratulations! You're paying attention. Reading *DOS For Dummies* by Dan Gookin (IDG Books Worldwide) is a good way to feel less confused. (Of course, so may hitting yourself on the head with a steel pipe, but reading *DOS For Dummies* won't hurt you.)

Opening or closing a catalog

To open a catalog you already created, follow these steps:

1. **Make sure that you're in the disk directory you want.**

   The current directory is shown at the top of the Navigator window.

2. **Click once on the Catalogs icon at the lower-left corner of the Navigator window.**

   The right side of the Navigator window now displays only catalog files in the current directory.

3. **Double-click on the icon for the catalog you want to open.**

   The Catalog window opens on your screen, with the catalog you selected as the current catalog.

To close a catalog, simply close the Catalog window. You can do that in the usual ways — by pressing Ctrl+F4 (hold down Ctrl and press F4) or by double-clicking on the Window Control button.

Adding something to a catalog

When you create a new table — or any other database item, such as a report — it goes into a catalog only if you remembered to *open* the catalog before you created it. What can you do if you forget to open the catalog you want and you have something sitting out on your hard disk that *should* be in the catalog, but *isn't?*

There are really two things to do. First, take comfort in the words of Roman Emperor Marcus Aurelius: "Tomorrow, you might die." Aurelius was no fun at parties, except when he did the lampshade-on-the-head trick, but he did have a way of putting things into perspective, especially about database problems.

Second, you can easily *add* a table or other database file to a catalog, even after you've created it. To add something to a catalog, follow these steps:

1. **Open the catalog to which you want to add something.**

2. **Click on Catalog in the menu bar to open the Catalog menu.**

3. **Select Add Item from the Catalog menu.**

    The Add Catalog File Item dialog box appears.

4. **In the dialog box, select the file you want to add to the catalog.**

5. **Click on the OK button.**

    The Add Item to Open Catalog dialog box appears.

6. **In the dialog box, type a description of the thing you're adding.**

7. **Click on the OK button.**

    You're done! The new item appears in the Catalog window.

The shortcut key for adding something to a catalog is Ctrl+A. If you want to bypass the Catalog menu, just hold down Ctrl and press A. Then follow Steps 4 through 7 in the preceding list.

Deleting something from a catalog

Deleting something from a catalog is even easier than adding something to a catalog. In the Catalog window, just click on the icon for the item you want to delete. Then press the Delete key on your keyboard. A dialog box appears, asking you to confirm that you want to delete the item from the catalog. If you're sure, just click on OK. It's done!

If you prefer, you can delete an item by clicking on it with the mouse to highlight it and then opening the Edit menu and selecting Delete.

Basic Steps for Creating a Table

After you know what fields you need in your table, it's time to begin creating your table in dBASE. Before you get into the specific, hands-on part of creating a table, you should know the basic steps in creating any dBASE table:

1. **Decide what fields you need.**

2. **In dBASE, create or open a catalog in which the table will be included.**

   This step is not absolutely necessary, but is highly advisable. If you don't open a catalog before creating a table, then dBASE won't keep track of which other database files your table goes with.

3. **In the left side of the Catalog window, double-click on the icon marked Tables.**

   The Table Structure window appears.

4. **In the Table Structure window, enter each field's name, data type, and width. If you're often going to be searching for data in the field, make it indexed.**

   In the index, *ascending* means in A..Z order, and *descending* means in Z..A order.

5. **Finally, save the table design and exit from the Table Structure window.**

   The new table will be visible in the Catalog or Navigator window.

Rules for dBASE Field Names

Earlier in this chapter, you worked out a table design by using descriptive names for its fields (Account Number, and so on). However, when you actually create the table in dBASE, you can't use just any old names for its fields. When you assign a field name in dBASE, you must follow these rules:

1. The field name cannot be more than ten characters long.

2. Only letters, digits (0 to 9), and underscores (_) are allowed.

3. The field name must begin with a letter.

4. Field names in dBASE are not *case sensitive.* In other words, uppercase or lowercase doesn't matter. FNAME is the same as fname is the same as fNAME.

Thus, *CUST_ID* is all right as a field name, but *CUST-ID* is illegal because it has a hyphen (rule 2). *Account Number* is illegal as a field name because it has a space (rule 2) and it's too long (rule 1). *2LiveCrew* is illegal as a field name because it doesn't begin with a letter (rule 3) and lacks talent (rule 5). Oops, there *is* no rule 5; forget that last part.

Because of these rules, you usually have to make some modifications in the field names you start out with. *Account Number* can be changed to *CUST_ID*, *First Name* can be changed to *FNAME*, and so on.

What the Heck Is a Data Type?

Each field in a dBASE table has a *data type* that you must specify when you set up the table. Why do you need to go to all that trouble? The reason is simple: The data type tells dBASE how to treat the field's data. For example, when you select Numeric as the data type, dBASE knows that it can do mathematical operations with the data in that field — something it can't do if you select Character (text) as the field type. In dBASE, you can specify any of the following data types:

- ✓ *Character* is the data type used for plain text. Sometimes, you may also want to use it for numbers when you don't need to perform any calculations with the numbers. For example, you *could* add up all the telephone numbers or zip codes of bookstore customers, but why would you want to? Put numbers like these in a text field. (If you put numbers in a Character field, you need to pad the numbers with zeroes so that they'll end up in the correct order if you ever sort them to put them in numerical order. See Chapter 15 for an explanation of how to do this.)

- ✓ *Numeric* is the data type used when you need to perform mathematical operations on the data and the data is all whole numbers (1, 5, 181, and so on). You can use a field like this to keep track of how many orders a customer places, for example.

- ✓ *Memo* data type is for free-form text. Most dBASE fields hold a specific amount of information, but a memo field can hold up to 32,000 characters — about eight typed, single-spaced pages of text. You might use a field like this to keep miscellaneous notes about each customer: family birthdays, book preferences, or a log of telephone calls. (In fact, you will add a memo field to the sample Customers table when you get to Chapter 10.)

- ✓ *Logical* data types are for keeping track of yes/no situations, such as "Is this customer's payment overdue?"

- ✓ *Date* data type is — oh, all right — a Date field is for holding dates and times, such as the date of a customer's last order.

- ✓ *Float* data type is used for numbers with decimal points, such as dollar amounts.

One drawback of computerized database management — even with dBASE — is that once they've been created, fields are limited to a specific size. You can't have one record with a 10-character First Name field and another record with a 1,000-character First Name field. (You can *change* the size of the field, as you learn in a later chapter, but then the fields are limited to the *new* size.) The exception is when you use a memo field. A memo field is stored in a special way that lets it hold a variable amount of data.

Hands-On: Creating the Custdata Table

In this section, you actually create a dBASE table to hold customer records for the Caveat Emptor bookstore. The table will be called *Custdata.* There are two reasons for the name: first, the table holds customer data; and second, the dBASE software comes with a table called *Customer,* which means that Borland already took the best name for our table.

This exercise assumes that you've already created the *Caveat* catalog as described in Chapter 2. However, if you didn't, you can still follow the steps, even though you should create the catalog first. To create the new table, follow these steps:

1. **Start dBASE by double-clicking on the dBASE icon in the Windows Program Manager.**

2. **Make sure that you're in the disk directory you want.**

   The current directory is shown at the top of the Navigator window.

3. **Click once on the Catalogs icon at the bottom-left corner of the Navigator window.**

   dBASE displays the catalogs available in the current disk directory.

4. **In the Navigator window, double-click on the catalog icon labeled Caveat.**

   The Catalog window opens with *Caveat* as the current catalog.

5. **In the left side of the Catalog window, double-click on the Tables icon.**

   The Table Structure window opens, as shown in Figure 4-1.

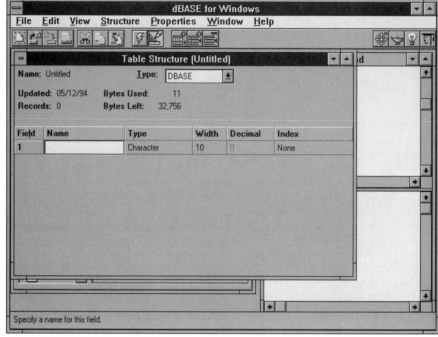

Figure 4-1:
The Table
Structure
window.
This is
where you
define the
fields for a
table.

Creating the table's fields

For each field in the table, you need to specify a field name, data type, width, and whether the field is indexed. Unlike the name of a catalog, which can't be more than eight characters long, field names can be up to ten characters long. The only characters allowed for field names are letters, digits, and underscores.

To specify the first field of the sample table, type **cust_id** in the first column of the first line, making sure you include the underscore between **cust** and **id**, because spaces aren't allowed in field names. Then press Tab. dBASE creates a field named *CUST_ID*. As soon as you press Tab, the second column seems to come to life. The word *Character* appears, along with a little button at the right side of the blank.

The little down-arrow button is called a *list-box button*. If you click on it, dBASE displays a list from which you can select the field's data type. Anytime you see a little button like this at the right side of a blank, its purpose is for opening a list box.

Click on the button at the right side of the blank. dBASE shows you a list of the data types you can assign to a field. In this case, you want to use the type dBASE already picked — Character. Simply click on the button again to close the list. If you accidentally selected another type, just open the list again and click on Character.

The whys of data types

If you have an inquiring mind, you may wonder why CUST_ID is a character-type field even though the field holds account numbers. You may also wonder whether a statue of Elvis is really on Mars. This book doesn't cover Mars or the Elvis question, but CUST_ID is a character field because account numbers aren't arithmetical. Normally, you specify a numeric data type for a field only if you're going to add, subtract, or perform other arithmetic operations with the numbers that the field contains.

There's no law saying that you can't make CUST_ID a numeric field, and there are some advantages to doing so (see Chapter 15). But there are also advantages in making it a character field; plus, it's traditional, and you know how popular "traditional values" are these days.

Now press Tab again. The cursor moves to the Width column. Press Delete to delete the 10 and type **5** for the width. (If the number 10 is highlighted in reverse video, you can simply type **5**, and dBASE automatically deletes the old value.)

You may wonder why I told you to call the field *CUST_ID* instead of *Account Number*. The reason is that *CUST_ID* is shorter and fits more easily when the data is displayed in a row-and-column table.

Telling dBASE if the field should be indexed

The last column of the Table Structure window tells dBASE if you want the field indexed. The first thing to know about this column is that you *don't* need to know much about it for now. The second thing to know (if you're one of those type-A overachievers who can't relax for a single second) is that when you index a field, it helps dBASE keep your records in order and find stuff faster. If you had a large customer database, you'd want to index the field.

Go ahead and open the list box, just as you did in the Data Type column. In the list, click on Ascend as the index type.

Adding another field

Now add a second field to the sample table. Press Tab; the cursor automatically moves down to the first column of the second row. Type **FNAME** in the first column. Press Tab to move to the Type column.

For this record, accept the suggested data type — Character. You don't need to open the list box this time. Press Tab until dBASE moves the cursor down to the first column of the next line.

Defining the rest of the fields

After you're in the first column of the next line, dBASE is ready for you to enter data for another field. Define the rest of the fields in your sample table as follows:

Name	Type	Width	Indexed
LNAME	Character	15	None
MRMS	Character	5	None
SALUTATION	Character	15	None
ADDRESS	Character	25	None
CITY	Character	15	None
STATE	Character	5	None
ZIP	Character	10	None

Remember that you should use the Number data type only when you will be performing mathematical operations on the data in the field. That's why the ZIP field, like the CUST_ID field, is a Character data type, even though it contains numbers. Another advantage to making the Zip field a Character data type is that you can use it for customers who live in countries that use letters in their postal codes, such as Canada

Saving the Table Design

After you define all your fields, you have just one more thing to do — but it's a biggie. You need to save your table design.

To save the table design, click on File in the menu bar at the top left of the screen and select Save from the menu. The Save Table dialog box appears, as shown in Figure 4-2.

If you prefer to bypass the menu when you're saving the table structure, you can press Ctrl+S, the shortcut key for saving a design (or anything else).

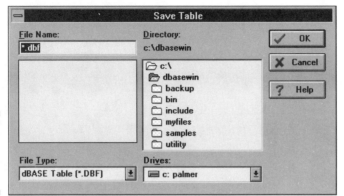

Figure 4-2:
The Save
Table
dialog box.

Type **Custdata** in the File Name blank. Then click on the OK button at the right side of the dialog box.

Just as a catalog is a file on your PC's hard disk, a table is a file on your PC's hard disk. Therefore, a table name has the same MS-DOS restrictions as a catalog name: letters, digits, underscores, and a few special characters, but no commas, periods, or spaces, with a maximum of eight letters and no differentiation between uppercase and lowercase.

Now, dBASE asks you for a description of the table. In the dialog box, enter **Bookstore customer records** and then click on OK.

That's it! You've defined your first database table in dBASE. Close the Table Structure window by double-clicking on the Window Control button in the top left corner of the window. Be sure that you double-click on the button for the Table Structure window, not for the dBASE main window.

When the Table Structure window closes, you see the Catalog window again. Now, however, the Customer table is listed in the window.

If you want to take a break, shut down dBASE and put on your roller blades. Unless you have no sense of balance, in which case roller blades would be dangerous, so you might try rock-climbing instead. On second thought, why not just have a cup of coffee and watch the news?

Chapter 5

Putting Data in Your Table

· ·

In This Chapter

▶ Opening the Table Editor window

▶ Entering customer data

▶ Editing records and fixing mistakes

▶ Moving around in the Browse window

· ·

*1*f you've been reading the chapters of this book in sequence, you've already seen how to plan a database, design a table, and set up the table's fields. What you *haven't* seen is how to put data in the table. (You also haven't seen the pile of candy bar wrappers that have accumulated under your boss's desk in the last 15 years, but that's another story.)

What you need to do now is to put some customer data into your table. It's not hard — in fact, compared to entering data in old-style database managers, it's incredibly easy. You do, however, need to pick up a few tricks along the way. In this chapter, therefore, you learn exactly how to enter data into a table. The example Caveat Emptor Bookstore database helps illustrate the steps you need to take.

Before you can put data in a table, you need to

✔ Know your way around dBASE (Chapter 3).

✔ Create the table (Chapter 4).

You *should* also have created a catalog (Chapter 2) and put the table in the catalog (Chapter 4).

To follow along with the book's example database, you need to have already

✔ Created the Caveat catalog (Chapter 2) and the Customer table (Chapter 4).

✔ Changed the current directory to the main dBASE directory (Chapter 4).

If you're putting data into your own real-life table, just read this chapter to get the basic ideas. Then follow the steps using your own table instead of the one in the book.

Preparing to Add Data to a Table

First, you need to start dBASE and then open the Caveat catalog by following these steps:

1. Click the Catalogs icon at the lower left corner of the File Viewer window.

The right side of the File Viewer window now shows the available catalogs in the current disk directory.

2. Double-click the icon for the Caveat catalog.

The Catalog window opens on your screen, with the Caveat catalog selected.

3. Click the Maximize button at the top right corner of the window to make the Catalog window fill the screen.

In the Catalog window, you should now see an icon for the Customer table.

4. Right-click (click with the right mouse button) the Customer table icon.

The SpeedMenu appears, as shown in Figure 5-1.

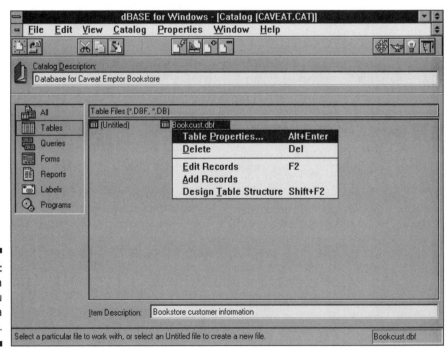

Figure 5-1:
Using a
SpeedMenu
to add data
to a table.

If the Customer table icon doesn't appear in the Catalog window, you probably just forgot to open the Caveat catalog before creating the table. No problem! Just open the Catalog menu and choose Add Item, or press Ctrl+A, the Add Item shortcut key. Then, in the Add Catalog File Item dialog box that appears, double-click on the Customer table. That adds the table to the Caveat catalog. (For more detailed instructions on adding an item to a catalog, see Chapter 4.)

Using the dBASE SpeedMenus

You can access a SpeedMenu by clicking, with the right mouse button, on the icons for all different kinds of dBASE files. The choices available on a SpeedMenu depend on the type of file involved. Notice that the shortcut key for most menu choices is listed at the right side of the SpeedMenu. In this example, you clicked the icon for a table, so you have the following menu choices:

Table Properties: This command enables you to enter or change your description for the table as well as see its current size and location on your disk. *Shortcut key:* Alt+Enter.

Delete Selected Item: Choosing this command enables you to delete the item you clicked. *Shortcut key:* Delete.

Edit Records: If you've already entered data in your table, this command enables you to change it. For example, if you added some terrible, awful things about one recalcitrant customer who absolutely *refused* to buy a first-edition copy of *Serious Journalism* by Geraldo Rivera, well, you just may want to change those hasty comments to nicer ones lest the customer somehow learns of them and has *you* investigated by Geraldo. *Shortcut key:* the F2 function key.

Add Records: This command enables you to add data to your table. (You'll use this in a sec.) *Shortcut key:* none.

Design Table Structure: This command enables you to change the structure of the table — that is, you can use this command to change what information the table contains. (You learned how to define a table structure in Chapter 4.) *Shortcut key:* Shift+F2.

Later, if you want to see how the SpeedMenus affect other types of files, you can change the current directory to DBASEWIN\SAMPLES. Then you can right-click sample files for tables, forms, reports, queries, and other dBASE objects to open SpeedMenus for each type. Of course, if you work through this entire book, you eventually create all these different file types yourself, and the SpeedMenus work on these newly created files, too.

Form, Browse, and Columnar Layouts

The point of this chapter, after all, is to learn how to add records to a table, so after you open the SpeedMenu, choose <u>A</u>dd Records. (You can do so either by clicking the menu choice or by pressing the key for the underlined letter — in this case, *A*.) After you choose the command, the Table Records window appears, as shown in Figure 5-2.

Figure 5-2:
The Table
Records
window,
showing an
empty
record
displayed in
Form Layout.

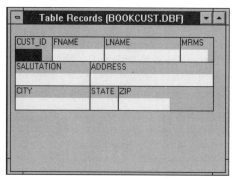

The way the Table Records window looks after it first opens is called *Form Layout.* Form Layout is one of three layouts you can use to enter or edit records in a table. These three choices are as follows:

- ✓ *Form Layout*, in which dBASE displays all the *fields* (slots for data items) contained in one record.

- ✓ *Browse Layout*, in which dBASE can display multiple records in a row-and-column format, as shown in Figure 5-3. (There are no records shown in the figure because no records have yet been added to the sample table.)

- ✓ *Columnar Layout*, which is very similar to Form Layout, except that the fields are displayed in a single column down the left side of the window, as shown in Figure 5-4.

Figure 5-3:
Browse
Layout
displays
multiple
records in
row-and-
column
format.

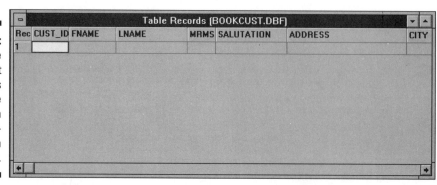

Figure 5-4:
Columnar
Layout
displays all
fields of a
single
record in a
column
down the
left side of
the window.

You can switch from one layout to another by opening the View menu and choosing Browse Layout, Form Layout, or Columnar Layout.

You can switch between Form Layout and Browse Layout by pressing F2. In this case, the key works as a *toggle,* like a light switch. If you start in Form Layout and press the key once, you switch to Browse Layout. Press it again, and you switch back to Form Layout. Press it one more time, and you're back in Browse Layout. Unfortunately, the F2 toggle works to switch you only between Browse Layout and Form Layout. To switch to Columnar Layout, you must do so through the View menu.

Using the Browse Layout

In this chapter, you enter data by using the Browse Layout window, so switch to it if you aren't there already. Then click the Table Records window's Maximize button to make the window fill the screen. Your screen should now look something like that shown in Figure 5-5.

Across the top of the window, just under the SpeedBar, you can see a field name at the top of each column. The box under the field name CUST_ID is highlighted because that's the first place dBASE puts anything you type. Along the top border of the window, dBASE displays the name of the current table.

The other major item to notice is the group of buttons on the right side of the SpeedBar. If they look to you like the forward and reverse buttons on a tape player, it's no accident. After you enter some records, these buttons enable you to move forward and backward through your table while it's displayed in the Table Records window. These buttons and their functions are shown in Figure 5-6. They work exactly the same, whether you're using Browse, Form, or Columnar Layout.

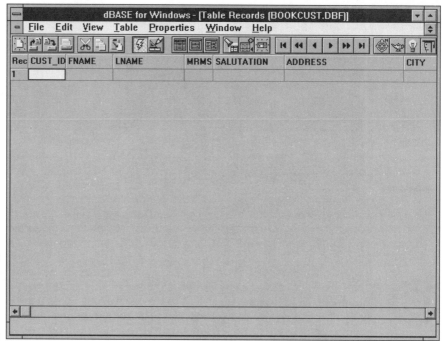

Figure 5-5:
Preparing to
enter data in
a table.

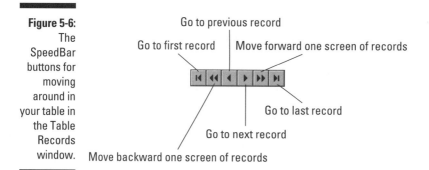

Figure 5-6:
The
SpeedBar
buttons for
moving
around in
your table in
the Table
Records
window.

Entering Customer Data

The best way to learn how to enter data is simply by doing it. This section, therefore, walks you through the steps of entering data into the Caveat database.

In Browse Layout, the intersection of a column and a row is called a *cell,* just like in a spreadsheet program such as Quattro Pro or Lotus 1-2-3.

Basic steps for entering data

The basic procedure for entering data in the Browse Layout is simple. Just follow these steps:

1. **Type the data you want in the first column of the first row.**

2. **Press Tab.**

   dBASE moves you to the next column on the same row.

3. **Type the data for that column and press Tab again.**

4. **After you reach the end of the row, just press Tab again.**

   dBASE automatically moves you down to the first column of the next line.

5. **After you finish entering your data, close the Table Records window in the usual way.**

   dBASE automatically saves everything you typed.

To move to the next row without entering data for all the columns in the current row, just press the down-arrow key on your keyboard. You can use the arrow keys or the mouse to move up or down in Browse Layout any time you want.

Hands on: entering data in the Customer table

Right now, the highlight is in the Cust_ID column. Because this is the first customer record, type in **00001** for the customer ID.

Notice that as soon as you finish typing **00001**, dBASE beeps and moves you to the next column (that is, the next field). That's because you typed five digits, which filled up the CUST_ID field. (Remember that in Chapter 4, you gave this field a width of 5.) Now, in the FNAME field, type **James** and press Tab. Voila! — dBASE automatically moves you to the next field.

Padding numbers

If you're wondering why I told you to enter the leading zeros, it's because dBASE needs them to put the customer account numbers in the correct order. Because CUST_ID is a character field instead of a numeric field, simply entering the numbers as 1, 2, 3, and so on, would mean that if it sorted the records by CUST_ID, dBASE would put 10 before 2, 21 before 3, and so on because 1 (the first character in 10) comes before 2, and so on. (For a complete explanation, see Chapter 15.)

Every time you *finish* entering a record — that is, after you complete a row in the Browse Layout and move to the next row — dBASE saves that record to your PC's hard disk. That way, even if the electricity goes off and your computer shuts down, the only data you can lose is the data you're currently entering in the record.

Go ahead and enter the rest of the data for this record. (If you make any mistakes typing, don't worry about them right now. You learn how to correct mistakes a little later.) To enter the last name, type **West** and press Tab. For MRMS, type **Prof.**; and for the salutation, type **Jimbo**.

To complete the sample record, enter the following data: For the address, type **Mythic University**; for the city, type **Martinsville;** for the state, type **CA;** and for the ZIP code, type **98035.**

What's the focus?

Whenever you click the mouse or press a key, dBASE sends the result of your action to the place on the screen that has the *focus*. This concept sounds pretty technical, but it's actually very simple in practice. Usually, the place with the focus is highlighted or contains a blinking cursor. In this example, the focus is in the current cell of the Browse Layout. If you start typing, dBASE places your text in that cell.

After you pressed Tab after typing **Mythic University**, the window automatically "moved to the right" across the Browse Layout, bringing the next column (ADDRESS) into view. Whenever you move past the edge of the current screen, dBASE automatically moves the window so that you can see more of the Browse Layout. The same thing happens if you fill up more rows than can fit on the screen: The Table Editor window moves down when you want to see additional rows beyond the bottom of the screen.

After you type the ZIP code and press Tab, dBASE automatically moves you down to the next line. Sometimes, depending on the circumstances, it also displays a dialog box asking if you want to add records. If that happens, just click Yes. Either way, dBASE moves you down to the first column in the next row of the Browse Layout, where you can enter the next record. You also see the same dialog box if you're using Form or Columnar Layout.

This table actually contains 15 records, which are listed in Appendix A. You can enter as many or as few as you want, but for now, just enter the four additional ones listed here. In a later chapter, you change the structure of this database, which requires a little extra typing to change any records you've already entered.

You must pad out the CUST_ID numbers with zeroes. Otherwise, dBASE gets mixed up if you ever want to sort your records by CUST_ID numbers.

To continue building the Customer table, enter the following four records. A couple of the records have deliberate mistakes in them, so don't worry about them.

CUST_ID	00002
FNAME:	Harriet
LNAME:	Smith
MRMS:	Ms.
SALUTATION:	Ms. Stowe
ADDRESS:	14 Parakeet Lane
CITY:	New York
STATE:	NY
ZIP:	10087

CUST_ID   00003

FNAME: Jules

LNAME: Twombly

MRMS: Mr.

SALUTATION: Jules

ADDRESS: The AB Hotel

CITY: Las Vegas

STATE: NV

ZIP: 34567

CUST_ID   00004

FNAME: Arnold

LNAME: Harris

MRMS: Mr.

SALUTATION: Arnie

ADDRESS: 101 Fifth Avenue

CITY: Boise

STATE: ID

ZIP: 23413

CUST_ID   00005

FNAME: Teri

LNAME: Lane

MRMS:	Ms.
SALUTATION:	Ms. Lane
ADDRESS:	5678 15th St., #5-A
CITY:	Santa Barbara
STATE:	CA
ZIP:	93101

After you finish entering the last record, your screen should now look like the one shown in Figure 5-7 — only bigger. (Don't sweat any minor differences.)

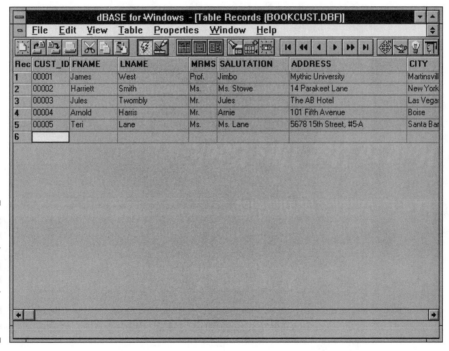

Figure 5-7:
The Customer table in Browse Layout after entering five records.

Moving around in the Browse Layout

In your sample Browse Layout, try experimenting a bit with moving around in your Browse Layout. (Refer to Figure 5-6 if you need help with any of the SpeedBar buttons.) For example, try to perform the following tasks:

✔ Move to the first record by clicking the First Record button at the left end of the SpeedBar.

✔ Move to the last record by clicking the Last Record button.

✔ Move to the fourth record by clicking the Previous Record button. Notice that the record number (displayed in the bottom left corner of the screen) changes.

✔ Move to record number three by pressing the up-arrow key.

✔ Move to the FNAME column by pressing Tab.

✔ Move to the ZIP column by pressing Ctrl+End. (Hold down the Ctrl key and press the End key.)

✔ Move to the Cust_ID column by pressing Ctrl+Home.

✔ Move to the LNAME column by clicking in it with the mouse.

Table 5-1 summarizes the tricks for moving around the Table Editor window.

Table 5-1	How to Move around in the Table Editor Window
To Move to This Position	**Do This**
First record in table	Click the First Record button at the left end of the SpeedBar.
Last record in table	Click the Last Record button.
First column in table	Press Ctrl+Home.
Last column in table	Press Ctrl+End.
Next column to the right	Press Tab or Enter.
Next column to the left	Press Shift+Tab. (Hold down the Shift key and press Tab.)
Up a row	Press the up-arrow key.
Down a row	Press the down-arrow key.
Up 26 rows	Press the PgUp key.
Down 26 rows	Press the PgDn key.
First record	Press Ctrl+PgUp. (Hold down the Ctrl key and press the PgUp key.)
Last record	Press Ctrl+PgDn. (Hold down the Ctrl key and press the PgDn key.)

In database and spreadsheet jargon, the little box formed by the intersection of a row and a column is called a *cell*.

And *that* brings us to the very important topic of editing data in a table. To prepare for the next section, move to the top left corner of the Browse Layout. Then sit up straight (remember: poor posture is a leading cause of computer backaches!) and get ready for some fun.

If you were using some other database packages, this would be the point at which you'd need to save your work. But in dBASE, you don't need to worry: It's already been done for you!

Editing Data and Fixing Mistakes

As occasionally happens, you made a couple mistakes as you entered the data in your sample table, so now you need to correct them. (Oh, all right, *you* entered everything just as you were supposed to, but the Big Boss is going to get mad at somebody about the errors, so I'm putting the blame on you. After all, I can't really afford to lose this job; I've got two cats and five credit cards to support. You understand. Don't you?)

Replacing text completely

In the second record of the sample table, Harriett's last name should be *Stowe*, not *Smith*. You know Harriet: she wrote the book *Uncle Tom's Cabin.* To avoid getting a stern letter from her agent, correct it by following these steps:

1. **Using the mouse, click in the LNAME column of Harriet Stowe's row.**

   The cursor moves to the LNAME cell with the word *Smith*.

2. **Tap the Home key to move the cursor to the beginning of the cell.**

   The cursor should now be to the left of the *S* in *Smith*.

3. **Press Ctrl+Shift+right arrow. (Hold down Ctrl and Shift at the same time and press the right-arrow key).**

   dBASE highlights the entire name.

4. **Type Stowe.**

   The new text automatically replaces the highlighted cell contents.

Editing text without replacing it

If you want to edit the data in a cell without replacing it completely, you can do so in either of two ways. You can either click in the cell with the mouse, or use the arrow and Tab keys to move to the cell. As soon as you're in the cell, just type and delete as needed. As always, dBASE saves the changes you make as soon as you move out of the current row in the Browse Layout.

To see how the editing process works, suppose that the address you entered for Jules Twombly in the third record is wrong. He doesn't actually live at the AB Hotel in Las Vegas — that's a nice enough hotel, of course, but it's said to be frequented by gangsters, computer book writers, and Wayne Newton impersonators. Instead, Jules lives at the ABC Hotel, a $2,500-a-night joint on the Las Vegas Strip.

To edit the Address cell, follow these steps:

1. **Press the down-arrow key once.**

   Notice that dBASE saves the new version of Harriet Stowe's record.

2. **Press Tab three times.**

   The cursor moves to the ADDRESS cell.

3. **Press the right-arrow key six times.**

   The cursor should be just to the right of the *B* in *AB*.

4. **Type** C **and then press the down-arrow key once.**

   The highlight moves down to the next row, and dBASE saves the changed version of Jules' record.

Editing keys in dBASE

What? Edit *keys*? How do you do that?

No, wait. You misunderstand. I don't mean that you actually *edit* keys in dBASE — I mean that dBASE provides you with editing *keys*. You can use these keys to edit text and other data in Browse Layout cells.

After you open a cell for editing, you can move around the cell and edit its contents by using any of the key combinations listed in Table 5-2.

Table 5-2	dBASE Editing Keys
To Do This	*Press These Keys*
Delete data in a field	Ctrl+Shift+right arrow to highlight the data; then type new data or press Del
Move to the beginning of a field	Home
Move to the end of a field	End
Move left one space	Left arrow
Move right one space	Right arrow
Move right one word	Ctrl+right arrow (hold down the Ctrl key and press the right-arrow key)
Move left one word	Ctrl+left arrow
Copy highlighted data to the Windows Clipboard	Ctrl+Insert
Paste data from the Windows Clipboard to the current cell	Shift+Insert
Undo the last editing change	Alt+Backspace (or choose Undo from the Edit menu)

Along with these keys or key combinations, dBASE provides a few other editing keys that apply to special situations. You get the chance to use those later in the book.

Closing the Customer Table

Now that you're finished entering and editing your customer data, you can close the table and take a break. To close the table, simply double-click the Window Control button at the top left of the table's window. (Make sure *not* to click the dBASE main window button unless you want to close dBASE, too!) If you're not yet a proficient double-clicker, you can also close the window by clicking the Window Control button once and then choosing Close from the Control menu.

If you have trouble double-clicking the mouse quickly enough, you may want to reconfigure Windows to enable you to double-click it more slowly. You can do this by opening the Windows Control Panel (that's in the Main program group) and selecting the Mouse icon. For full details about this procedure, see *Windows For Dummies* (IDG Books Worldwide).

Chapter 6

Looking at Your Data

· ·

In This Chapter

▶ Jazzing up the Browse window

▶ Changing column headings

▶ Changing column widths

▶ Moving columns

▶ Moving around in the Browse window

· ·

*C*reating catalogs and tables, entering and editing data, and bungee jumping are all fine ways to spend a few hours. But at some point, you've got to be able to *see* the data in your database. Otherwise, it does you about as much good as an accordion in a rap group. In this chapter, you learn to change a table's Browse window so that you can see everything you need at a glance.

Before you can change how your records are displayed in the Browse window, you need to have done the following:

   ✔ Created a table (Chapter 4) and put some data in it (Chapter 5)

   ✔ Learned how to display and edit your data in the Browse window (Chapter 5)

   ✔ Learned the basics of moving around in the Browse window (Chapter 5)

If you're looking at data with a Browse window in your own real-life database, just read this chapter to get the basic ideas. Then follow the steps with your own database instead of the one in this book.

Changing the Look of Your Browse Window

If you want to make your Browse window easier to read — or you just don't like the way it looks — you can easily do a Browse window makeover. You can change the width of columns, make rows taller or shorter, and even change the order of columns.

To get some practice at changing your Browse window layout, open the Caveat database you created in earlier chapters. Using the right mouse button, click on the Bookcust table and, in the SpeedMenu, select Edit to display the table's Browse window, shown maximized in Figure 6-1.

You can do a number of things to improve this Browse window:

✔ Make the Browse window easier to read by changing the headings of columns to make the headings more meaningful — for example, *Cust ID* instead of *CUST_ID, First Name* instead of *FNAME,* and *MrMs* instead of the forbidding *MRMS.*

✔ Reduce the width of the several columns (CUST_ID, FNAME, LNAME, SALUTATION, and so on) that are wider than they need to be.

✔ Move the MRMS column to the left of the first and last name columns.

You can make other changes as well, but these are a good start.

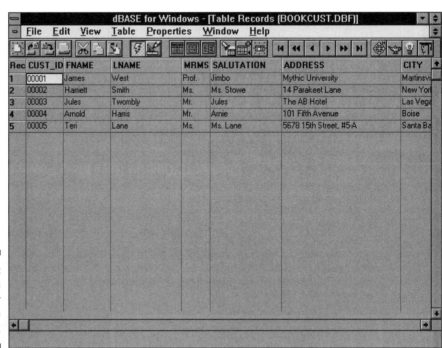

Figure 6-1:
The
Customer
Browse
window.

Changing column headings

Changing column headings in the Browse window is fairly easy. The basic steps are as follows:

1. **Open the Properties menu and select Table Records Window.**

   The Browse Inspector dialog box appears. At the right side of the dialog box there should be a list of fields in the current table. If you don't see a field list, click on the tab marked *Fields* at the bottom left corner of the dialog box.

2. **In the field list, click on the field whose column heading you want to change.**

   None of this affects the field name itself. Only the title of the column in the Browse window changes.

3. **Click on the Properties button below the field list.**

   The Field Properties dialog box appears. At the top left corner of the dialog box is a blank labeled *Heading*.

4. **In the blank, type the new text that you want for the column heading.**

5. **Click OK to close the Field Properties dialog box.**

   dBASE returns you to the Browse Inspector dialog box.

6. **Click OK to close the Browse Inspector dialog box.**

   dBASE returns you to the Browse window. The column heading for the field you selected has been changed to the new text.

Hands on: changing Bookcust table column headings

Now apply those steps to the Browse window for the Bookcust table. You're going to change the *CUST_ID* column heading to *Cust ID,* the *FNAME* heading to *First Name,* and the *LNAME* heading to *Last Name.* With the Bookcust table displayed in the Browse window, follow these steps:

1. **Open the Properties menu and select Table Records Window.**

   The Browse Inspector dialog box appears, as shown in Figure 6-2. If your screen doesn't look like the figure, click on the Fields tab at the lower left corner of the dialog box.

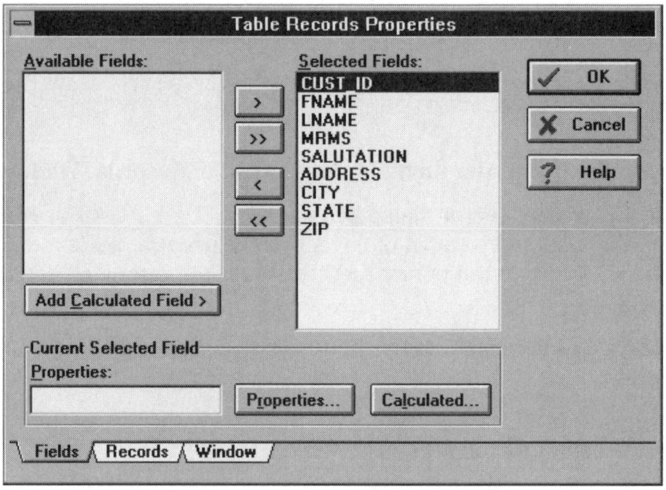

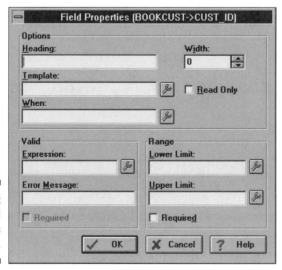

Figure 6-2:
The Browse
Inspector
dialog box.

2. **Make sure that the CUST_ID field is highlighted in the field list.**

   If the CUST_ID field isn't highlighted, click on it with the mouse.

3. **Click on the Options button underneath the field list.**

   The Field Properties dialog box appears, as shown in Figure 6-3.

Figure 6-3:
The Field
Properties
dialog box.

4. In the Heading blank, type Cust ID.

5. Click on OK.

dBASE returns you to the Browse Inspector dialog box.

6. Click on OK again.

dBASE returns you to the Browse window. The column heading for the CUST_ID field has been changed to *Cust ID*.

Use the same method to change the column headings for the *FNAME* column (to First Name), the *LNAME* column (to Last Name), and the MRMS column (to MrMs).

Changing Column Widths

You can change a column's width in two ways. The first is quick and easy but not very precise, and the second is precise but involves a couple more steps.

Changing column widths using the mouse

The first method is simply to drag a column's right border with the mouse. To do this, move the mouse onto one of the vertical lines that separate the columns. Notice that the mouse pointer changes into a double-headed left-and-right arrow, which means that you can drag a column border to resize the column.

To try this method out, do the following:

1. Position the cursor on the vertical line that serves as the right border of the Cust ID column.

Notice that the mouse cursor changes into a double-headed left-and-right arrow.

2. Hold down the left mouse button and slowly roll the mouse to the left.

As you do, the column border moves to the left, causing the column to become narrower. Stop when the mouse cursor almost touches the *D* in *Cust ID*.

3. Release the left mouse button.

The column has narrowed to fit the caption and the data.

You can use this same method to widen a column, the only difference being that you drag the border to the right instead of to the left.

This method is easy and straightforward. The problem is that it's very hard to get exact column widths.

The column width in the Browse window has no effect on the field length in the table. Making a column narrower doesn't reduce the amount of data you can put in a field, and making it wider doesn't increase the amount of data you can enter. The only reason to change column widths (and row heights) is to make the Browse window easier to read.

Changing column widths with more precision

To change a column to a precise width, you need to use the Browse Inspector dialog box. This dialog box allows you to enter a numeric width for the column — for example, if you want the First Name column to be *precisely* ten characters wide, no more, no less. (Of course, if you're that obsessive about everything, maybe you should relax for a while and watch *American Gladiators* on TV — or maybe not.) The basic steps are as follows:

1. **In the Browse window, open the Properties menu and select Table Records Window.**

   The Browse Inspector dialog box appears. There should be a field list at the right side of the dialog box. If not, click on the Fields tab at the lower left corner of the dialog box.

2. **Make sure that the field you want is highlighted in the field list.**

   If the field isn't highlighted, click on it with the mouse.

3. **Click on the Options button underneath the field list.**

   The Field Properties dialog box appears.

4. **In the Width blank, enter the column width that you want.**

5. **Click on OK.**

   dBASE returns you to the Browse Inspector dialog box.

6. **Click on OK again.**

   dBASE returns you to the Browse window. The column width has been changed to precisely the width that you selected.

Now, apply those steps to narrow the columns for FNAME, LNAME, SALUTA-TION, ADDRESS, CITY, and ZIP fields, all of which are wider than they need to be. Just experiment until you find the widths you like best.

When you changed the width of the column for the FNAME field, were you surprised that it wasn't listed as *First Name,* which you entered as a column heading in the previous section of this chapter? Remember that when you change a field's column heading, it affects only the column heading in the Browse window and has no effect on the field name itself.

If you've narrowed the columns, you should now be able to see more of the data from your sample Browse window on-screen. The ADDRESS, CITY, and STATE columns are all there. Only the ZIP column might still be cut off by the right edge of the screen. If so, use either of the two methods you just learned to make the STATE field narrower so that all the columns will be visible on-screen.

 Because changing column widths in the Browse window doesn't affect the underlying table, you can make the columns narrower than the data that's in them. For instance, in this book's example table, Teri Lane's address is pretty long. If you narrowed the ADDRESS column much, you couldn't see all of her address. However, the whole address would still be in the table — so you can print it, view it in Form Layout view, or widen the column again to make the whole address visible.

Because it's so easy to narrow and widen columns in the Browse window, you can do whatever suits your fancy at the moment. If you come back after lunch and don't like the new width, you can change column back to the way it was. (Which, of course, you *can't* do with your waistline after that pig-out lunch you just had at the pizza place. As database guru E.F. Codd sagely observed, "Once on the lips, forever on the hips.")

Widening a column

You can widen a column with the same methods that you use to narrow a column: drag the right border or use the Column Width dialog box.

In the Browse window for this book's example table, try narrowing the AD-DRESS column until it's too narrow to show all of Teri Lane's address. Then widen it again, using any method you like. You'll see that Teri's address is still there, in all its pristine glory.

Moving Columns

You may want to make one other change to the sample Browse window layout. (Or you may not, but this is America, and database diversity, like your MTV, is guaranteed by the Constitution.) The MrMs column may work better placed to the left of the First Name column.

Just as resizing columns (and rows) has no effect on the size of the fields in the underlying table, moving columns has no effect on the order of fields in the table. Moving a column only changes the placement of the column in the Browse window.

To move a column, move the mouse pointer onto the title cell at the top of the column until the cursor changes into a grasping hand. (Well, actually just a picture of a grasping hand; this isn't an Edgar Allen Poe story.) Then hold down the left mouse button.

Still holding down the left mouse button, drag the mouse slowly in the direction you want to move the column (left or right). As you do so, you'll see the column you're dragging move with the mouse pointer across the Browse window. When the column is finally where you want it to be, release the mouse button.

That may sound a little confusing, but once you see how the process works, it's not. Try it yourself by moving the MrMs column in the sample Browse window to the left of the First Name column, as shown in Figure 6-4.

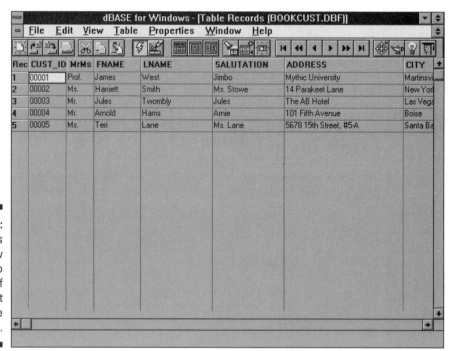

Figure 6-4:
The MrMs column now appears to the left of the First Name column.

Saving Your Changes

dBASE automatically saves changes in the layout of a Browse window when you close the window. So you're done!

If you want to take a break, shut down dBASE and plop down on the couch. There's a good rerun of *Gilligan's Island* starting right about now. Otherwise, turn the page and head for the next chapter. (The Skipper would be proud of you, little buddy.) Did I ever tell you my theory that Gilligan was alone on the island, and that all the other characters were hallucinations, each representing a different aspect of Gilligan's own tortured psyche?

Chapter 7

Get Help Whenever You Need It

● ●

In This Chapter

▶ How to use context-sensitive Help

▶ Using the Help table of contents and hypertext

▶ How to search for a Help topic

▶ How to use Interactive Tutors

● ●

*T*here's an old saying: If you teach someone how to fish, then ... no, wait, that's not it. If you give someone a fish, pack it in dry ice ... no, that's not it, either. Anyway, the point is, this book teaches you how to use the most important features of dBASE. But what if you forget something and don't have this book handy, or you used the pages of this book to wrap fish?

That's when the powerful dBASE Help System comes in handy. It enables you to *teach yourself* new skills as you need them. In dBASE, you can:

✔ Browse through Help topics at random by using the Table of Contents.

✔ Use the context-sensitive Help feature to get help with whatever you're working on at the moment.

✔ Click on Search to get help on any topic you can name.

✔ Use Interactive Tutors to get step-by-step instructions for database tasks, even as you're doing them.

✔ Use Experts and let dBASE do most of the work *for* you.

In the spirit of teaching you how to fish — or at least how to find out things for yourself — this chapter takes you step by step through the dBASE Help System. Experts are covered in separate chapters.

Getting Help in dBASE

The most obvious place to look for help is the Help menu, which is always at the upper right corner of the menu bar.

If you select Contents or press Shift+F1, dBASE displays a screen that lists all of the major topics in the Help System, as shown in Figure 7-1.

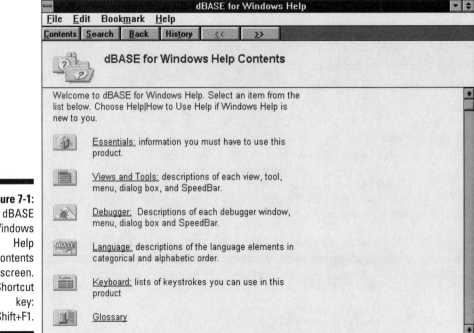

Figure 7-1:
The dBASE
for Windows
Help
Contents
screen.
Shortcut
key:
Shift+F1.

What the other Help menu choices mean

Some of the functions of the items on the Help menu are obvious. The functions of the following items may not be quite so obvious:

  ✔ Search lets you search for help on specific topics, such as data types or creating a table. See "Searching for a Topic" later in this chapter for more information.

  ✔ Views and Tools is a different kind of table of contents for the dBASE Help System (see Figure 7-2). It displays the different tools and database items that you can use in dBASE. To get help on any of them, just click on the picture or the underlined text, called *hypertext*. dBASE either shows you a list of help topics or takes you directly to a screen with help on that item.

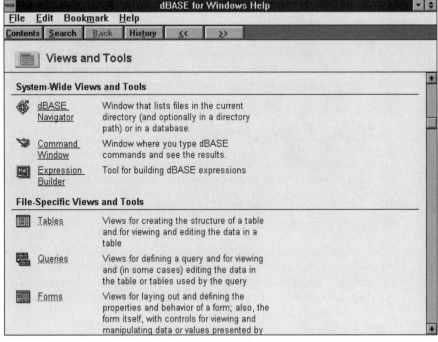

Figure 7-2:
Getting help
through the
Views and
Tools
choice on
the Help
menu.

✔ Language can help you on the dBASE programming language. If you're a real heavy-duty computer type, you can use this language to create your own database programs that run within dBASE. However, you don't need to use this language, or even know anything about it, to use dBASE.

✔ Keyboard opens a window that shows you every shortcut key you can use in dBASE. A shortcut key is actually a key combination, meaning that you hold down one key and press another. These key combinations let you bypass the menus to save time. For example, if you have a table displayed in a Browse window, you can search for an item in your table either by opening the Table menu and selecting Find Records (that takes two steps) or by pressing Ctrl+F (that's one step).

✔ Experts lets you use the various dBASE Experts. If you're not sure how to do something, and would prefer to have dBASE do most of the work *for* you, just select this menu choice to see if there's an Expert available. Experts ask you questions about what you want to do, and then the Expert does the task for you while you sit there munching on a chocolate bar and being lazy.

✔ Interactive Tutors takes you through step-by-step lessons on how to do various things in dBASE, such as designing a table or setting up a report. Like this book, the Tutors can use either its own example database or your own real-life database.

✔ <u>H</u>ow to Use Help opens a window with instructions on using the Help System. If you forget to read this chapter or leave this book at home, you can use this menu choice to find your way around.

✔ <u>A</u>bout dBASE for Windows tells you what version of dBASE for Windows you're using. It also tells you how much computer memory is free and some other techie stuff that you don't need to worry about.

Using hypertext links

Virtually every screen in the dBASE Help System has *hypertext*. No, the term doesn't refer to very, very nervous text. When you see a topic that you want to read about, you just click on the topic, and dBASE takes you directly to a Help screen about that topic. The new Help screen has more hypertext, which lets you jump to other screens, and so on.

Hypertext is always underlined. If the underline is a solid line, it means that clicking on the item takes you directly to another help screen. If the underline is a broken line, it means that clicking on the item shows you a hypertext list of Help screens. Whenever the mouse pointer is on a hypertext item, the pointer arrow changes into a pointing hand.

dBASE remembers the location and size of the Help window from the last time it was displayed. If you want the Help window to appear in a certain location or to be a certain size, you can drag it around the screen and resize it with the mouse. dBASE displays the window in its new size and/or location until you change the window again.

The following steps put the Table of Contents and hypertext through their paces to show you how they work. If you quit dBASE after the last chapter, start it up again and open the Caveat database you created in earlier chapters. Then do the following:

1. **Open the <u>H</u>elp menu and click on <u>C</u>ontents.**

   The Help Contents window opens.

2. **Notice the mouse cursor.**

   The cursor, which is usually an arrow, turns into a little pointing hand when it's over some of the text in the window. When the cursor turns into a hand, it's pointing at hypertext.

3. **Click on the hypertext <u>V</u>iews and Tools.**

   dBASE takes you to a window that shows tools you can use, as shown previously in Figure 7-2.

Any time you see the cursor turn into a pointing hand, you know that it's over a hypertext item. To see more about the item, just click the left mouse button.

Try clicking on hypertext items a few more times to jump from one Help screen to another. Don't worry. dBASE leaves a trail of bread crumbs so that you can find your way back to the starting screen if you need to! To back up, you simply select Back, which is explained in the next section.

Using the Help buttons

Take a closer look at the buttons that appear at the top of every Help screen: Contents, Search, Back, History, and two buttons marked with double arrows (see Figure 7-3).

Figure 7-3:
Help screen
buttons.

The Contents button

If you move from the Help Contents screen to another screen (as you just did by using hypertext links), clicking on the Contents button takes you back to the Contents screen.

The Search button

You can use the Search button to search for the Help topic you need. You learn how to use it in the next section.

The Back button

If you move from your starting Help screen to another screen, clicking on the Back button retraces your steps. It takes you back the way you came, one Help screen at a time.

The History button

If you click on the History button, dBASE displays the little window shown in Figure 7-4. It lists the previous 40 Help topics you've seen. You can use the scroll bar on the right side of the window to move down the list if all the items aren't visible in the window. To go to a Help topic, just double-click on the topic in the list.

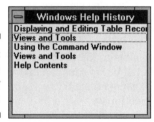

Figure 7-4:
The Help
History
window.

The arrow buttons

If you click on the arrow button marked >>, dBASE displays the next Help
screen. The arrow button marked << takes you to the preceding Help screen. If
you're at the last screen in a series, there isn't a next screen, so the >> button
doesn't do anything if you click on it. The same thing applies if you're at the
first screen in a series: There isn't a preceding screen, so clicking on the <<
button doesn't do anything.

Normally, the label on a button or menu choice is displayed in solid black type.
Sometimes, however, the text is displayed in gray letters that are a little hard to
read, indicating that the button or menu choice doesn't apply to what you're
doing at the moment.

Using the Help menus

Just like most windows, dBASE Help windows have a menu bar at the top that
provides you with several extra tricks.

Creating bookmarks

Have you ever used a bookmark? It's a little slip of paper, an index card, or
maybe a mackerel, that you put between the pages of a book so that you can
instantly find your place again. Well, you can do the same thing with dBASE,
except that you can't use the mackerel.

The following steps take you through the process of setting a bookmark and
returning to it. If you're not currently at the dBASE Help Contents screen, click
on Contents to return to the screen.

Suppose that you wanted to put a bookmark on the Help window for adding
records to a table. To do that, follow these steps:

1. **Click on Views and Tools at the left side of the Help window.**

   dBASE takes you to the Views and Tools Help window.

2. In the lower right part of your screen, click on Tables.

dBASE shows you a little hypertext list of Help screens for tables.

3. Click on Displaying and Editing Table Records.

A window appears for this topic.

4. In the window, click on Table Records Window Tasks.

A new window appears that shows information about this topic.

5. Click on Bookmark in the menu bar to open the Bookmark menu.

6. Click on Define in the Bookmark menu.

The Bookmark Define dialog box appears, as shown in Figure 7-5.

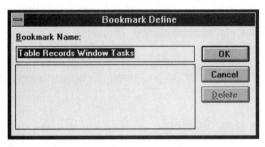

Figure 7-5:
The
Bookmark
Define
dialog box.

7. To create the bookmark, click on OK in the dialog box.

There are just three more steps in this demonstration (originally, there were 39 steps, but we didn't want to get into any trouble for copyright infringement).

8. Click on Contents to return to the Help Contents screen.

9. Click on Bookmark in the menu bar to open the Bookmark menu.

The menu is different this time. Instead of offering only one menu choice, Define, the menu now has a second choice: 1 Table Records Window Tasks.

10. Click on the second menu choice, 1 Table Records Window Tasks.

dBASE takes you directly back to the screen where you placed the bookmark. Stay right there: You're going to do something else that's really incredible.

Annotating Help screens

Another impressive feature of the dBASE Help System is that you can attach little notes to Help topics. You can record your thoughts on a Help topic — either as a reminder to yourself or as a suggestion for other people who may be entering data on your PC.

To see how this feature works, add a note to the current Help topic. Follow these steps:

1. **From the _E_dit menu, select _A_nnotate.**

   The Annotate dialog box appears.

2. **Enter your note.**

   The cursor is already in the correct part of the dialog box for you to enter text. Type the following: **It's better to use forms when you're entering data, but using the Browse window is okay.**

3. **Click on _S_ave.**

As soon as you save the annotation, a little paper clip icon appears in the top left corner of the Help window. Whenever you see the paper clip, you know that a note is attached to the current Help screen. Click on it, and the note appears. To close the note window, just click on Cancel Then click on _C_ontents to return to the Help Contents screen.

If you ever want to delete an annotation, just open the note window and click on the _D_elete button.

Getting help about the Help System

It probably won't surprise you, but the Help System gives you information about _every_ feature in dBASE — even the Help System itself!

To get "Help on Help," you can either select _H_ow to use Help from the _H_elp menu, or if you're in a Help window already, just click on the _H_elp menu in the menu bar. A menu appears, with the following options:

- ✔ **_H_ow to use Help** explains how to use each different Help feature, just as I'm doing in this chapter.
- ✔ **Always on _T_op** tells dBASE to keep the Help window displayed on-screen at all times.
- ✔ **_A_bout Help** displays a screen that shows the current version of the Help System. You can ignore this menu choice.

Printing Help screens

If you want a paper copy of a particular Help topic, you can print one by selecting _P_rint Topic from the Help window's _F_ile menu. Make sure that you have selected a printer and that the printer is turned on and ready to print.

Any time you see a menu choice that has a letter underlined, such as Print Topic, the underlined letter is the hot key for that menu choice. To activate the menu choice without opening the menu, press Alt plus the underlined letter.

Searching for a Topic

dBASE also enables you to search for a Help topic, which is another easy-to-use but powerful feature. You can get to the Search dialog box (shown in Figure 7-6) in two ways:

- ✔ If you're not already in the Help System, select Search from the Help menu.
- ✔ If you are in the Help System, click on Search in the top of the window.

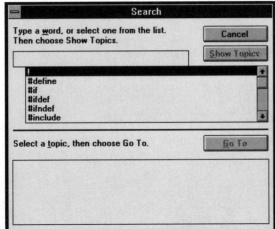

Figure 7-6:
Use the Search dialog box to find the Help topics you need.

Suppose that you are setting up a table and aren't sure which data type to use for a particular field. You can search for help on data types by following these steps:

1. **Open the Search dialog box.**

   The cursor is automatically positioned in the blank where you type the topic you want to search for.

2. **Enter the search topic.**

   For this example, type **data.** As you type, the list box underneath the blank automatically moves to the topics that relate to data.

3. Select a subtopic.

In the box, double-click on the data type topic. In the lower list box, dBASE displays all topics relevant to that subtopic, as shown in Figure 7-7.

4. Double-click on the Help topic (in the bottom list) that you want to see.

For the purposes of this example, double-click on data type, definition. dBASE takes you to a Help screen with advice on that topic.

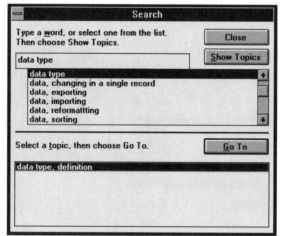

Figure 7-7:
The Search
dialog box
displays
relevant
Help topics.

You can search for any Help topic in exactly the same way.

Using Interactive Tutors

Interactive Tutors and Experts are the final stop on your tour through the dBASE Help System. These Tutors go beyond just giving you general information; they take you step-by-step through whatever you need to get done.

The main difference between Tutors and Experts is that Tutors give you step-by-step instructions on what to do, while Experts actually do most of the work for you. Experts are covered, where appropriate, in other chapters of this book.

To use an Interactive Tutor, select Interactive Tutors from the Help menu. The main Interactive Tutors window appears. On the left are topics for which Tutors are available. If you click on a topic, dBASE displays a list of Tutors you can use for that topic.

Suppose that you want to learn about setting up a table. In the Tutors main window, click on Building a Database. A list of tutors for that topic appears on the right. Click on the Tutor for Database Basics. dBASE automatically displays a series of Tutors at the lower right corner of the screen, with your work area still showing on the left side of the screen (see Figure 7-8). As you go along working with your table, click on the appropriate button in the Tutor window to receive instructions on what you should do next.

If you don't need a Tutor anymore, you can get rid of it by closing the Tutor window. To close a Tutor window, click on the X button. That returns you to the main Tutors menu. To quit the Tutors and return to dBASE, click on the Quit button.

Play with the dBASE Help System until you have a feel for it. Then you can use it any time you need to get instant information about dBASE!

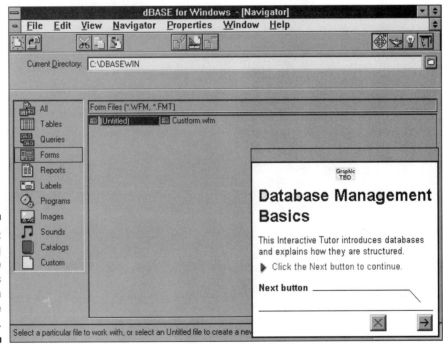

Figure 7-8:
Following
step-by-step
instructions
from an
Interactive
Tutor.

"YES, I THINK IT'S AN ERROR MESSAGE."

Chapter 8

Redesigning Your Table

. . . .

In This Chapter

▶ Adding fields

▶ Moving fields

▶ Deleting fields

▶ Changing fields

. . . .

*H*ardly anything is perfect on the first try. Mozart supposedly could knock out a perfect string quartet in an afternoon, but music historians now believe that the story was probably concocted by his publicist. The philosopher Ludwig Wittgenstein thought he'd come up with a perfect solution for metaphysical problems when he wrote his first book, *Tractatus Logico-Philosophicus,* but by the next morning he sobered up and wished that he'd written a detective novel instead. Other than Mozart's string quartets and Wittgenstein's apodictic philosophical ramblings, the only perfect things in life are chocolate-almond ice cream, the Los Angeles Lakers, and the Violent Femmes' *Why Do Birds Sing?* CD.

It's next to impossible to set up the perfect table on your first try. Just when you think you've set up the Customer table perfectly, your boss walks in and requests some changes. He knows that you are a whiz and is sure that you can make the changes quickly and easily. And guess what? With dBASE, you *are* and you *can*.

Before you can redesign a table, you need to

   ✔ Create the table.

   ✔ Understand basic table concepts such as fields and data types.

   ✔ Eat a good, healthy breakfast: none of that greasy stuff — no eggs and bacon or pancakes with lots of syrup — just wholesome American grains, skim milk, a little piece of fruit, and dry toast for a totally pleasure-free dining experience.

To carry out the steps by using the book's example database, you need to have created the Customer table (Chapter 4): the data for this table is in Chapter 5. If you're redesigning a table in your own real-life database, just read this chapter to get the basic ideas and then follow the steps using your own table instead of the one used in this book.

What Changes Can You Make?

What can you change about your table? In a word, *anything you want.* (Okay, that's three words; so sue me.) You can change the definition of fields that you created, add fields, move fields, delete fields, and Marshall Fields. In this chapter, you learn how to do all these things because your boss suddenly has *lots* of good ideas that he wants you to put in the database design.

Adding Fields

Adding new fields is one of the most common operations you'll do in dBASE. It's not as common as squeezing into a parking space that's too small, but it is still pretty common.

Why redesign your database?

If you need to redesign a database, don't beat yourself up about it (unless you just like doing that sort of thing). In most cases, changes aren't needed because of anything you did wrong but because your database users change their minds about what they want, get an idea for a new feature they want you to add, or didn't explain what they really need in the first place.

In fact, the most common reason for database design changes is users not explaining what they really need in the first place, and this problem is probably the most avoidable of all three scenarios. When you're designing a database for anyone other than yourself, require users to be clear about what they want. If they refuse—well, this book doesn't sanction violence, but ...

As with other database-creation tasks, the best way to learn how to change the fields in your database is to work through a few examples. With that in mind, the following sections show you how to make changes to the sample bookstore database you've been working on since Chapter 2. If you're working with a real-life database, you can follow along, making the same moves (where appropriate!) with your own database.

If you haven't already done so, start up dBASE and open the Caveat catalog. Using the right mouse button, click on the Customer table and, from the SpeedMenu, select Design Table Structure. The Table Designer window appears on your screen. Maximize the window so that it looks like Figure 8-1.

Sometimes, you'll see the phrase "right-click." This just means "Click with the right mouse button."

Adding a field to a table design *doesn't* add any data in the new field. If the table already contains records, you need to go back and add the data into the new field for those records.

---

dBASE for Windows - [Table Structure [CUSTOMER.DBF]]

File   Edit   View   Structure   Properties   Window   Help

Name: CUSTOMER.DBF   **Type:** DBASE

Updated: 04/17/94   **Bytes Used:** 106
Records: 6   **Bytes Left:** 32,661

Field	Name	Type	Width	Decimal	Index
1	CUST_ID	Character	5	0	Ascend
2	FNAME	Character	10	0	None
3	LNAME	Character	15	0	None
4	MRMS	Character	5	0	None
5	SALUTATION	Character	15	0	None
6	ADDRESS	Character	25	0	None
7	CITY	Character	15	0	None
8	STATE	Character	5	0	None
9	ZIP	Character	10	0	None

Customer.dbf   Excl

Figure 8-1:
The Table Designer window.

Adding a field at the end of the table

Suppose that Honest Janis — the bookstore owner for whom you've been creating the sample database — wants to add a phone number field to the table. This seems like a good idea because the bookstore sometimes needs customer phone numbers.

The easiest place to add the field is at the end of the table, underneath the line for the ZIP field. Easy is good, so I'll show you how to do it that way. To add the phone number field, follow these steps:

1. **In the Table Designer window, click in the line under the bottom (ZIP) field.**

   An empty line opens up, indicating that dBASE is ready to receive a new field.

2. **Enter the field name.**

   Type **PHONE** and then press Tab or click in the Type column of the same row.

3. **Specify a data type.**

   What data type should you use? Remember that even though the field will contain phone numbers, you aren't going to do any arithmetic with the numbers. Therefore, just accept the default data type of Character.

4. **Specify the field width.**

   In the Width column, type **13** and press Tab.

5. **Save the modified table design.**

   Open the File menu and select Save. Alternatively, you can click on the Save button in the SpeedBar. That's the third button from the left end.

 The Save button on the SpeedBar

 The Save button is just a SpeedBar shortcut. Instead of opening the File menu and selecting Save, you just click on the Save button in the SpeedBar.

Inserting a field in the middle of the table

Adding a field at the end of a table is pretty easy. Now, you learn how to insert a field in the middle of the table by making yet another revision to the infamous Customer table. The field you insert will hold the date of the customer's first purchase.

The basic technique is this: Click in the line for the field that's *just below* where you want to insert the new field. Then open the <u>S</u>tructure menu and select <u>I</u>nsert Field. An empty row opens above the field where your cursor is located. After that, you simply define the field in the normal way.

To insert and define the new field in the sample table, follow these steps:

1. **Click in the line for the PHONE field.**

   You're going to insert the new field above the PHONE field.

2. **Open the <u>S</u>tructure menu and select <u>I</u>nsert Field.**

   A blank row should open above the PHONE field.

3. **Enter the field name.**

   Type **FIRSTSALE** and then press Tab to move to the Type column.

4. **Choose a data type.**

   Click on the list-box arrow on the right side of the blank. In the list that appears, select Date by clicking on it.

   When the highlight is in the Data Type column, you can select the data type by pressing the key for its first letter. To select Memo, for example, press the *M* key on your keyboard; for Date, press *D;* and so on.

5. **Enter a width for the table.**

   Tab to the Width column and enter **13**.

6. **Save the modified table design.**

   Click on the Save button in the SpeedBar. Your screen should look something like Figure 8-2.

Moving Fields

In general, the order of fields in a table isn't that important. As you learned in Chapter 7, you can rearrange the order of columns in the Browse window. However, the table's field order does control the order in which fields are *normally* displayed in Browse windows, forms, reports, and so on. At times, you may want to change the order by moving a field.

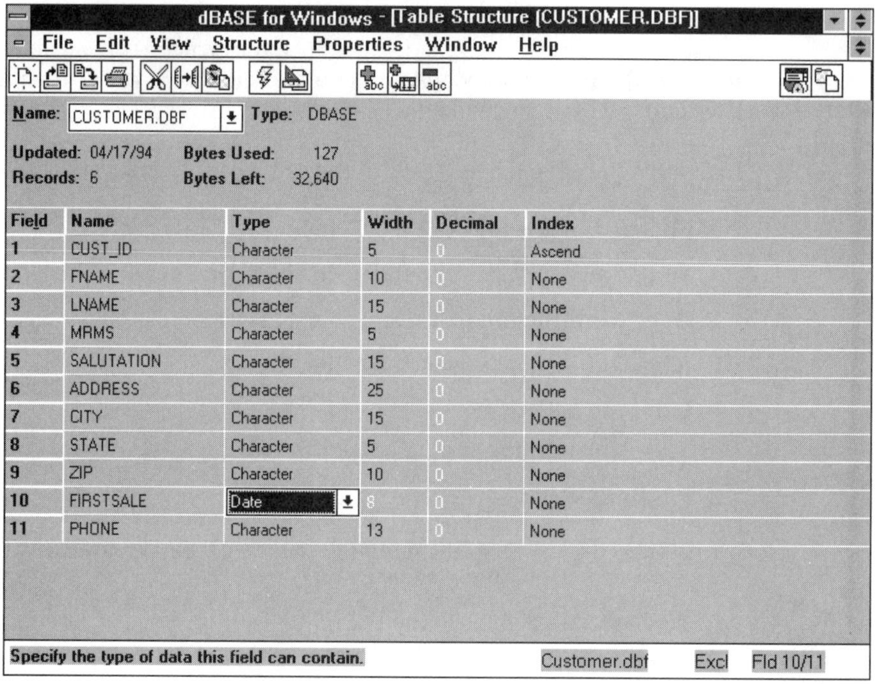

Figure 8-2:
The sample
table after
you've
inserted the
PHONE and
FIRSTSALE
fields.

To see how it's done, move the FIRSTSALE field in the sample table so that it comes just after the CUST_ID field and just before the FNAME field. Follow these steps:

1. Select the row for the field you want to move.

To do that, move the mouse pointer along the row you want until it's in the far left column of the Table Designer window. That's the column labeled Field, as Figure 8-2 illustrates. When the mouse pointer is in the proper position, the pointer becomes a little hand — actually, just a picture of a little hand, but you get the idea. If you're working with the book's example database, move the mouse pointer (hand? paw? Oh, to heck with it!) into the Field number column at the left end of the line for the FIRSTSALE field.

2. Hold down the left mouse button and drag the field up or down.

In the book's example, drag the FIRSTSALE field upward. Stop when it's right under the row for the CUST_ID field. As you drag the field up or down, you'll see it change position in the table design, following the mouse pointer, or the mouse hand. Don't mice have paws, anyway? Can somebody check on that?

3. Release the mouse button.

This "drops" the field in its new location (KER-CHUNK!). FIRSTSALE should now be above the FNAME field and below the CUST_ID field.

Remember that if you simply want to rearrange the order of the columns in the Browse window, you don't have to change the order of the fields in the table. You can change the order or width of columns in the Browse window without making any changes in the table design itself.

Deleting Fields

Imagine that shortly after you finish moving the FIRSTSALE field to its new location, Honest Janis changes his mind. He decides that the table doesn't need a FIRSTSALE field after all, so you need to delete the field from the table. But you're not frustrated: Janis has promised that if the database is ready on schedule, he'll buy you a first edition of this book. (Come to think of it, you already *have* a first edition of this book, so why are you working so hard?)

Sweet and generous person that you are, you decide to delete the field anyway. And it's the easiest thing you've done yet.

To delete a field, just follow these steps:

1. Click in the row for the field you want to delete.

For the sample table, click in the row for the FIRSTSALE field.

2. Open the Structure menu and pick Delete Selected Field. Alternatively, you can just press Ctrl+D on your keyboard.

dBASE deletes the selected row.

3. Click on the Save button in the SpeedBar.

dBASE saves your modified table design. Your screen should now look something like Figure 8-3.

If you already have records in your table, you may lose data when you change a field, especially if you're changing its size or data type. Before making any changes in your table design, it's a good idea to copy your database file to another directory as a backup and make your changes to the original.

```
┌─────────────────────────────────────────────────────────────────────┐
│ ─          dBASE for Windows - [Table Structure [CUSTOMER.DBF]]   ▼│♦│
│ ─   File   Edit   View   Structure   Properties   Window   Help      ♦│
│ ┌──┬────┬────┬──┬──┬──┬──┐ ┌──┐ ┌──┐ ┌────┬────┬───┐         ┌──┬──┐│
│ │  │    │    │  │  │  │  │ │ ⚡│ │  │ │ ⊞  │ ⊞  │ ─ │         │  │  ││
│ └──┴────┴────┴──┴──┴──┴──┘ └──┘ └──┘ └─abc┴abc┴abc┘         └──┴──┘│
│ Name: CUSTOMER.DBF        ♦  Type:  DBASE                            │
│                                                                       │
│ Updated: 04/17/94    Bytes Used:    119                             │
│ Records: 6           Bytes Left:  32,648                            │
│ ┌─────┬───────────────┬──────────┬───────┬─────────┬──────────────┐ │
│ │Field│ Name          │ Type     │ Width │ Decimal │ Index        │ │
│ ├─────┼───────────────┼──────────┼───────┼─────────┼──────────────┤ │
│ │ 1   │ CUST_ID       │ Character│ 5     │ 0       │ Ascend       │ │
│ │ 2   │ [FNAME    ]   │ Character│ 10    │ 0       │ None         │ │
│ │ 3   │ LNAME         │ Character│ 15    │ 0       │ None         │ │
│ │ 4   │ MRMS          │ Character│ 5     │ 0       │ None         │ │
│ │ 5   │ SALUTATION    │ Character│ 15    │ 0       │ None         │ │
│ │ 6   │ ADDRESS       │ Character│ 25    │ 0       │ None         │ │
│ │ 7   │ CITY          │ Character│ 15    │ 0       │ None         │ │
│ │ 8   │ STATE         │ Character│ 5     │ 0       │ None         │ │
│ │ 9   │ ZIP           │ Character│ 10    │ 0       │ None         │ │
│ │ 10  │ PHONE         │ Character│ 13    │ 0       │ None         │ │
│ └─────┴───────────────┴──────────┴───────┴─────────┴──────────────┘ │
│                                          Customer.dbf      Excl      │
└─────────────────────────────────────────────────────────────────────┘
```

Figure 8-3:
The
Customer
table design
after you
deleted the
FIRSTSALE
field.

Changing Fields (Or Fooling with Field Properties)

You can do a lot more than just add, move, and delete fields in dBASE. One of the most powerful things you can do is apply *field properties,* which control how your data is entered and displayed. For example, you can make all the letters in a field display in uppercase; you can add formatting characters to a phone number field; or you can even tell dBASE to check for data entry errors.

If you're proceeding from the previous section, close the Table Designer window and return to the Caveat catalog window. Right-click on the Customer table and, in the SpeedMenu, select <u>E</u>dit Records. The Browse window appears on your screen. Maximize the Browse window so that it fills the entire screen.

You make changes in the table's basic structure in the Table Designer window. For changes in the field properties, however, you use the Browse window.

Turning on automatic uppercase

Suppose that you're asked to change the LNAME field in the Customer table so that it automatically displays the customer's last name in all uppercase letters. This change saves the data-entry person some work. It also ensures that no matter who enters a customer record, the last name always appears in upper-case letters.

In order to make the LNAME field automatically change letters to uppercase, you need to fool around with its field properties.

This is not scary: You already set the width of each field, which is a sort of field property, when you designed the table. To set this other property, just follow these steps:

> **1. Open the Properties menu and select Table Records Window.**
>
> The Table Records Properties dialog box appears, as shown in Figure 8-4.

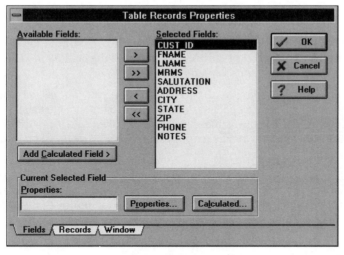

Figure 8-4:
The Table
Records
Properties
dialog box.

> **2. In the field list at the right, click on the field (LNAME) you want to uppercase.**
>
> **3. Click on the Properties button under the field list.**
>
> The Field Properties dialog box appears. Notice that at the left, there's a blank labeled Template.

4. **Type an "at" sign and an exclamation mark (@!) in the Template blank.**

5. **Click on OK to close the Field Properties dialog box.**

6. **Click on OK to close the Browse Inspector dialog box.**

The Browse window now displays the field you selected in all uppercase letters.

And that's it! The next time someone enters a customer record, dBASE will automatically convert the customer's last name to uppercase letters. No more using the Caps Lock key and then forgetting to turn it off.

Setting field properties

In the preceding section you assigned a *field property* to the LNAME field. Making dBASE change letters to uppercase is only one of the things you can do in the Field Properties dialog box. You'll use the template property again in the next section when you add formatting characters to the PHONE field. Here's a summary of what the field properties are and what they do:

- ✔ *Heading* lets you specify the caption at the top of the Browse window column for the currently selected field in the top part of the screen. If you don't fill in this property, dBASE simply uses the field name. This property was demonstrated in Chapter 6.

- ✔ *Template* enables you to do two things. First, you can restrict what type of data can be put into specific slots of a field. Second, when all the values in a field have the same format, you can put boilerplate formatting characters into the field. In the next section, you use this property to jazz up a phone number field.

- ✔ *When* is a fairly advanced property. It lets you keep anyone from changing the data in a field unless certain conditions are true. Don't worry about this one too much, unless your life is just soooo boring that you have nothing better to do.

- ✔ *Width* lets you control the width of a field's column in the Browse window. It has no effect on the *actual* size of the field (how much data it can hold). It controls only how the field is displayed.

- ✔ *Read-only* prevents anyone from changing the data in a field.

- ✔ *Valid* is a slightly more advanced property that lets dBASE check newly entered data to make sure it's all right.

✔ *Low Range* lets you set a minimum value for a numeric field. For example, if you're creating a database for a bookstore that doesn't carry books that sell for less than $10, you can make $10 the minimum value in a price field for an inventory table.

✔ *High Range* lets you set a maximum value for a numeric field.

Using templates to insert formatting characters

The most important thing to understand about *templates* is that they're different from the *plates* used for high-class foods, such as Chicken Kiev, or even from the soggy paper plates used for pizza. You use templates to control and format the data in a field. (You can still eat pizza if you want. Just don't put it on a template.)

You've used a template once already, to make the letters in the LNAME field display in uppercase. Now, you'll use a slightly different template trick to make the PHONE field easier to read by adding parentheses and hyphens. Follow these steps:

1. **Display the table in the Browse window.**

2. **Open the Properties menu and select Table Records Window.**

   The Browse Inspector dialog box appears, as shown in Figure 8-4, earlier in the chapter.

3. **In the field list, click on the field (PHONE) whose properties you want to change.**

4. **Click on the Properties button under the field list.**

   The Field Properties dialog box appears. Notice that at the left, there's a blank labeled *Template*.

5. **Type** (999)999-9999 **in the Template blank.**

6. **Click on OK to close the Field Properties dialog box.**

7. **Click on OK to close the Browse Inspector dialog box.**

   It's done! If you click on the horizontal scroll bar at the bottom of the window, you can scroll right in the Browse window and see that the formatting characters have been added to the PHONE field.

You did two things when you specified the mask for the PHONE field:

▶ You put some formatting characters in the field: parentheses to enclose the area code and a hyphen to separate the parts of the phone number.

▶ By filling the rest of the field with 9s, you told dBASE that only digits or spaces can be put in the field. No letters or other characters are allowed.

There's more to learn about templates, but that's plenty for now. The main thing to remember is that if you need to format data that has the same structure in every record or restrict data to digits or spaces, you can use a template to do it.

Filling in Phone Numbers

As a final housekeeping detail, open the Customer table in the sample database and fill in the PHONE fields for the five records you previously entered. Notice that as soon as you click in the PHONE field, the template appears.

As you type the phone numbers, you don't need to type the parentheses and hyphens because dBASE puts them in the field for you. Type *only* the numbers:

James West	415 555 4678
Harriet Stowe	212 555 2345
Jules Twombly	201 555 6213
Arnold Harris	321 555 9876
Teri Lane	805 555 1234

You don't have to worry about creating the perfect database on your first attempt because dBASE makes it so easy for you to make revisions. Now that you've redesigned the sample table to Honest Janis's liking, shut down dBASE and enjoy his good mood.

Part II
Finding and Playing with Your Data

The 5th Wave   **By Rich Tennant**

"MISS LAMONT, I'M FILING THE CONGREGATION UNDER 'SOULS', MY SERMONS UNDER 'GRACE' AND THE FINANCIAL CONTRIBUTIONS UNDER 'AMEN'."

In this part . . .

*B*asic skills are important. If you didn't know how to make change, balance a budget, or write your name, you'd have few career options except to run for Congress.

But basic skills, which are covered in Part I, can take you only so far. This part teaches you about the more advanced stuff you can do with dBASE. You learn how to change a table design, create on-screen forms that explain your database and catch errors, and search for data.

And if you *still* want to run for Congress, well, that option is always open to you.

Chapter 9
Adding and Using Memo Fields

• •

In This Chapter

▶ Adding a memo field

▶ Entering a memo

▶ Viewing and editing a memo

• •

Memo fields are powerful but controversial. Really. They're so controversial, in fact, that until now, you could learn about them only at certain monasteries in Asia where they shave your head, feed you steamed rice, and make you sing the theme song from *The Brady Bunch* in Chinese. Most database books don't cover memo fields. The authors are afraid.

However, the proprietor of our bookstore (your boss Janis) spent some time in one of those monasteries — don't worry, his hair grew back. So in this chapter, you learn how to create and put data into memo fields. Don't tell anyone that you have this information: The other Kung Fu masters would punish Janis severely for revealing it.

Before you can create a memo field, you need to have

▸ Created a table (Chapter 4).

▸ Learned basic database concepts, such as records, fields, and data types.

▸ Learned to juggle three razor-sharp, 18-inch long knives while you tap dance. (*Optional:* tap dance in clown shoes.)

To do the dance steps (tap, jazz, or ballet) with this book's example database, you need to have

▸ Created the Customer table (Chapter 4).

▸ Entered data in the table (Chapter 5).

▸ Modified the table and added new data (Chapter 8).

If you're adding a memo field to a table in your own real-life database, just read this chapter to get the basic ideas. Then follow the steps with your own database instead of the example database that I've been using in the book.

Adding a Memo Field

All fields in every record of a table, *except* for memo fields, must be the same size. You can't set up a Character field (for example, a First Name field) to have a width of 10 characters in one record and 200 in another.

Memo fields are different from other fields in two ways:

- ✔ Memo fields can vary in size and are designed to hold different amounts of data in different records.

- ✔ Memo fields can be a lot larger than other fields. Character fields can hold a maximum of 254 characters (letters, digits, and so on). A memo field's size is limited only by the size of your PC's hard disk. If your PC has a very big hard disk — say, 10 or 15 feet in diameter — you can create enormous memo fields (but you'll have trouble carrying the PC through the door into your office).

Even though memo fields are different from other fields, you add memo fields to a table in the same way you add any other type of field. You can check this by adding a memo field to the Customer table in the example bookstore database. Open the Caveat catalog, get into the Table Designer window (by clicking on the Customer table with the right mouse button and selecting Design Table Structure), and follow these steps:

1. **Click in the row at the bottom of the table design, right under the PHONE field.**

2. **For the field name, type** NOTES.

3. **For the Type, open the list box and select Memo.**

 4. **Save the table design by clicking on the Save button in the SpeedBar.**

5. **Close the Table Designer window.**

 Memo fields can vary in size and hold so much data because dBASE stores their contents in a file separate from the table itself. Instead of trying to cram an unknown but possibly huge amount of text into the table itself, dBASE places a *pointer* in the table's memo field that shows where dBASE stored the text. When you open a memo field, dBASE follows the pointer, retrieves the data, and displays it on-screen.

The text contained in memo fields is kept in a file with the same name as the table, but ending with the letters *DBT*. Thus, if a table is named *CUSTOMER*, the associated memo file would be called *CUSTOMER.DBT*. A *DBT* file is only created if a table has memo fields.

Entering a Memo

The great thing about memo fields — apart from their sentimental association with *The Brady Bunch* song — is that you don't really need to put anything in them. You can store many notes in the memo fields of some records and not put any at all in others.

The basic steps for entering a memo are as follows:

1. **Open the table in the Table Editor window.**

   You can display the table in Browse, Form, or Columnar Layout. Generally, it's easiest to enter memo text if you have the table displayed in Form Layout.

2. **Double-click on the memo field of the record you want to edit.**

   The Memo Editor window appears on the screen.

3. **Type the text you want in the Memo Editor window.**

   You can use most standard keyboard techniques, such as the arrows, Backspace, and Delete keys.

4. **Double-click on the Window Control button for the Memo Editor window.**

   dBASE displays a dialog box asking if you want to save the text you entered in the memo field.

5. **To save the text, answer Yes.**

   dBASE saves your text and closes the Memo Editor window. It then returns you to the table, where you can edit another record if you want.

Now try entering some notes in a memo field. Right-click on the Customer table in the Catalog window and select Edit Records. Click on the Form Layout button in the SpeedBar to switch from the Browse window to a Form window that shows one record at a time. Your screen should look something like Figure 9-1. (The circle-slash mark means there isn't any text in the memo field.)

Whenever you have a table displayed in the Browse window, you can switch to Form Layout or Columnar Layout by clicking on the appropriate button in the SpeedBar. Then, if you wish, you can switch back to Browse Layout by clicking on the Browse button. All three buttons are next to each other in the center of the SpeedBar.

Double-click on the NOTES field and the dBASE Memo Editor window appears. Type the following in the window: **A good customer for many years.** When you're finished, close the Memo Editor window and answer Yes in the dialog box when it asks if you want to save the memo text. dBASE returns you to the Customer table.

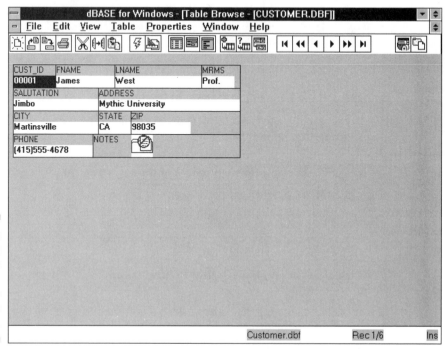

Figure 9-1:
Getting
ready to
enter data
into the
NOTES
memo field.

Now try entering a longer memo. In the SpeedBar, click twice on the Next Record button to move to the record for Jules Twombly. Double-click on the NOTES field and, in the Memo Editor, type the following:

> **Jules is a heck of a guy. Always pays his bills on time and has excellent taste in books. Not at all afraid of those Kung Fu masters. Wife: Becky. Two daughters: Lori and Sarah.**

When you finish typing, the Memo Editor should look like Figure 9-2. Close the Memo Editor and save the text. Notice that the memo field no longer has the circle-slash mark on it. That's because the memo field now has some text in it.

If you change your mind while you're entering text in the Memo Editor and don't want to save the text, you can simply close the window and answer No in the dialog box.

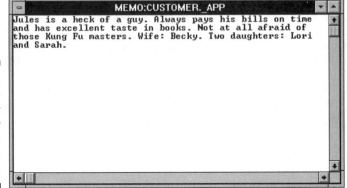

Figure 9-2:
The Memo
Editor
window
after you
enter some
text.

Viewing and Editing a Memo

You can open the memo field for viewing or for more editing in exactly the same way as when you enter the memo text. Just double-click on the memo field to open the Memo Editor.

Try it with the memo field in the record for James West. Follow these steps:

1. Double-click on the NOTES field in James West's record.

Remember that how the table is displayed doesn't matter. These steps work equally well in Browse, Form, or Columnar Layout.

2. In the Memo Editor, click just to the left of the *g* in *good*.

4. Edit the memo.

Type **really.** The memo should now read: *A really good customer for many years.*

5. Holding down Ctrl, press the right-arrow key three times.

The cursor should be on the first letter of the word *many*.

6. Press Delete repeatedly to erase the text *many years*.

In its place, type **a long, long time.**

7. Save the changes.

Close the Memo Editor window and answer Yes in the dialog box.

To select text for deletion in the Memo Editor, position the mouse at the beginning of the text you want to select. Then, holding down the left mouse button, drag the mouse until all the text you want to delete is highlighted. If you're a keyboard whiz, you can also select text one word at a time by holding down *both* Shift and Ctrl and then pressing the right- or left-arrow key.

That's all there is to creating, entering, and editing memo fields! Close the Table Editor window. If you're going straight on to the next chapter, get ready to learn about on-screen forms. And watch out for those Kung Fu masters.

Chapter 10

Creating Your Own Forms

● ●

In This Chapter

▶ What are forms good for? Lots!

▶ Using the Form Expert

▶ Types of forms you can create

▶ Selecting a form's style

▶ Moving around your table with a form

▶ Entering data with a form

● ●

*F*orms are a part of modern life. There's the brilliant, graceful form your best friend's daughter exhibits in her ballet recital (deny it at your own risk!); the form that the "earth was without, and void" you hear about in church; the Tai Chi forms that your spouse is always bugging you to try; and, of course, the dreaded IRS Form 1040.

None of these forms has anything to do with dBASE forms. dBASE forms, in fact, are much more useful than any of them, except maybe the one about the earth having form, which is *really* useful because it keeps us from flying off into space. In dBASE, forms give you another way — a very *powerful* way — to enter and view the stuff in your database.

Before you can create a form, you need to have:

  ✔ Created a table. A form is used to enter data into or display data from a table; without the table, you've got *nada*. Well, that's not quite true: you've got your health and good looks.

  ✔ Put data in the table. Okay, you don't really *have* to do that, but with no data, there's nothing to look at with the form.

  ✔ Learned basic database concepts, such as table and field.

To do the steps with the book's example database, you need to have created the Customer table (Chapter 4) and put data in it (Chapter 5). You should also have created and opened the Caveat catalog (Chapter 2).

If you're creating a form for your own real-life database, just read this chapter to get the basic ideas. Then follow the steps with your own table instead of the one in the book.

What Are Forms Good For?

Saying that "forms are powerful," that they "get your wash 44 percent brighter," or that they perform other miracles doesn't tell you all that much. That's TV-commercial talk, which means that it says nothing. So what are forms and what good are they?

So far, you've learned that you can use the dBASE Browse window to enter and view all records in a table. Although the Browse window is good for viewing lots of records at the same time in a row-and-column format, it does have some important disadvantages:

> ✔ You can view many records at a time, but you normally can't view all the data in each record because some of the columns disappear off the right side of the screen. This problem is addressed somewhat by the simple Form and Columnar views, but you can improve on these.

> ✔ Apart from the column captions, you can't put text in a Browse window to explain the meaning of each field. If new employees are entering data, they may be confused. In a simple table like the one you created for the book-store customers, this limitation isn't much of a problem. In more complex databases, it can be a *serious* problem.

> ✔ It's just not as easy to enter records using a Browse window as it would be if the screen looked more like a paper form, with captions, blanks, and explanatory text.

Customized forms let you overcome all these disadvantages. Usually, you'll create forms that display all fields for one record on-screen at the same time, include explanatory text, and look very much like paper forms. If you're an absolute dBASE genius (which you will be by the time you finish this book), you can put list boxes and other controls on a form to make it even easier to use. You also can include photos, graphics, and even sound recordings.

Calling Up a Form Expert

Like most things in dBASE, creating a form is easy. In this section, you learn just how easy it is by creating a sample form for entering records into the Customer table. There are two ways to create a form in dBASE. One is easy and very flexible, the other is even easier but slightly less flexible:

✔ You can tell the dBASE Form Expert to create a form *for* you. This is the easiest way to create a form, and for most purposes, is the best way to create a form. The Form Expert asks you what table to use, what fields to use, how to arrange them, and how the form should look. If you don't like the design created by the Form Expert, you can then modify it to suit your taste.

✔ You can lay out the form "by hand." When you do it this way, dBASE gives you a blank on-screen form. You tell dBASE which table the form should work with and then put the fields you want in the locations you want on the form. (You can also use a query instead of a table, but that's not important here. Queries are covered in Chapter 13.) This approach takes a few more steps but gives you the most flexibility in how your form looks and works. You'll learn some of these "by hand" techniques in Chapter 14.

In this chapter, you learn how to create a form using the dBASE Form Expert, a surprisingly simple task. Here are the basic moves you make:

1. Open the Catalog for your database.

This ensures that the form you create will be included in the catalog.

2. Click on the Forms icon at the left side of the Catalog window.

Any forms you've already created are shown in the right side of the Catalog window. In the right side of the window, there is a form icon labeled Untitled.

3. Double-click on the Untitled form icon.

The first form-creation dialog box appears on your screen, as shown in Figure 10-1. Notice that there are two radio buttons near the top of the dialog box. The radio button for Expert Assistance is already selected, so unless you click in the other radio button (marked Blank Form), dBASE will automatically start up a Form Expert to help you. To get a blank form that you can lay out "by hand," click in the Blank Form radio button and then click on the Next button.

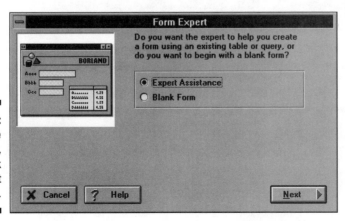

Figure 10-1:
To use Form Expert, simply click on the Next button.

4. Click on the Next button.

In the next dialog box, shown in Figure 10-2, dBASE asks which table or query you want to use with the form.

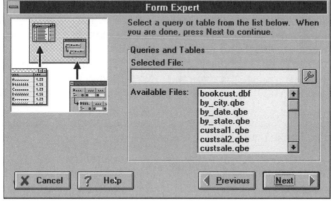

Figure 10-2: dBASE asks which table or query you want to use with the form.

5. In the Available Files list, double-click on the table or query you want to use.

The name of the file you selected should appear in the Selected File blank.

6. Click on the Next button.

In the next dialog box, shown in Figure 10-3, dBASE asks which fields you want to include on the form. If you're planning to use the form for data entry, it's best to include all the fields.

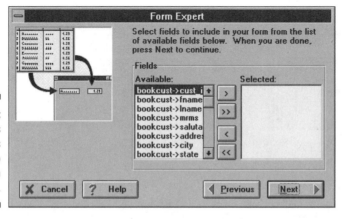

Figure 10-3: dBASE asks which fields you want to include on the form.

Between the Available list and the Selected list, there are four buttons. The top button, with a single right-pointing arrow, takes the currently high-lighted field in the Available list and selects it for inclusion on the form — that is, moves it into the Selected list.

The second button, with a double right-pointing arrow, moves *all* the fields from the Available list into the Selected list.

The third button, with a single left-pointing arrow, deselects the field currently highlighted in the Selected list. In other words, it deletes the field from the Selected list and moves it back into the Available list.

The fourth button, with a double left-pointing arrow, deselects *all* the fields in the Selected list and moves them back into the Available list.

7. Select the fields you want for the form; then click on the Next button.

A new dialog box appears, as shown in Figure 10-4, asking what kind of layout you want for your on-screen form. You have four choices, each of which is illustrated at the top left corner of the dialog box.

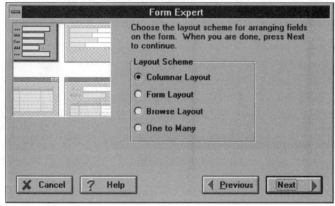

Figure 10-4:
dBASE asks
which
layout you
want to use
for the form.

Columnar Layout arranges the fields and field labels in a column, aligned with the left edge of the screen.

Form Layout arranges the fields and labels as they might appear on a printed form.

Browse Layout arranges the fields in pretty much the same way they'd appear in a Browse window.

One to Many layout is a specialized layout for multi-table forms. Don't worry about this one.

8. Select the layout you want for the form and then click on the Next button.

The next dialog box, shown in Figure 10-5, lets you choose the size, color, and style of text (such as the form title) on your form. It also lets you select the background color for the form and for the field blanks. There are several things to notice about this dialog box.

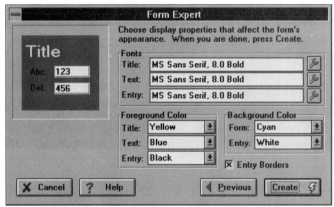

Figure 10-5:
dBASE asks
about the
text styles,
sizes, and
colors you
want to use
on the form.

At the top left corner, dBASE shows you a preview of what the form will look like if you create it with the current text size, color, and so on.

The Fonts group, at the top right of the dialog box, lets you pick the text size, font, and style for the form's title, any text that appears on the form, and the table data that will be displayed in the field blanks. Notice that at the right end of each blank, there's a wrench button. By clicking on the button, you open another dialog box that lets you make your choices for each text item on your form.

The Foreground Color group controls the color of the letters in each different text item (such as title and field labels). Each blank in this group has a simple down-arrow button at its right end. By clicking on the button, you can open a list box in which you can select the color you want for each item.

The Background Color group controls the color of the form's background. It works the same way as the Foreground Color group.

The Entry Borders check box lets you tell dBASE if you want a line around each field blank on the form. The field blanks are where the table data will appear.

9. Select the text sizes, styles, colors, and other stuff in the dialog box. Then click on the Create button.

The dBASE Form Expert works for a few moments and then displays your form layout on the screen, as shown in Figure 10-6. If you want, you can now modify the form layout.

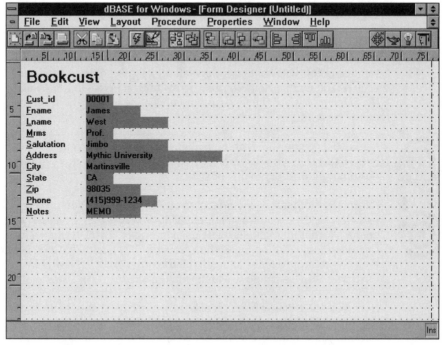

Figure 10-6:
dBASE
creates and
displays the
layout of
the form.

10. Save the form design by opening the File menu and selecting Save.

You're done! Now you or anyone else can use the form to enter or view data in the table.

Hands on: Creating a Form

Now you'll create a form for the book's example database. If you want to create a form for your own database, just follow along, making the same moves with your own database.

First, start up dBASE again and open the Caveat catalog. In the left side of the Catalog window, click on the Forms icon. Then double-click on the Untitled form icon in the right side of the Catalog window. The first dialog box appears, as shown in Figure 10-1, asking if you want Expert Assistance. Because you do, simply click on the Next button.

In the next dialog box, shown in Figure 10-2, the Expert asks which table or query it should use to create the form. At the right side of the dialog box is a list of tables and queries. In the list, click on the Bookcust table; when you do, its name should appear in the blank above the list. Then click on the Next button.

Selecting and arranging fields

In the next dialog box, shown in Figure 10-3, the Expert asks which fields it should include from the Customer table. Normally, if you're going to use a form for data entry, you want to include all the table's fields on the form. Therefore, click on the double right-pointing arrow button between the Available list and the Selected list. All the fields should now appear in the Selected list. Click again on the Next button.

If you change your mind about a choice you made in an earlier dialog box, the Form Expert lets you backtrack by clicking on the Previous button at the bottom right of every dialog box.

A form doesn't have to include all the fields in a table. You can include as many or as few fields as you want. For entering new records, though, it's best to create a form that includes all fields in the table. If you created a form for the Customer table that only had the Last Name, City, and ZIP Code fields on it, then you'd have to enter data into all the other fields by switching to the Customer Browse window, which would make the form a waste of time.

Next, you see a dialog box that asks how the Expert should arrange the fields on the form. At the right side of the dialog box, as shown in Figure 10-4, are radio buttons you can click to select a field layout. After you've chosen the field layout you want, click on the Next button.

The next dialog box, shown in Figure 10-5, lets you choose the size, style, and color for the form's text. As before, there are list boxes on the right and previews on the left. Click on the buttons at the right to see what the different options look like. Then select the ones you like best.

That's all the information you need to provide! The Form Expert is now ready to create your form. In the dialog box, click on the Create button. dBASE works for a few seconds, and presto! Your new form design appears on-screen, as shown earlier in Figure 10-6.

The final step is to name the form design and save it. To do this, open the File menu and select Save Form. The Save Target File dialog box appears. In the File Name blank at the top left corner of the dialog box, type **CUSTFORM**. Then click on OK. dBASE saves the form on your PC's hard disk.

Previewing your form

To see what your form will look like when it's used — or to start using it yourself — click on the Run Form button in the SpeedBar.

Moving Around in the Table

In this section, you learn about moving around *in* the Customer table when you're looking at it with a form. That's different from moving around *under* a table, which is sometimes good for picking up loose change or the odd contact lens.

But rest easy: Moving around your table with a form is very similar to moving around it with a Browse window. You just use the buttons in the SpeedBar. Here are the moves to make (see Figure 10-7 for the buttons to click):

✔ **To move to the first record:** Click on the First Record button in the SpeedBar or press Ctrl+PageUp on your keyboard.

✔ **To move to the last record:** Click on the Last Record button in the SpeedBar or press Ctrl+PageDn.

✔ **To move to the next record:** Click on the Next Record button in the SpeedBar or press the PageDn key.

✔ **To move to the previous record:** Click on the Previous Record button in the SpeedBar or press the PageUp key.

✔ **To move to a specific record number:** Open the Form menu and select Go to record number, or press Ctrl+G. In the dialog box, type the number of the record you want and click on OK.

Figure 10-7:
Use these buttons to move around in the table while using a form.

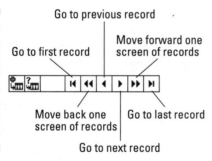

Go to previous record

Go to first record

Move forward one screen of records

Move back one screen of records

Go to last record

Go to next record

Play around with the buttons and key combinations a few times just to get the feel of them. It's easier than you probably expected.

Entering Data with a Form

Entering data with a form is just as easy as entering data with a Browse window. To enter data using a form, follow these steps:

1. **In the Catalog window, click on the Forms icon at the left.**

   The Catalog window displays all the forms you've created for the current database.

2. **Right-click on the icon for the form you want to use.**

3. **In the SpeedMenu, select <u>R</u>un Form.**

   The Form window appears. This window is where you can enter new records using the form.

4. **Open the Form menu and select Add record, or press Ctrl+ A.**

   dBASE creates a new, blank record after the current last record in the table. The new record is displayed in the form. All of its fields are blank, because you haven't yet entered any data. The cursor is in the first field.

5. **Enter data in the first field.**

   Type the appropriate data in the first field. If you fill the first field, dBASE automatically kicks you into the next field. Otherwise, just press Tab to go to the next field.

6. **Enter data in each field of the new record. When you've entered all the data for that record (whether or not you use all the fields), press Ctrl+A to add another record.**

   The new record is automatically saved, and a new, blank record appears displayed. You can now enter data for another record.

7. **When you're finished, close the Form window.**

   dBASE returns you to the Catalog. If you want to verify that the data you entered is in the table, you can display the table in a Browse window.

Now that you've learned yet another valuable dBASE skill — creating and using forms — get up and stretch your legs. Better yet, make those legs walk you down to the nearest ice cream store and indulge in some chocolate almond. Consider it a "form" of reward for your hard work.

Chapter 11

Finding Stuff Fast in Your Database

● ●

In This Chapter

▶ Different ways to find stuff

▶ Finding stuff the easy way

▶ Looking for parts of words

▶ Searching for things that *sound like* something

▶ Replacing stuff the easy way

● ●

*B*efore you can find stuff in a database, you need to have

✔ Created a table (Chapter 4).

✔ Put some data in the table (Chapter 5) so that you have something to find.

✔ Learned about fundamental database concepts, such as table, field, and data type (Chapters 1 and 2).

✔ Found your glasses so that you can see the PC screen.

In order to do this chapter's steps with the book's example database, you need to have

✔ Created the Caveat catalog (Chapter 2).

✔ Created the Customer table (Chapter 4).

✔ Put customer records into the table (Chapter 5).

If you're searching for data in your own real-life database, just read this chapter to get the basic ideas. Then follow the steps with your own database instead of the one in this book.

Finding things is a problem for everyone. You can't find your car keys, or your checkbook, or your mother-in-law's sense of humor. You can't find the nerve to ask your boss for a raise. You can't find your youthful idealism. And you can't find any good TV shows on Sunday night.

One thing you *can* find — you hope — is information in your database. And with dBASE, it's as quick and easy as you could imagine. If the information you need is something simple, such as the data on all customers who have the last name *Trump,* you can use the Find Records menu choice. Just open the Table menu, select Find Records, pick the last name field in the list at the lower left, type the word **Trump,** and receive your answer. If what you're looking for is more complicated, dBASE helps you create a *query* to find whatever you need. For example:

✔ With Find Records, you can display the records for all the customers who live in California.

✔ With Find Records, you also can display the records for all the customers who have the letters *an* anywhere in their last name, address, or city.

✔ With Replace Records, you can search for every occurrence of Minneapolis and replace it with Albuquerque (which would mightily annoy your customers in Minneapolis).

✔ With a simple query, you can display only the first and last name fields of the records for customers whose zip code is 90210.

✔ With a more complex query, you can display the records for all the customers whose names contain the letters *an,* have the zip code 90210, and are professors at the University of California. And so that you don't have to redo the query every time you need the information, you can save it to reuse later, just like fast-food hamburgers you pop into the freezer (but without the cholesterol).

Both ways of finding information have advantages and disadvantages. Using the Find Records menu choice is fast and easy, but you can look for (or find and replace) only one thing at a time: a last name, a string of letters, or a ZIP code, for example. Using a query is a bit more involved (though still easy), but you can look for combinations of things, display only the fields you want, and save the query to use again later.

If you ever see the word *string* in a computer book, it has nothing to do with the stuff you use to tie up a box. In computer jargon, a string is just some text, like "Sister Susie sells seashells by the seashore." (Most strings are a little easier to say five times fast.)

This chapter covers everything you need to know about using the Find Records and Replace Records menu choices. You learn about queries in the next chapter.

Finding Stuff the Easy Way

The easiest way to find stuff in your database is to use the Find Records menu choice. The basic steps are as follows:

1. **In the Table Editor, display the table you want to search.**

   You can display the table any way you want: in Browse, Form, or Columnar view. It makes no difference for the search.

2. **Open the Table menu and select Find Records.**

   The Table menu is available only when a table is displayed in the Table Editor. Selecting Find Records displays the Find Records dialog box.

3. **In the Find Field list, select the field you want to search.**

   You select a field by clicking it. For example, if you are looking for a customer record with the last name of Smith, you click on the LNAME field.

4. **In the Find What blank, type the text you want to find.**

   If you're looking for a customer record with the last name of Smith, type **Smith**.

5. **In the check boxes, select the search options you want.**

   The check boxes are the little square blanks marked Match Case, Anywhere in Field, and Soundex. These options are explained in the next section.

   An option is turned on if there's an X in its check box. You can turn an option on or off by clicking its check box.

6. **Start the search by clicking on the Find Next button.**

   This action tells dBASE to find the first (if any) record that matches what you're looking for. You can then look at the Table Editor window, where the record will be shown. To find the next matching record, just repeat Step 6. When there are no more matching records or you get to the end of the table, dBASE tells you.

It may surprise you to learn that the Find menu choice activates a dBASE command, but the command itself isn't called *Find*. Instead, it's the dBASE *Locate* command. If you've worked with older versions of dBASE, this will help you understand how the Find menu choice works. If you haven't worked with older versions of dBASE, this knowledge probably won't do you a single bit of good, even if you live to be 100 years old.

Options in the Find Records dialog box

The great thing about the options in the Find Records dialog box is that they're all standard equipment — they come with dBASE and don't cost you a penny more! (If you feel guilty about getting free options, send me a check, and I'll forward it to the dealership.)

The Find Records dialog box is shown in Figure 11-1. If text has been entered in the Find What blank, you can see the Find Next button. This button is grayed out when the blank is empty.

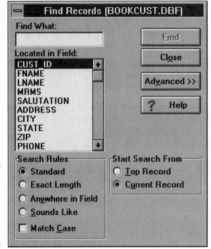

Figure 11-1:
The Find
Records
dialog box.

The following are the standard-equipment options in the Find Records dialog box:

- *Match Case* tells dBASE to pay attention to whether letters are uppercase or lowercase. Normally, this option is turned on unless you turn it off. If it's turned on, you'll see an X in the check box for the option. If Match Case is not turned on and you enter **joe** in the Find What blank, dBASE searches for not only joe, but Joe, JOE, joE, and so on. If Match Case is turned on, dBASE searches only for exact matches (in other words, joe).

- *Anywhere in Field* tells dBASE to look anywhere in the field. Normally when you search for something, dBASE looks for it only at the beginning of the field. For example, suppose you're looking for a name that contains the letters *ge*. Unless you turn on the Anywhere in Field option, dBASE finds

Gerald (which starts with the letters *ge*) but not Jorge (which contains *ge*, but not at the beginning of the field). If you check Anywhere in Field, however, dBASE finds both names.

✔ *Soundex* is pretty fancy stuff. It lets you search for things that sound like what you type in the Find What blank. Suppose that you have only an approximate memory of a customer's name: it begins with *H*, ends with *t*, and there's an *r* in there somewhere. By checking the Soundex option, you can type **hrt** in the Find What blank. dBASE searches for anything that sounds something like that: Hart, Harriet, and so on. It would not look for His Royal Highness Prince Charles, but that's probably not someone you would be searching for in your job anyway, unless you work for a tabloid newspaper.

Using wildcards: not needed here

Previous versions of dBASE let you use *wildcard* characters in doing a search. For example, if you want to find all the records in which a customer's first name begins with *J*, enter J* (the letter *J* plus an asterisk). This search finds Joe, Jill, Johann, Jeremy, and so on. If you have something more specific in mind, you can use the ? (question mark) wildcard. Enter J???, and dBASE searches for all first names that begin with *J* and have exactly four letters (one for each question mark). Thus dBASE would find John, Joan, and Jill, but not Jeremy, Johann, or Jorge.

The current version of dBASE for Windows does not use these wildcard characters with the Find Records menu choice. Instead, if you want to search for something that begins a word or text

string, type the text that you know in the Find What blank of the Find Records dialog box. Thus, if you type J in the Find What blank, dBASE finds all the records for the selected field that have text beginning with *J*.

If you want to search for something that's not at the beginning of the field, just check the Anywhere in Field checkbox in the Find Records dialog box. With this box checked, you can enter **ri** in the Find What blank, and pick the first name field, and dBASE will find all the records in which the first name field contains *ri*, including records for Harriet Stowe and Teri Lane.

For more information about wildcards, see Chapter 12.

Hunting down the hidden options

There are two important search options that aren't in the Find Records dialog box: *Exact* and *Near*. No, they aren't really hidden; it just seems that way. They're in the Desktop Properties dialog box for the reason that they apply to many kinds of database searches, not just those using the Find Records dialog box. The Desktop Properties dialog box is shown in Figure 11-2.

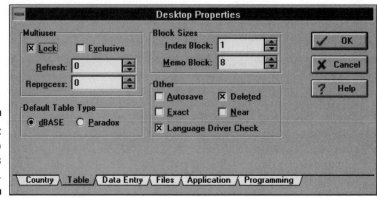

Figure 11-2:
The Desktop
Properties
dialog box.

Here's what the Exact and Near options do:

> ✔ *Exact* tells dBASE to look only for records that have an exact match of the search text. Normally, this is turned off, meaning that if you're searching for the text *jo*, dBASE searches for jo, jolly, Jolene, and so on in the field you selected. If you turn on Exact, then dBASE searches only for the exact text that you type.

> ✔ *Near* tells dBASE that if it can't find exactly what you type, then it should display any records that contain something similar to what you type. dBASE uses this setting if you don't tell it to use the Exact option.

If you want to change the Exact or Near options, you have to get to the Database Settings dialog box. Here's how to find it:

1. **Open the Properties menu and select Desktop.**

   The Desktop Properties dialog box appears. Along the bottom of the dialog box are little tabs, similar to the tabs that stick up from the tops of file folders.

2. **Click on the tab labeled Table.**

   In this part of the dialog box, you can change the Exact or Near option as you desire.

3. **To make the changes you selected, click on OK to close the dialog box.**

   If you change your mind, just click on Cancel.

Hands on: Finding a Customer Record

To get some experience with the Find Records operation, try using it in the sample Customer table you created in earlier chapters. Suppose that you want to find the records of all customers who live in California. To do so, follow these steps:

1. **Make sure that the Caveat catalog is opened.**

   Remember that a catalog's job is to keep together all the items that pertain to a given database. But if you don't open the catalog before you start working, it won't do you any good! (See Chapters 2 and 4 if you need a review of catalogs.)

2. **In the Catalog window, double-click on the icon for the Customer table.**

   The Table Editor should appear on your screen. Normally, it shows the Customer table in Browse view.

3. **Press F2 to switch to Form view.**

   Now you can see an entire record on the screen at once.

4. **Open the Table menu and select Find Records.**

   The Find Records dialog box appears on your screen.

5. **Drag the dialog box out of the way so you can see all of the record.**

   Your screen should look something like Figure 11-3.

6. **In the Find What blank, type CA. (Don't type the period.)**

   dBASE knows what you want to search for.

7. **In the Find Field list, click on STATE to select that field.**

   dBASE knows what field you want to search. You might need to click on the scroll bar to move downward in the list. (If you're hazy about how to use scroll bars, see IDG's *Windows For Dummies* by Andy Rathbone.)

8. **Click on the Find Next button.**

   dBASE finds the first record with *CA* in the STATE field. That's the record for James West, or "Jimbo" as he's known to his friends, family, and parole officer.

9. **Click again on the Find Next button.**

   dBASE moves to the record for Teri Lane, who lives in Santa Barbara, California. If you haven't been there, it's notable that Santa Barbara is the home of Isla Vista, where you'll find UCSB, rated as the top party school in North America. (It also has outstanding academics, but who cares about that?)

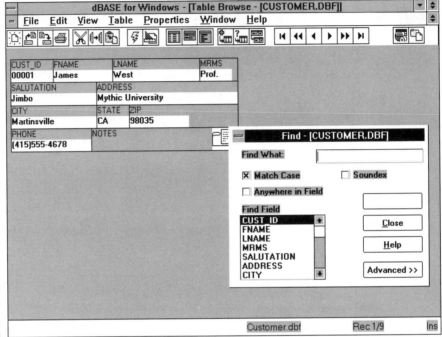

Figure 11-3:
Your screen
should look
something
like this
after you
drag the
dialog box
to the side.

10. Click one more time on the Find Next button.

There are no more records with *CA* in the STATE field. dBASE beeps at you and displays a dialog box titled Alert that says Value not found. (see Figure 11-4). Originally, the box said Danger Will Robinson! but Borland (which makes dBASE) didn't want to get sued by the Jupiter 2's robot.

dBASE searches *down* from your current position in the table. So if you aren't looking at the first record in the table (Record Number 1, for James West), press Ctrl-PgUp to move to the top of the table.

In theory, when you use the Find Records menu choice, dBASE starts searching from the first record in your table. In practice, however, that doesn't always happen. If you're viewing a record in the middle or near the end of a table and you do a Find Records, dBASE may not search above the current record. That means if you're at record number 15 and the data you're searching for is in record number 9, your search will come up empty because dBASE normally searches downward in the table.

To be safe, therefore, you should always go to the first record in the table before doing a Find. In older DOS versions of dBASE, you did this by typing the rather quaint-sounding GO TOP command. You can still use this command if you like, but you can also go to the first record by pressing Ctrl-PgUp or by opening the Table menu and selecting Top Record.

Figure 11-4:
dBASE has
reached the
end of the
table. There
are no more
records of
people living
in California.

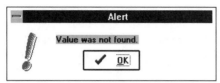

Finding Something Buried in a Field

Suppose that you've been working for three nights straight and, in your semicomatose state, you vaguely remember a customer whose first name has two *R*s in it somewhere. That's it; you don't remember anything more.

Bleary-eyed, hands trembling, you open the Table Editor, go to the first record, and open the Find Records dialog box. Do that now. If you can't make your hands tremble, the situation will lack drama, but the search works just as well. To do the search, follow these steps:

1. **In the Find What blank, type RR. (Don't type the period.)**

   This action tells dBASE what you want to search for.

2. **In the Find Field list, click on FNAME to select that field.**

   This action tells dBASE where you want to search.

3. **Click in the check box next to Match Case to uncheck it.**

   dBASE looks for all occurrences of *rr*, regardless of capitalization.

4. **Click the checkbox next to Anywhere in Field to check it.**

   dBASE searches for all occurrences of *rr*, no matter where they appear in the field.

5. **Click on the Find Next button.**

   dBASE finds the first record with *rr* in the FNAME field. That's the record for Harriet Stowe, who is virtually unknown today but was once famous as the author of *Uncle Tom's Cabin* and other great works of American literature.

6. **Click again on the Find Next button.**

   dBASE beeps and displays a dialog box that says `Value not found.` Because Harriet Stowe was the only customer with the *rr* in her name, you know that she's the one you wanted to find.

Finding and Replacing Stuff

You can replace things in your table just as easily as you can find them. For example, suppose that you find that all the customers whose records indicate that they live in California actually live in New Jersey. You can tell dBASE to go through the table, look at the STATE field of each record, and change every occurrence of *CA* to *NJ,* the abbreviation for New Jersey. Here's how to do it:

1. **In the Catalog window, double-click on the icon for the table you want.**

   In this case, it's the Customer table. The Table Editor should appear on your screen. Normally, it shows the Customer table in Browse view.

2. **Press F2 to switch to Form view.**

   Now you can see an entire record on the screen at once.

3. **Make sure you're at the first record in the table.**

   If you aren't, press Ctrl-PgUp to jump to the top of the table.

4. **Open the Properties menu and select Replace Records.**

   The Replace Records dialog box appears on your screen (see Figure 11-5).

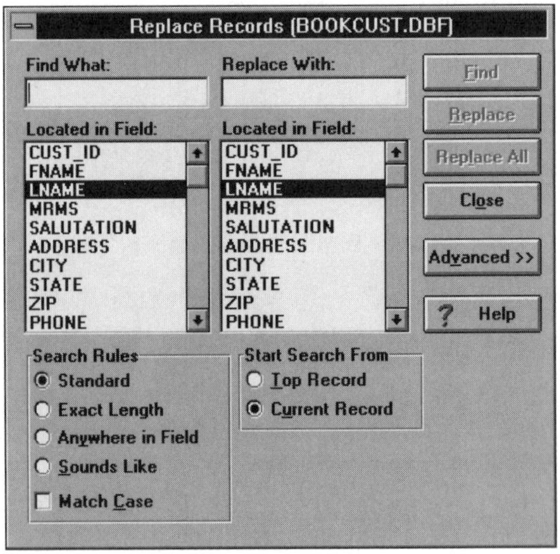

Figure 11-5:
The Replace
Records
dialog box.

5. **Drag the dialog box out of the way so you can see all of the record.**

6. **In the Find What blank, type the value you want to find and replace.**

   In this case, type **CA**. (Don't type the period.)

7. **In the field list under the Find What blank, select the field you want to search.**

   In this case, select the STATE field so that dBASE searches in that field.

8. **In the Replace With blank, type the replacement text.**

   In this case, type **NJ** to let dBASE know what to replace the original value with.

9. **In the field list under the Replace With blank, select the field where the new value should go.**

   In this case, select the STATE field again.

10. **Click on the Replace All button.**

    dBASE tells you how many matching records it found and asks if you want to commit your changes, which just means "Are you sure about this?"

11. **If you're sure, click on OK.**

    dBASE replaces the original value in all the table's records.

Do You Have to Index?

One thing you may hear, sooner or later, is that *indexing* a field makes database searches go faster. Indexing is covered in Chapter 15. But should you always index the fields you want to search?

The answer is no. In a small database — say, 1,000 records or fewer — almost any search goes quickly. In a larger database, however, a search goes faster if you search on an *indexed* field.

Don't feel, however, that you must index a field before you search for stuff in it. Unless your database is larger than 1,000 records, indexing a field probably won't make much difference in search speed.

Now, if you can find the energy, go get some fresh air. It's not good to sit cooped up all day in front of the computer. Even when you're working with dBASE.

"HOW'S THAT FOR FAST SCROLLING?"

Chapter 12

Queries Have More Power to Find Stuff

● ●

In This Chapter

▶ What is a query, anyway?

▶ Three steps for perfect queries

▶ Doing a simple query

▶ Saving a query to use later

▶ Reusing a saved query

● ●

*Y*ou have to put up with lots of weird words every day. For example, there's *microprocessor* (a boss who's always looking over your shoulder); *short meeting* (you should forget about getting anything done for the rest of the afternoon); *revenue enhancement* (which never seems to enhance *your* revenue); and even *epistemology* (the study of plant stems — always a favorite at parties). Well, get ready for another one: *query*.

In the last chapter, you learned how to use the F̲ind Record menu choice. Although it's quick and easy, it has some disadvantages. First, you can search for only one thing at a time. Second, you can't view just the fields that interest you. Third, you can look only for matches of one kind. In a sales table, for example, you can look for all records in which the price is *exactly* $10 but not for all records in which the sale price is less than *or* more than $10.

In this chapter, you learn how to find information in your database using queries. Queries require a little more effort than using the F̲ind Record menu choice, but they deliver a lot more power. You can handle it: You're psycho-epistemologically well-integrated (ready).

To understand the ideas in this chapter, you should know the concepts of a table, fields, and data types (Chapter 3). To practice using queries with this book's database, you can use the Sales table you'll create in this chapter.

If you're creating a query for your own real-life database, just read this chapter to get the basic ideas. Then follow the steps with your own table instead of the one in this book.

Query is just a fancy word for a question you ask dBASE about a table or database. *Running a query* just means asking the question. Without queries, you couldn't find your data as easily. And without words like *query*, database experts couldn't get paid $100 an hour.

Three Steps for Perfect Queries

Before you get into the specific steps of doing a query, it's important to understand the big picture, which is illustrated by Figure 12-1. When you set up a query, you are doing three things:

- ✔ You specify the fields you want to search. For example, if you want the records for all customers named Smith who live in ZIP code 90210, you tell dBASE to search the LNAME (last name) and ZIP fields.

- ✔ You specify what you're looking for. For the example just described, you'd tell dBASE to show you all the records in which Smith is in the LNAME field and 90210 is in the ZIP field.

- ✔ You specify what fields you want to see in the answer. You may not want to see all the fields of the records found by the query. When you run a query, you must tell dBASE which fields you want to see when it displays the answer.

Figure 12-1:
What
happens
when you
create and
run a query.

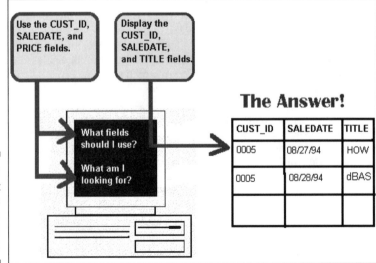

You can also specify the order in which you want dBASE to display the records (A to Z or Z to A), but that's optional.

Because queries are often more complicated than simple searches you do with the Find Record menu choice, it would be a pain in the neck if you had to redo them every time you needed to get the same information from your database. Therefore, you can also save queries and reuse them whenever you want.

How to Create a Query in dBASE

You may want to work through the hands-on example of creating a query later in the chapter, but here are the basic steps for creating a query in dBASE:

1. **In the left side of the Catalog window, click on the Queries icon.**

   dBASE displays all the currently available queries in the right side of the Catalog window. In addition to the available queries (in other words, those already created), you'll see an icon labeled Untitled.

2. **Double-click on the Untitled query icon.**

   dBASE displays a dialog box asking which table you want to search for data.

3. **In the dialog box, select the table you want to use.**

   As soon as you select a table, dBASE displays the Query Designer window, which contains a *skeleton* of the table's structure. The skeleton is basically just a horizontal field list. In the skeleton, you pick the fields you want to include in the query. You also tell dBASE if you want it to sort the records it finds in any particular order, such as by last name or account number.

4. **Pick the fields you want to see in the answer.**

   You pick the fields by clicking in the little boxes on the second row of the table skeleton, as shown in Figure 12-2. Clicking in a box selects that field and tells dBASE to display that field in the query answer. If you want to see all of the table's fields in the query answer, click in the little box on the left end. When you click in any of the boxes, a check mark appears in that box to show that the field is selected for display.

   If the field you want isn't currently shown on the screen, you can use the left- and right-arrow buttons at the left end of the table skeleton to scroll the fields left and right.

Click here if you want
the query answer to
display all fields in the table.

Click in these boxes
to select the fields to
display in the query.

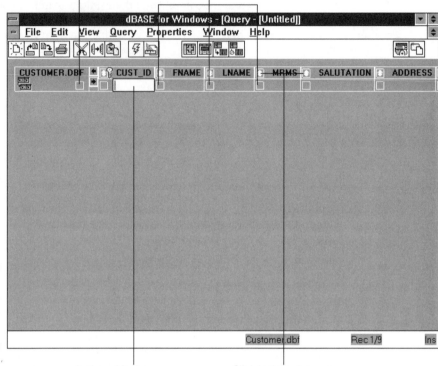

Figure 12-2:
The Query
Designer
window.

In these blanks, you
enter the stuff the query
should be looking for.

Click in these boxes to
sort records by the
fields you choose.

5. If you want the records sorted in the query answer, tell dBASE how to sort them.

You do this by clicking on the Sort button of one or more fields, as shown in Figure 12-2. When you click on the Sort button, a list box is displayed as long as you hold down the left mouse button. As you move the mouse pointer up and down in the list box, the message line at the bottom of the window tells you what each option is. When you've highlighted the option you want, release the left mouse button. The list box closes and your selection is made. If you want to change it, just reopen the list box and pick something else.

What sort of thing is sorting, anyway?

To *sort* records means to put them in order. For example, you can sort customer records in alphabetical order by last name or in numerical order by ZIP code. You can sort sales records in order by the date the sale was made, in numerical order by dollar amount, or alphabetical order by the book title.

Sorting can be done in *ascending* (A through Z, 1 through 10) order or *descending* (Z through A, 10 through 1) order. There are also some fine points about uppercase and lowercase letters, which you can generally ignore. Sorting is explained in more detail in Chapter 16.

For example, if you want to see the query answer in alphabetical order by last name, click the Sort button of the LNAME field, pick Ascending sort from the list box, and release the mouse button.

6. Tell dBASE what you're looking for.

You do this by entering a value in the blank under a field name. To get into a particular blank, just click in it with the mouse. There are some special rules for entering values in field blanks, which are explained in the next section. For example, if you are looking for a customer whose first name is Teri, you enter **$"Teri"** into the first name (FNAME) field blank. Be sure to include the quote marks.

 7. Run the query and look at the answer.

Running the query means that you tell dBASE to look for records matching what you told it in Step 6 and then display the records on the screen as a query answer. You run the query by clicking on the button that looks like a lightning bolt, otherwise known as the Run query button, in the middle of the SpeedBar. As soon as you click it, dBASE finds the records that match what you're looking for (if there are any) and displays them on your screen in a query answer.

8. Save the query and then head for the beach. Surf's up!

Save the query by opening the File menu and selecting Save. If you prefer, you can click the Save button in the SpeedBar. dBASE displays a dialog box asking you to name the query. The rules for naming the query are the same rules as for naming a table or any DOS disk file: a maximum of eight letters, digits, or underscore characters, and no spaces or punctuation marks are allowed. After you've saved the query, it's time to hit the waves. Don't forget your sunscreen!

Editing data in the query answer

Normally, the answer to a query contains *live* data, which means that you can edit the data just as though the data were displayed in the Table Editor window (explained in Chapter 5). However, if you sort the data on more than one field, dBASE copies the original table data for the query answer. You still get the answer you want, but you can't edit the data.

Sorting *on a field* just means using that field to put the records in order. Thus, if you sort on the last name field, the records in the query answer are in order by last name. Sorting on more than one field means using multiple fields to order the records. If you sort on last name and first name, then overall, the records will be in order by last name. But within each group of records with the same last name — for example, you might have 15 customers with the last name Jones — the records will be in order by first name: Alice Jones, Bruce Jones, Carol Jones, Dan Jones, and Engelbert Jones.

Changing the order of fields in the answer

Normally, the fields in the query answer appear in the same order as they appear in the table. In this book's example Bookcust table, this means that the fields in the query answer appear in the order CUST_ID, FNAME, LNAME, and so on. This order stays the same even if the query answer doesn't display all the fields.

But suppose that you want the query answer to display the fields in a different order — for example, CITY, LNAME, and FNAME? Can you change the order of the fields in the query answer? Yes!

Anyway, it's easy to rearrange the order of the fields in the query answer. All that you need to do is drag a field into the position you want. For example, if want to move the MRMS field (see Figure 12-2) to the left of the FNAME field in the query answer, do the following:

1. **In the table skeleton, position the mouse pointer on the field you want to move.**

   In this case, that's the MRMS field.

2. **Hold down the left mouse button.**

That's the button that's on the same side as your left hand. No, wait, is it the one on the same side as your right hand? Hmm ... left mouse button, right hand ... no, it's the button on the same side as your middle hand. Of course, that's only if you live next to a toxic waste dump; otherwise, it's your left hand. If you figured it all out by yourself, give yourself a big hand (any side you want).

3. **Drag the mouse horizontally in the direction you want to move the field.**

   The field you're moving is dragged along with the mouse pointer. In this case, drag the mouse to the left. The MRMS field follows the mouse.

4. **When the field is where you want it to be, release the left mouse button.**

   dBASE drops the field into its new location in the table skeleton. When you run the query, the answer fields appear in the new order.

How to Search for Stuff

In principle, searching for stuff is easy. All you do is enter what you're looking for in the appropriate field blank in the table skeleton.

In practice, it's a little more complicated: not much more complicated, but a little. You have to combine what you're looking for with dBASE *operators* so that dBASE knows exactly how to look for your data. Table 12-1 provides a list of the operators you can use.

Table 12-1	dBASE Operators
Operator	*What It Means*
>	greater than
<	less than
=	equal to
<>	not equal to
>=	greater than or equal to
<=	less than or equal to
$	contains
Like	pattern match

Using the query operators

Some of the operators are pretty obvious. If you've studied a little math — as most of us have — you know what >, the *greater than* operator, means. To search for a number in a field that's greater than 10, for example, you enter **>10** in the table skeleton's blank under that field name.

The only operators that really aren't quite so obvious are the operators for *not equal to, contains,* and *pattern match.* Table 12-2 provides some examples of how the operators work.

When you're looking for text, you have to enclose the text in quotation marks and combine it with an operator. For example, **$ "Teri"** searches for all records that contain *Teri* in the search field, no matter what else is also in the field; **= "Teri"** searches for all records that contain *Teri* and nothing else in the field.

You can also use the greater than, less than, and other relational operators with text. Entering > **"B"** tells dBASE to look for all records where the field begins with a letter after *B* in the alphabet.

Table 12-2	How Query Operators Work
What You Type	*What dBASE Looks For*
="Teri"	Any record with *only* Teri in the field. Nothing else can be in the field.
$ "Teri"	Any record containing Teri in the field, no matter what else is in the field.
> 10	Any record containing a number greater than 10 in the field.
<> 9.95	Any record *not* containing the number 9.95 in the field.
Like "*ne"	Any record containing text that ends in the letters *ne.* The asterisk is what's called a *wildcard;* wildcards are explained in the next section.

Using wildcards

Sometimes, you're not exactly sure what you're looking for. You may remember only that a person's name begins with *J,* or more specifically, that it's a four-letter name beginning with *J* and ending with *n.* Wildcards are a way of telling dBASE that it should ignore any letters except the ones you've specified. The asterisk (*) wildcard tells dBASE that it should ignore any number of letters, while the question mark (?) wildcard tells dBASE to ignore only one character.

That description may seem a little abstract, but wildcards are easy to understand when you see an example. Table 12-3 provides some examples of wildcards in action.

Table 12-3	How Wildcards Work
If You Enter	*dBASE Looks For*
J*	Any text beginning with the letter *J*. In a customer table, dBASE may find the names John, Jane, Jim, Jonathan, Joseph, Joan, Jurgen, Jorge, and Juanita.
J*n	Any text beginning with *J* and ending with *n.* dBASE may find John, Jonathan, and Jurgen.
J??n	Any text beginning with *J*, then having two letters you don't know, and ending with *n*. dBASE could find John and Joan.
J???	Any text beginning with *J* and followed by any three letters. dBASE would find John, Jane, and Joan.

Important Points to Remember

Several things about setting up a query in the Query Designer are important to remember:

- The fields you search and the fields shown in the answer aren't necessarily the same. Just because you search for data in a field doesn't mean it has to appear in the query answer.

- You can search on one or more fields, but you don't *have* to search for data in *any* fields. You can use a query just to see your records in order or to display only certain fields. Searching for data in more than one field is explained in the next chapter.

- You can have the query answer display one or more fields. You can display all the fields or just the ones you want.

- You can rearrange the order of the fields in the answer. You do that by dragging the fields around in the table skeleton.

- You can sort the answer records on one or more fields.

- If you sort on more than one field, the query answer data isn't live data: it's *read-only,* which means you can't change the data in a table by changing it in the query answer.

✔ Unless the answer is read-only, you can edit the data in the query answer. You can change all the customers' first names, for example, so that they are humorous, as long as your customers have a very good sense of humor.

✔ The Run Query and Design Query buttons in the SpeedBar let you design a query and then click on the Run Query button to see if the query works properly. If the query doesn't run correctly, you can click on the Design Query button to switch back to the Query Designer window, where you can make some changes and then run the query again. You can keep repeating the process until the query works exactly the way you want.

Drudge Work Alert! Setting Up a Sales Table

To see the full power of queries, you first need to set up another sample table. This table will record all book sales at Caveat Emptor, the bookstore owned by Honest Janis introduced in Chapter 2. If you've been playing hooky (hookey? hockey? hooey?) since you finished Chapter 11, start up dBASE again and open the Caveat catalog. Then create the Sales table with the fields listed in Table 12-4. Don't worry: You'll use the table a great deal later in the book.

You learned how to set up a table in Chapter 4, so there's no point in repeating the information here. If you're a little hazy on the subject, follow the instructions in Chapter 4. Note also that when you see *N/A* below, it means that something is not applicable. For example, for the SALEDATE field, the Field Size column in Table 12-4 contains N/A because dBASE automatically sets the field size of a Time/Date field.

Table 12-4	Fields for the Sales Table			
Name	*Type*	*Width*	*Decimal*	*Indexed*
CUST_ID	Character	5	N/A	Ascend (Yes)
SALEDATE	Date	N/A	N/A	No
TITLE	Character	50	N/A	No
AUTHOR	Character	25	N/A	No
PRICE	Float	8	2	No

Save the table under the name *Sales*. When dBASE prompts you for a description, enter **Book sales table**.

Now enter the following five records into the Sales table. (If you want to put in more records, Appendix A lists all ten records for this table.) Because it contains numeric data, the Sales table is better for illustrating the power of queries than the Customer Records table.

CUST_ID: 00004
SALEDATE: 8/21/94
TITLE: How to Write a Computer Book
AUTHOR: Obscurantis, Jargon
PRICE: 2.95

CUST_ID: 00001
SALEDATE: 8/25/94
TITLE: In Praise of Idleness
AUTHOR: Russell, Bertrand
PRICE: 12.95

CUST_ID: 00002
SALEDATE: 8/26/94
TITLE: Getting Your Husband Off His Lazy Butt
AUTHOR: Russell, Mrs. Bertrand
PRICE: 12.95

CUST_ID: 00005
SALEDATE: 8/27/94
TITLE: How I Turned $25 Cash into a Successful Business
AUTHOR: Fleiss, Heidi
PRICE: 24.95

CUST_ID: 00005
SALEDATE: 8/28/94
TITLE: Access 2 For Dummies
AUTHOR: Palmer, Scott
PRICE: 19.95

Creating a Simple Query

Now that you've created the Sales table, it's time to do a simple query. This one will do just a little more than you can do using the Find Record menu choice. In the next chapter, you learn how to do more powerful queries. At this point, you should have the Caveat catalog opened and the Catalog window on-screen. Click on the Query icon on the left side of the Catalog window, as shown in Figure 12-3.

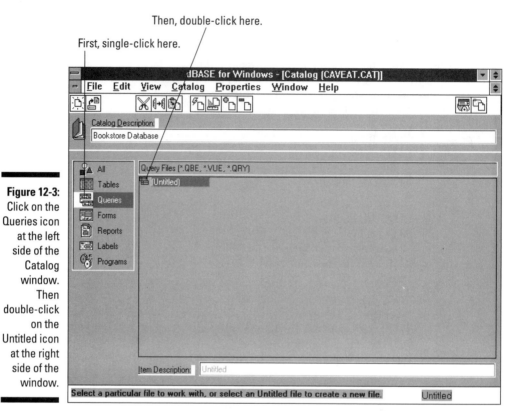

Figure 12-3:
Click on the
Queries icon
at the left
side of the
Catalog
window.
Then
double-click
on the
Untitled icon
at the right
side of the
window.

No queries exist yet, so the right side of the Catalog window is empty except for
the Untitled icon. To create a query, double-click on the Untitled query icon on
the right side of the window. When you do this, dBASE displays a dialog box
asking which table to use. Select the Sales table and click on OK. Then the
Query Designer window appears, as shown in Figure 12-4. Click on the window's
Maximize button so that the window fills the whole screen.

To select the fields for the query answer and tell dBASE what you're looking for,
follow these steps:

1. **Click in the field selection boxes for CUST_ID, SALEDATE, TITLE, and
   PRICE.**

   These are the little boxes in the second row of the table skeleton, underneath each field name. When a field is selected for display, a check mark
   appears in the field selection box.

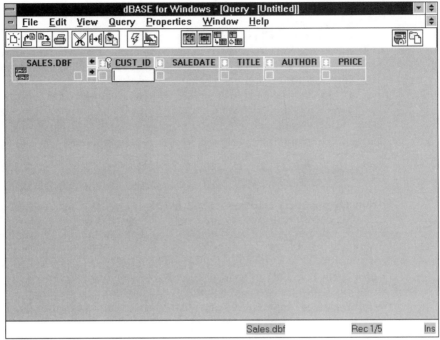

Figure 12-4:
The Query
Designer
window.

2. Enter the query condition.

You want to find all book sales where the price of the book is greater than
$10. Therefore click in the blank under PRICE in the table skeleton and
type **> 10.** The table skeleton should look like the one shown in Figure 12-5.
Do not, absolutely, *don't,* include the dollar sign. The dollar sign has a
special meaning in queries, and it's *not* a unit of currency.

Figure 12-5:
How the
table
skeleton
should look
after you've
done Steps
1 and 2.

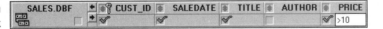

What you did in the preceding example was use a *relational operator* (greater than) to prepare for a search that you can't do by using the Find Record menu choice. Instead of telling dBASE to search for a specific text string or number, you asked it to look for records in which the price has a certain relation to $10 — in this case, a price that's greater than $10. You'll learn even more about relational operators in the next chapter — unless you run away and join the circus, in which case you'll be much too busy cleaning out the animal cages. Don't ask what you'll be cleaning out of them. Trust me, you'll have more fun learning about queries.

Running the query

Running the query is the easiest part of all. Do you see the lightning bolt button on the SpeedBar, shown in Figure 12-4? That's the Run query button. Click on it, and dBASE finds all the Sales records that match what you specified in the query.

dBASE displays the query answer in a Browse window. In the answer, you see only the fields you requested and only the books that satisfy the query — that is, the ones costing more than $10. The answer window is shown in Figure 12-6.

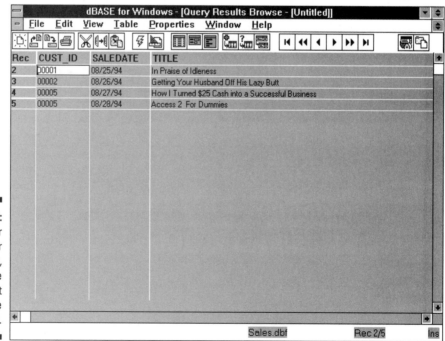

Figure 12-6:
The answer to your query (sorry, not the query about which horse to bet).

The answer window for a dBASE query doesn't have any special name. Different
database managers call the answer window different things. Paradox calls it an
answer table, and Access calls it a *dynaset.* If for some reason you ever use
another database manager, you'll need to know that little bit of jargon. The
window title of a query answer is Query Results Browse — you can use that as a
name if you like.

Saving the query

The last step in the query process is saving the query, which is almost as easy
as running the query. Open the File menu and select Save. The Save File dialog
box appears, as shown in Figure 12-7. If it looks familiar, that's because it's
basically the same dialog box you used to name the form and the tables you
created earlier in this book.

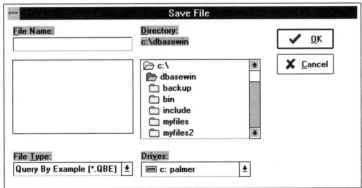

Figure 12-7:
The Save
File dialog
box.

For the query name, type **OVER10.** Then click on the OK button. Finally, close
the Query window by double-clicking on the Window Control button in the
top left corner. (As usual, make sure that you don't accidentally click on the
Window Control button for dBASE; the button you want is the one underneath
the button in the top left corner of the screen.) dBASE returns you to the
Catalog window. (The shortcut key for closing the window is Ctrl+F4.)

Rerunning a query

The sample query you just created was fairly simple. When you get to be a real
dBASE guru, you undoubtedly will want to create bigger databases and more
complex queries — and to run the same query more than once. It would be
wasteful and time-consuming to set up the same query each time you want to
run it.

That's why dBASE makes it so easy to rerun a saved query. To rerun a query, just double-click on its icon in the right side of the Catalog window. The query answer should appear, just as before.

At the moment, the Over10 query is displayed in the Catalog window. If you were to rerun the query right now, dBASE would list the same book sales in the query answer. Suppose, however, that six months have passed since you ran the query the first time, and lots of new sales have taken place. No problem — you still have the query you created when you were getting started with dBASE. Simply rerun the query, and all those new books sales will be included in the query answer.

That's it for now! You worked hard in this chapter and you deserve a break. Hmm … *90210* looks pretty good tonight … maybe Steve will hack into another computer! Naaah … he's turned into a regular good guy lately. Oh, well …

Chapter 13

Using Logical Operators and Replacing Data

In This Chapter

▶ Using logical operators for multiple-condition queries

▶ Doing calculations in a query

▶ Changing data with Replace Record

*T*he phrase *logical operators* sounds scary, as though it might mean having your appendix taken out by a bunch of Vulcans. Logical operators are really just familiar words like *and, or,* and *not.* They were invented by George Boole, an English mathematician who lived from 1815 to 1864. That's why they're also called *Boolean operators.*

Before that time, nobody knew about logical operators, which made daily life rather difficult. If someone wanted to go to the store for a frozen pizza *and* a bottle of gin, he or she had to make two trips. People who needed to get a pound of liverwurst *or* a bag of potato chips *and* a six-pack of soda were often so befuddled by the problem that they gave up and entered a monastery or convent, where the food was lousy, but at least they weren't required to make change.

Sometimes, history even shifted as a result. Marie Antoinette said, "Let them eat cake," after which she was beheaded by a mob of starving French peasants. What she meant to say was "Let them eat cake *and* steak *and* french fries, *and* have a nice bottle of wine." But because she didn't know about logical operators, she couldn't finish the sentence.

To understand the ideas in this chapter, you should know the concepts of a database (Chapter 2), a table (Chapter 4), and a query (Chapter 12). To create queries with the example database in this book, you need to have created the the Sales table (Chapter 12) as well as put data in the Sales table (Chapter 12).

If you're creating queries with your own real-life database, just read this chapter to get the basic ideas. Then follow the steps with your own database instead of the one in this book.

Creating Multiple-Condition Queries

In addition to making it easier to go to the store, logical operators are used to create queries that look for more than one thing at a time — also known as searching for *multiple conditions*. For example, you may want to look for every book sale that occurred before August 27th *and* was for more than $5. dBASE makes it simple.

Using AND and OR: the basics

Creating a query with multiple conditions is just like creating the simple queries you learned about in Chapter 12, except that you put more than one condition in the table skeleton.

When you use multiple conditions, you use the logical operators AND and OR to combine the conditions. For example, if you're looking for every customer who lives in Chicago and is named Smith, no person who lives outside Chicago or has a non-Smith name matches your search. On the other hand, if you look for people who live in Chicago or are named Smith, then your search will look for

- ✔ Any customer who lives in Chicago but is not named Smith.
- ✔ Any customer who does not live in Chicago but is named Smith.
- ✔ Any customer who lives in Chicago and is named Smith.

Life was hard in the old days, but we did multiple-condition queries, anyway . . .

Multiple-condition queries haven't always been this easy. In older versions of dBASE as well as most other data managers, you had to type things like

```
Display fname, lname, city for
  zip = "90210" .and. lname =
  "spelling".
```

But these days, almost all database managers have adopted the simple *query by example* (QBE) approach used by dBASE.

That last example may have surprised you a little. Normally, if you're going to the store OR going to the movies, you mean you'll do one or the other, but not both. That's called an *exclusive* OR. But in dBASE — just like all other database managers — OR is *inclusive.* That means if you search for records that match A or B, you'll find records that match A, B, or *both.*

Combining conditions with AND

Using AND conditions is easy. You simply enter each condition in the appropriate field on the same line of the Query Designer window's table skeleton, as shown in Figure 13-1.

Figure 13-1:
Entering two AND conditions to find all sales records where the sale date is after August 22, 1994 and the price is greater than $3.00.

SALES.DBF		CUST_ID	SALEDATE	TITLE	AUTHOR	PRICE
			> {08/22/94}			> 3.00

Enter AND conditions on the
same line of the table skeleton.

Everything else works the same as in the single-condition queries you learned about in Chapter 12. The basic steps are as follows:

1. **In the left side of the Catalog window, click on the Queries icon.**

   dBASE displays all the currently available queries in the right side of the Catalog window. In addition to the available (in other words, those already created) queries, there's an icon labeled Untitled.

2. **Double-click on the Untitled query icon.**

   dBASE displays a dialog box asking which table you want to search for data in the query.

3. In the dialog box, select the table you want to use.

As soon as you select a table, dBASE displays the Query Designer window, which contains a skeleton of the table's structure. (A skeleton is basically just a horizontal field list.) In the skeleton, you pick the fields you want to include in the query. You also tell dBASE if you want it to sort the records it finds in any particular order, such as by last name or account number.

4. Pick the fields you want to see in the answer.

You pick the fields by clicking in the little boxes on the second row of the table skeleton, as shown in Figure 12-2 of Chapter 12. Clicking in a box selects the field named above it and tells dBASE to display that field in the query answer. If you want to see all of the table's fields in the query answer, click in the little box on the left end. When you click in any of the boxes, a check mark appears in that box to show that the field is selected for display.

If the field you want isn't currently shown on the screen, you can use the left- and right-arrow buttons at the left end of the table skeleton to scroll the fields left and right.

5. If you want the records sorted in the query answer, tell dBASE how to sort them.

You sort by clicking on the Sort button of one or more fields, as shown in Figure 12-2. As long as you hold down the left mouse button, dBASE displays a list box. As you move the mouse pointer up and down in the list box, the message line at the bottom of the window tells you what each option is. When you've highlighted the option you want, release the left mouse button. The list box closes and your selection is made. If you want to change it, just reopen the list box and pick something else.

For example, if you want to see the query answer in alphabetical order by last name, click the Sort button of the LNAME field, pick Ascending sort from the list box, and release the mouse button.

6. Tell dBASE what you're looking for: in this case, the AND conditions.

You do this by entering a value in the blank under the name of each field you want to search, as shown in Figure 13-1. To get into a particular blank, just click in it with the mouse. You need to follow some special rules for entering values in field blanks. (These rules are explained in Chapter 12.) For example, if you were looking for a customer whose first name is Teri, you would enter **$"Teri"** into the first name (FNAME) field blank.

 7. Run the query and look at the answer.

Running the query means that you tell dBASE to look for records matching what you told it in Step 6 and then display the records on the screen as a query answer. You run the query by clicking on the Run query button in the middle of the SpeedBar. dBASE finds all the records that match what you're looking for (if there are any) and displays them on your screen.

8. **Save the query and then head for the mall. There's a sale at The Gap!**

   Save the query by opening the File menu and selecting Save, or by clicking on the Save button in the SpeedBar. dBASE displays a dialog box asking you to name the query. The name must follow the same rules as the name for a table or any other DOS disk file, with a maximum of eight letters, digits, or underscore characters, and no spaces or punctuation marks. Once you've saved the query, it's time to get some new threads. Your dog wouldn't be seen with you in public with what you've got on right now.

Hands on: querying the Sales table

If you took a break after the preceding chapter, get back into dBASE and load the Caveat catalog. In this section, you'll create a sample query that searches for all the records in the Sales table that have books sold after August 22 for more than $3. I'll take you through the process one step at a time so that you can see what's happening. If you're doing a query with your own table, just follow along with these steps:

1. **Open the Query Designer window, selecting the Sales table for the query.**

2. **In the blank under SALEDATE, enter** > {08/22/94}.

   Don't include the period. Notice that you must surround the date with curly braces.

3. **In the blank under PRICE, enter** > 3.00.

4. **Check the square box at the left end of the table skeleton's second line.**

   This causes check marks to appear under all the fields, indicating that they will all be displayed in the query answer.

5. **Click on the Run Query button in the SpeedBar.**

   This runs the query and displays your answer. To simplify matters here, you're not worrying about sorting the records in the query answer.

Did you notice something interesting? You didn't have to worry about the AND operator. dBASE took care of it for you. When you set up multiple conditions on the same line, dBASE automatically links them together with AND. All that you have to do in a query is tell dBASE what you want. It does all the work, except for going to the store and serving dinner to the peasants.

If you want, you can save this query in the usual way: open the File menu, select Save, and name the query with a DOS filename.

Looking for Mr. Range of Values

Another way to use AND is to look for a range of values. You know how kids go through an awkward age — the time between their 13th birthday and when they get to be about 20 years older than you are now? Well, dBASE queries let you look for values that are between one value and another. But it isn't awkward at all, as you discover in this section.

Suppose that the owner of the bookstore decides that he wants to see all the records for sales that occurred between August 23 and August 26. You can look for such a range by combining two AND conditions in the same field, as shown in Figure 13-2.

Figure 13-2:
Entering
multiple
AND
conditions
for the same
field.

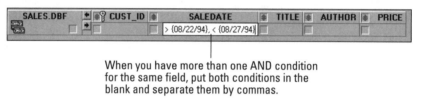

When you have more than one AND condition
for the same field, put both conditions in the
blank and separate them by commas.

Keep the following points in mind when entering multiple AND conditions:

- ✔ The first condition, **> {08/22/94}**, searches for all records with a sale date *after* (and not including) August 22.

- ✔ The second condition, **< {08/27/94}**, searches for all records with a sale date *before* (and not including) August 27.

- ✔ Because both conditions apply to the SALEDATE field, both must be in the SALEDATE column.

- ✔ Because both are AND conditions, both conditions must be on the same line of the table skeleton.

- ✔ When you have multiple AND conditions in the same blank, you put a comma between the conditions. In this case, the SALEDATE condition blank contains **> {08/22/94}, < {08/27/94}**.

You can use this same technique with other values, as well, including text values (such as ZIP codes) and numeric or float values (such as money). As an exercise, try setting up a query to find all books with prices between $10 and $20.

If you're still in the Query Designer window after creating the previous query, you may want to save this query under a different name.

Any time you need to save anything (a query, table, form, or even a whole database) under a different name, *always* select Save As from the File menu. If you make a mistake and select Save, dBASE saves the query (or whatever you're saving) under its current name and wipes out the old version of the query.

Combining conditions with OR

Combining conditions with OR works exactly the same as combining them with AND, except for one simple trick: the OR conditions go on different lines of the table skeleton.

What?! Different lines? But there's only one line for entering conditions, right? Nope: there can be as many condition lines as you need. To open up a new line, just display the table skeleton in the Query Designer window and then press the down-arrow key (see Figure 13-3). You can press the down-arrow key again to open up additional OR lines.

Figure 13-3:
Opening up
a new line
and using it
to combine
multiple OR
conditions.

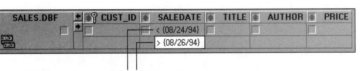

When you have multiple OR conditions
for the same field, put them on different
lines of the field's column in the table skeleton.

Suppose that you want to find records for all the sales made either before August 24 or after August 26. On the first line in the SALEDATE column, you enter the condition < {08/24/94}. On the second line, you enter the condition > {08/26/94}. (As usual, don't include the periods.)

You run and save the query in exactly the same way as any other query.

Putting OR conditions in different fields

You can also put OR conditions in different fields. Suppose that you want to find all the records for sales that either took place before August 24th or were for more than $15. You combine OR conditions just as before. The only difference is that the conditions are entered in different columns (see Figure 13-4) because one condition applies to the SALEDATE field and the other applies to the PRICE field.

You run and save the query in exactly the same way as any other query.

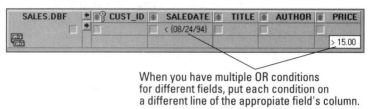

Figure 13-4:
Combining
OR
conditions in
different
fields.

When you have multiple OR conditions
for different fields, put each condition on
a different line of the appropriate field's column.

Doing Calculations in a Query

Did you know that the word *calculate* is derived from the Latin word *calculus,*
which is a word for a stone? Back in the old days — you know, like the 1950s —
nobody had PCs or pocket calculators. And because most people had only 14
fingers, they counted stones on the ground to do simple arithmetic. Really.
Honest.

dBASE doesn't require stones to do calculations, as you're about to learn. All
you need to do is set up your query in the normal way and then add a *calculated
field,* as shown in Figure 13-5.

To add a calculated field to a query, follow these steps:

1. **Set up a query in the normal way.**

   Select the table and fields that you want for the query answer, tell dBASE
   how to sort the data in the query answer, and enter any conditions you're
   looking for.

2. **Open the Query menu and select Create Calculated Field.**

   dBASE adds a calculated field to the Query Designer window.

3. **In the first line of the calculated field, delete CALC01 and enter the
   name you want.**

   dBASE calls the field in Figure 13-5 CALC01 because it's a calculated field
   (CALC) and it's the first calculated field that's been added to the query
   (01). You can delete this name by using Delete and then typing in the name
   you want.

4. **In the second line, enter the formula for your calculation.**

   For example, suppose that you want to see how much money each of the
   sales would have involved if you'd applied a ten percent discount to all
   your sales. In that case, you need to take the original price (contained in
   the PRICE field) and multiply it by 0.9. You enter **price * 0.9** as the formula
   — in this context, the asterisk means multiply. The operators you use in a
   formula are explained in the next section.

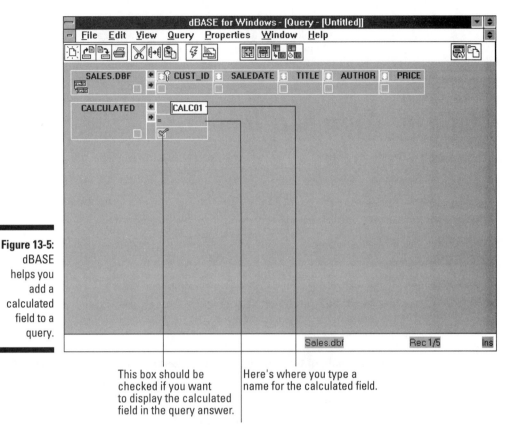

Figure 13-5:
dBASE
helps you
add a
calculated
field to a
query.

This box should be
checked if you want
to display the calculated
field in the query answer.

Here's where you type a
name for the calculated field.

Here's where you enter the
formula for the calculation.

5. Make sure that the selection box in the third line has a check mark. If not, click on it.

The check mark tells dBASE to display the calculated field in the query answer. Normally, dBASE has already checked the box because it assumes you want to display the calculated field.

6. Run the query by clicking on the Run query button in the SpeedBar.

dBASE displays the query answer, including the calculated field, on your PC screen.

Adding a new field in a query has no effect at all on the table you're using in the query. The calculated field exists only in the query itself, not in the table.

You can use standard arithmetic operators in a calculation: + for addition, − for subtraction, * for multiplication, and / for division. You also can use other dBASE mathematical operators; if you are really curious and want more information about these operators, see your dBASE for Windows manuals.

Replacing Data in a Table

You already know the *hard way* to replace data in a table. You open the Table Editor and, one record at a time, type in the new data.

But there's also an *easy way*. In the Table Editor, you can open the Table menu and use the Replace Record menu choice. In earlier versions of dBASE, as well as in dBASE 5 for DOS, you must create a query to do this. dBASE for Windows makes it much simpler.

The Replace Record menu choice works in the same way as a search-and-replace operation in a word processor. You tell dBASE what to look for and what to replace it with, and then dBASE scans through your table (in a field you specify) and replaces every occurrence of the original value with the new value. Here are the basic steps:

1. **In the right side of the Catalog window, double-click on the icon for the table you want.**

   dBASE opens the table in the Table Editor.

2. **Open the Table menu and select Replace Record.**

   The Replace dialog box appears, as shown in Figure 13-6.

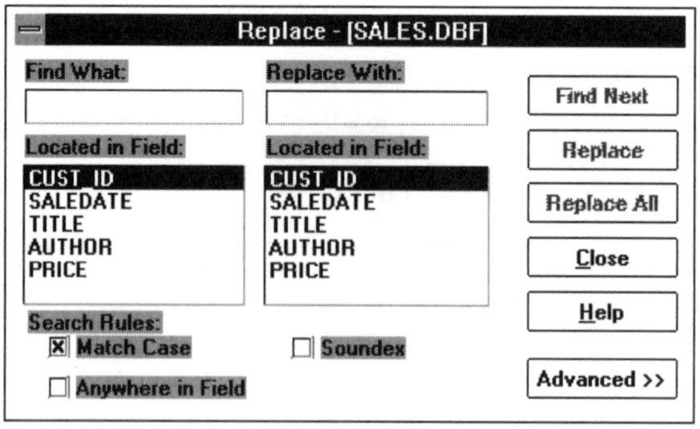

Figure 13-6:
The Replace
dialog box.

3. **Select the field you want to search.**

   You do this in the field list on the left, under the Find What blank.

4. **In the Find What blank, enter the value you want to replace.**

   In a text field, this could be a name, such as Jim; in a numeric field, it could be a number; and in a date field, it could be a date. If you want dBASE to replace whatever is in the field with a new value, you just type the field name in the blank. For example, if you want to replace every value in the Sales table's PRICE field, just enter **price** in this blank.

5. **Select the field in which the new value should go.**

   You do this in the field list on the right, under the Replace With blank. This is normally the same field as the one in the list on the left.

6. **In the Replace With blank, enter the new value you want.**

   This value can be text, a number, a date, or even a formula. For example, if you want to discount every amount in the Sales table's PRICE field by 10 percent, enter **price * 0.9** in the Replace With blank. You can use the same kind of formulas used anywhere else in dBASE, some of which are discussed earlier in this chapter.

7. **Click on the Replace All button.**

   dBASE does a search-and-replace operation in the field you specify, replacing every occurrence of the value in the Find What blank with the value in the Replace With blank.

As an exercise, open the Sales table and give all the customers a 10 percent discount. The way to do it is to use Replace Record to replace every amount in the PRICE field with that amount multiplied by 0.9.

That's it for this chapter! Take a break AND have a soda OR go to a movie. In the next chapter, you'll learn how to customize dBASE forms to make them even better!

Chapter 14

Hot Stuff! Customizing Your Forms

● ●

In This Chapter

▶ Modifying a form design

▶ Moving and resizing fields

▶ Changing and adding text

▶ Changing colors

▶ Changing the appearance of captions

● ●

*A*re you ready to be shocked and amazed? Sometimes, even database gurus (like you are becoming) don't do everything perfectly. The dBASE Form Expert itself, which you learned about in Chapter 10, slips up here and there. If you did the exercises in that chapter, the form design it created for you isn't quite perfect.

In this chapter, you learn the basic ideas and skills for customizing and modifying forms. The good news is that dBASE makes it easy for you to change the features of a form. This chapter discusses how to move the fields and their captions around on the form. Then you learn how to change a field's caption. Finally, you learn how to change the color scheme and appearance of the form.

Before you can customize a form, you need to have done the following:

✔ Created a table (Chapter 4) and put data in the table (Chapter 5)

✔ Created a form that you intend to customize (Chapter 10)

✔ Understood the concepts of a database (Chapter 2), a table (Chapter 4), and a form (Chapter 10)

To do the exercises with the form in this book, you need to have created the Customer table (Chapter 4), put data in it (Chapter 5), and created a form (Chapter 10).

If you're customizing a form you created for your own database, just read this chapter to get the basic ideas. Then use the ideas and techniques in this chapter to customize your own form.

Consider the form design created by the Form Expert, shown in Figure 14-1. The form looks … eaaahh, kind of okay, but it has definite shortcomings. For one thing, the fields and their captions are packed together too tightly. The form would be easier to read if the fields and captions were spread out a little. For another thing, the form title is just the name of the table you used to create the form: *Bookcust.* Likewise, the field captions are just the names of the fields. And the form would be more useful if the field captions were a little more descriptive.

In this chapter, you'll read about how to make all these changes. When you're finished, the form will look like Figure 14-2: not as good looking as a winning lottery ticket, but better than a phone bill with a surprising number of long-distance calls to your spouse's previous, um, friend.

Moving Fields and Captions

The simplest way to customize a form is to move fields and captions around. These are the basic steps for moving fields and captions on a form:

1. **Open the form you want to modify.**

   If you're already designing a form, you're already there. If not, you just need to open the catalog you want in dBASE and click on the Forms icon in the left side of the Catalog window. Then in the right side of the Catalog window, click on the icon for the form you want.

2. **Select the item that you want to move.**

   To select an item (field, caption, and so on) in the Form Designer window, just click on it with the mouse. When the item is selected, it's surrounded by a border with little black rectangles.

3. **Position the mouse pointer inside the border and then hold down the left mouse button.**

   You are ready to drag the item with the mouse.

4. **Drag the mouse in the direction that you want to move the item.**

   As you roll the mouse, the pointer turns into a grasping hand. The item stays with the hand as it moves on the screen. This action is called *dragging* the item, and no, it has nothing to do with Ru Paul (if you're in Generation X) or Uncle Miltie (if you're a Boomer).

5. **When the item is where you want it, release the left mouse button.**

   When you release the mouse button, dBASE drops the item at the new location.

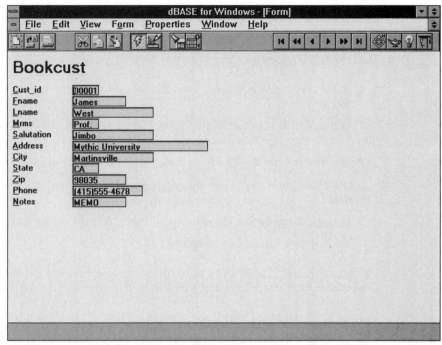

Figure 14-1:
The form
design
created by
the dBASE
Form Expert.
You can do
better.

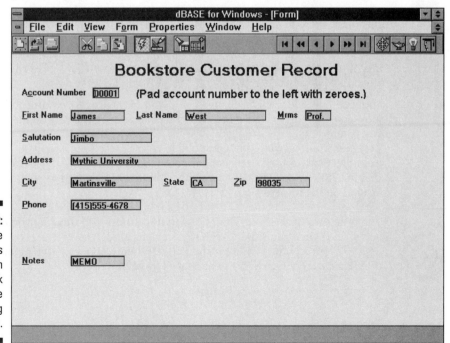

Figure 14-2:
How the
book's
sample form
will look
when you're
done jazzing
it up.

Moving stuff in the Custform

Now, it's time for a practical exercise. If you took a break after the last chapter, start up dBASE, open the Caveat catalog, and do the following:

1. **In the Catalog window, click on the Forms icon at the left side of the window.**

   In the right side of the window, dBASE displays all the forms that have been created for this database.

2. **Double-click on the Custform icon in the Catalog window.**

   dBASE displays the form as it will appear when it's used to enter or view data.

3. **If needed, maximize the window so that it fills the entire screen.**

   Your screen should look like Figure 14-1.

Moving fields and captions isn't difficult in principle. You just use the mouse to drag them from their old locations on the form to where you want them.

Fields, captions, and all the other things you see in a form design screen are called *controls*. Each control has properties that you can set, such as text, size, and any special jobs that the control is supposed to do. Although the forms you're creating here are simple, you can add push buttons, list boxes, and other advanced controls on the forms you design. Of course, that's after you finish this book and you are a real-life dBASE expert!

Dragging things around

Suppose that you want to change the layout of the Custform form so that it looks like the one in Figure 14-2. Apart from changing the text on the form — you'll get to that later — all you have to do is drag things around in the Form Designer window. Note that certain field labels have been changed — for example, Cust_id has been changed to Account number. You'll learn how to do that in a little while. For now, you only need to worry about moving things around on the form design.

The little dots in the Form Designer window form a grid that lets you align text, fields, and other items the way that you want. All you need to do is drag the item to approximately where it should be. When you release the mouse button, dBASE *snaps* the item to the nearest grid location.

To change the form, use the following steps and Figure 14-2 as your guide.

1. **Maximize the Form Designer window if you haven't already done so.**

   The Form Designer window should fill up the screen.

2. **One at a time, drag all the fields and captions except Cust_ID to the bottom half of the window.**

   The fields and captions are now out of your way while you arrange the form layout.

3. **Drag the Cust_ID field blank two vertical grid lines to the right.**

   You should now have room to change the field caption from *Cust_ID* to *Account Number.* Later, If you're not entirely satisfied with the position of the field blank, (after you've changed the caption) you can just drag the blank again until it's where you want it. Your screen should look something like Figure 14-3.

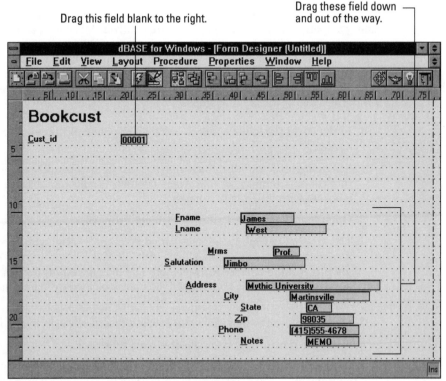

Drag this field blank to the right.

Drag these field down and out of the way.

Figure 14-3:
The Form
Designer
window,
showing
vertical and
horizontal
grid lines.

Notice that dBASE makes things easy for you — anything you move on screen automatically snaps into position along two of the window's grid lines.

3. **Drag the Fname caption until it's directly under the caption of the Cust_ID field.**

4. **Drag the Fname field blank so that it's on the same line as the caption.**

You're going to change the caption from *Fname* to *First Name,* so be sure to allow enough space between the caption and the field blank.

5. **In the same way, drag the other captions and field blanks into their new locations.**

When you're finished, the captions and field blanks should be in about the same positions as those in Figure 14-4.

Changing a Control's Properties

Everything on a form design is called a *control.* The fields are controls, the form title is a control, and the field captions are controls. Moreover, all controls have *properties.* In real life, things have properties, too: a brick has the properties of weight, hardness, shape, and color; a karate-chopping hand that breaks a brick has the properties of weight, shape, and color (black and blue). dBASE things have properties, too, but they're for doing database stuff. To change a control's properties, follow these basic steps:

1. **In the Form Designer window, click on the control that you want to change.**

For example, if you want to change the text in the Cust_ID caption, click on that caption. Remember that when a control is selected, it's surrounded by a border with little black squares.

2. **Open the View menu and select Object Properties.**

The Properties window appears on your screen, though you need to maximize it to see more than just a little bit of it. The properties it shows are those of the control you selected. The maximized Properties window is shown in Figure 14-5. Your screen may not look exactly like Figure 14-5, for reasons that I'll explain in a moment.

3. **Find the property that you want to change and click on that line.**

4. **Enter the new property or select it from a list box.**

A list box is a little drop-down list from which you can make selections with the mouse. If a property has a list box that you can use, a little button appears at the right end of the line after you click on the property's line. You can open the list box by clicking on the button.

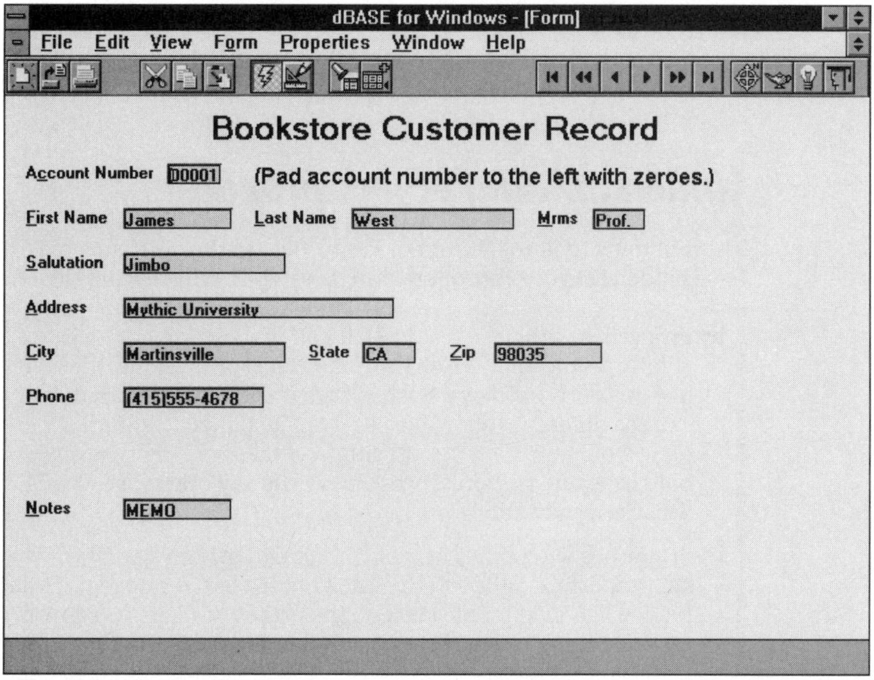

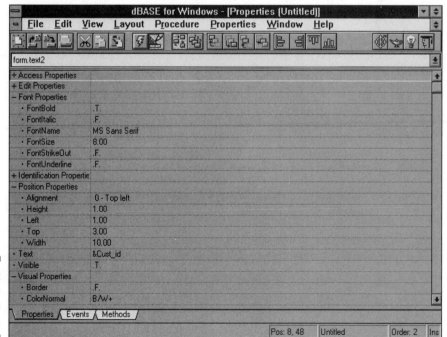

Figure 14-4:
How the book's sample Custform form will look when you're done jazzing it up.

Figure 14-5:
The Properties window.

5. Close the Properties window.

You should now be at the Form Designer window, where you can check the changes you made.

Understanding object properties

The first thing to know about the Properties window is that some properties have hidden lists of subproperties. You can tell "what's what" like this:

- Properties with a dash at the left end of their line have a list of subproperties that are already showing. For example, the Font Properties line in Figure 14-5 has a dash at its left end. Underneath it, indented, you can see different subproperties. Font just indicates the way text is displayed on your screen. Font subproperties include type size (font size), bold face, and the font style. Unless you say otherwise, dBASE uses MS Sans Serif as the style.

- Properties with a plus sign at the left end of their line *also* have a list of subproperties, although the list is hidden at the moment. To display the hidden list, just double-click on the property's line. As soon as the list appears, the plus sign turns into a dash.

- Properties with a dot at the left end of their line are single properties, without subproperties. For example, Text is just the text that's displayed in a caption on the screen. Whatever is in that line is what dBASE uses as the caption.

The property at the very top of the Properties window — in Figure 14-5 the line form.text2 — is the *name* of the control. If you're doing heavy-duty database programming, you need to know this; otherwise, it's just one of those interesting bits of knowledge, like the atomic weight of molybdenum or Sophie Tucker's birthday.

Changing text and fonts

Because you're going to be changing the text on the form, the main properties you'll use are the Text and Font properties. You can use the Properties window to change the location and size of stuff on a form, but it's more easily done by dragging with the mouse.

Now, you'll change a control's Text and Font properties. You can use the same basic technique to change other properties, as well. At the moment, say that you've decided that you can no longer endure that geeky *Bookcust* title for the form. You want to change it to *Bookstore Customer Record,* make the font more interesting, and move the title to the center of the top of the form. Follow these steps (if you're changing text in your own real life form, make the same basic moves with your own form):

1. **Click on the form text to select it.**

   In this case, click on the Bookcust form title.

2. **Open the View menu and select Object Properties.**

   The Properties window appears.

3. **Maximize the window so that it fills the whole screen.**

4. **Click on the line for the Text property.**

   dBASE highlights the current text, which is Bookcust.

5. **Type the new text that you want.**

   In this case, type **Bookstore Customer Records**. (Don't type the period.) You don't need to press Enter. As soon as you begin to type, dBASE automatically deletes the old, highlighted text.

6. **If the Font Properties line has a plus sign, double-click on the line.**

   dBASE displays the list of font subproperties.

7. **Click on the line for the font name.**

   As soon as you select the line, a little wrench button appears at the right end of the line. This is a list-box button.

8. **Click on the list-box button.**

   dBASE displays the Font dialog box, as shown in Figure 14-6. You can select the font, style, and size from the lists in the box. At the lower-right is a preview of what your text will look like if you go with the current font and size that you've selected.

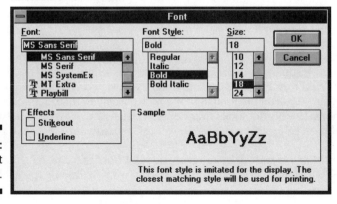

Figure 14-6:
The Font
dialog box.

9. **Change the font, style, and size as you wish.**

   In this case, change the font to Arial. You'll need to use the scroll buttons to move up in the list. If you're hazy about scroll buttons, a good resource is *Windows For Dummies* by Andy Rathbone (IDG Books Worldwide).

10. **Close the Font dialog box by clicking on OK.**

11. **Close the Properties window by double-clicking on its Window Control button in the top left corner of the window.**

    The title won't all be visible, so to see it on your form, resize the title by selecting it and then using the mouse to grab one of the blank squares on its right border and dragging it down and to the right.

    dBASE returns you to the Form Designer window.

You can change the other text items in your form in exactly the same way. When you change the field captions, notice something very interesting: each caption has an underlined letter. By holding down Alt and pressing that letter, a user of your form can go directly to that field. If you look in the Properties window, you see that the underlined letter in each caption is preceded by an ampersand (&). This ampersand tells dBASE to underline that letter in the field caption and use it as the field's hot key.

If you're following along with this book's example, use the same technique to change all the text in the form design so that it matches Figure 14-4. Don't worry about that extra bit of text to the right of the Account Number field blank. You'll learn how to insert text in a minute.

Resizing a control

One problem with adding more text is that the new text may not fit in the control's previous, smaller space. But that problem is easy to fix! First, select the control. If you just changed the control's properties, it should still be selected — surrounded by a border with little black squares. If the control isn't selected, just click on it.

Now, resize the border to make the control bigger. Position the mouse pointer over the black square in the middle of the border's right edge. The mouse pointer should turn into a horizontal double arrow. Then hold down the left mouse button and roll the mouse to the right, dragging the right border along with it. When the border looks big enough, release the left mouse button. If the border still isn't the right size, just repeat the process until you get it right.

You can shrink the control by dragging its right border to the left. This same technique works to resize any control on your form, including the field blanks.

To grab something with the mouse — whether it's a field or just one corner of a field — position the mouse pointer over it and hold down the left mouse button. To drag something with the mouse, grab the item and then continue to hold down the left mouse button while you move the mouse.

Changing a Form's Colors

Changing colors on a form is easy. With the form displayed in the Form Designer window, here are the basic steps:

1. **Select the part of the form whose colors you want to change.**

   This can be a field, text, or the whole form itself.

2. **From the View menu, select Object Properties.**

   The Properties window appears.

3. **If Visual Properties has a plus sign at its left end, double-click on it.**

   dBASE displays the visual subproperties list.

4. **Click on the ColorNormal line.**

   A list-box button appears at the right end of the line.

5. **Click on the list-box button.**

   The Choose Color dialog box appears, as shown in Figure 14-7. Notice that at the top left corner of the dialog box, the captions Foreground and Background appear. To the left of each caption is a little circle, called a *radio button*. If you click on a radio button, a little dot appears in it, showing that its function has been selected. When you first open the dialog box, Foreground is selected, indicating that the color you pick applies to text. If you click the Background radio button, the color you pick applies to the background. At the top right corner of the dialog box, dBASE displays a preview of what your currently selected colors will look like.

6. **With Foreground selected, click on the color box for the text color you want.**

7. **Click on the radio button for Background.**

8. **Click on the color box for the background color you want.**

9. **When you're satisfied, click on OK to close the Choose Color dialog box.**

10. **Close the Properties window.**

    dBASE returns you to the Form Designer window, where you can see the new colors that you've selected.

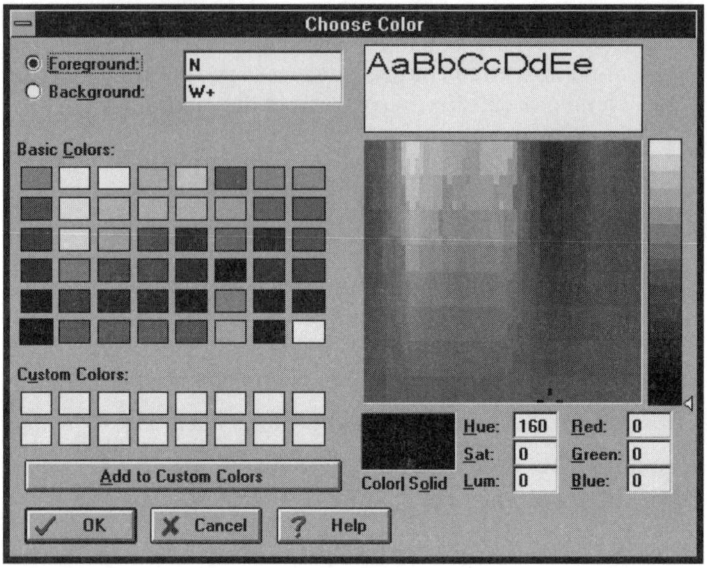

Figure 14-7:
The Choose
Color dialog
box.

Adding Text to a Form

Finally, you need to know how to add new text to a form. This technique is important because, using it, you can add other controls to a form, including really hot items like your own list boxes.

For this book's example form, the text in question is the reminder note next to the Cust_ID field, which tells the form's user to pad the account number to the left with zeroes. You can, of course, add any text anywhere in the field with this method:

1. In the Form Designer window, open the View menu.

If the menu shows a check mark next to the Controls choice, then the Controls window should be visible, as shown in Figure 14-8. If Controls isn't checked, then click on it with the mouse. The Controls window should appear.

Depending on how you have your dBASE windows set up, the Controls window might or might not be visible. It might appear and then disappear as it moves behind other windows. If you need the Controls window and it isn't visible, there are two things you can do.

First, open the View menu. If the menu choice for Controls isn't checked, then clicking on it should make the Controls window visible. If the menu choice *is* checked, then the Controls window is hidden behind another window. The easiest way to make it appear is simply to click on the Controls menu choice to uncheck it, then reopen the menu and click on the Controls menu choice again: this will make the window appear.

The next easiest way is to open the Window menu. If the Controls window is anywhere on your screen (hidden or not), there will be a menu choice for the Controls window. Just click on that menu choice.

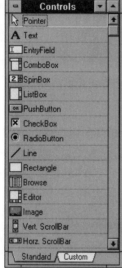

Figure 14-8:
The
Controls
window.

2. **Click on the line marked A Text.**

3. **In the Form Designer window, click where you want to put the new text.**

   In this book's example form, click just to the right of the Account Number field blank. A new text control appears where you click. It doesn't look like much yet, but it will.

4. **Open the View menu and select Object Properties.**

   The Properties window opens, with properties for the next text control.

5. **Maximize the Properties window.**

6. **In the Text line, enter the new text that you want.**

   If you wish, you can also change the font properties to make the text stand out more.

7. **Close the Properties window.**

8. **In the Form Designer window, resize the new text's border so that all of the text is visible.**

Saving a Form Design

You can save a form design by selecting Save from the File menu or clicking on Save in the SpeedBar. The Create File dialog box appears. Just enter the form name (maximum of eight letters) in the File Name blank and then click on OK. It's saved!

If you're doing this book's example form, save it as *CustForm.* Then relax for a bit. In the next chapter, you learn how to sort and index your data. (What the heck is that? Don't worry — it's going to be tons of fun!)

Part III
Organizing and Printing Your Data

The 5th Wave   By Rich Tennant

EXCUSE ME, MA'AM-ROYAL CANADIAN MOUNTED PROGRAMMERS-SOMEONE HERE REPORT A MISSING FILE?

In this part . . .

Putting data into a database is one thing. Parts I and II covered all the ways to do that. Organizing data and getting it *out* of a database are something else. This part shows you how to sort the data in your database in any way you like.

This part also shows you how to print out your data: either the quick-and-dirty way, by printing directly from a datasheet or form, or the the easy-but-pretty way, by creating simple reports.

Chapter 15

Sorting and Indexing, Even When You're Out of Sorts

In This Chapter

▶ Two ways to put stuff in order

▶ Sorting different kinds of fields

▶ Sorting on more than one field at a time

▶ When to use indexes (and what they are, too)

▶ Indexing on more than one field at a time

Consider your phone book. Or if you prefer, consider your neighbor's phone book, in case you get the urge to tear the phone book in half. If you look inside the phone book, you'll find all the names neatly arranged in alphabetical order. If they weren't arranged that way, it would be difficult to find a phone number when you needed one.

In this chapter, you'll learn two ways to put your dBASE data in order — in alphabetical order, numerical order, date order, or if you've got a dominance fetish, pecking order. If you have a dBASE table of names and addresses, like this book's example Customer table, you'll be able to see your records not only by the order they were put in the table but also by last name, city, ZIP code, or any other field you choose. Just don't tear the thing in half.

To understand the ideas in this chapter, you should know the concepts of a database (Chapter 2) and a table (Chapter 4). To do the exercises with the example database in the book, you need to have created the Sales table (Chapter 12).

If you're sorting records in your own real-life database, just read this chapter to get the basic ideas. Then use the ideas and techniques in this chapter to customize your own database.

Doing Simple Sorts

When you see the term *simple sort,* you may think of Jethro Clampett or Ernest P. Worrell. Although these fictional characters are indeed simple sorts, they're a different kind of simple sort from those you do in dBASE. In dBASE, a simple sort puts records in order by one field, such as sale date or last name. Later in this chapter, you'll learn how to sort your records on more than one field.

To sort your records, you need to put them in order by a particular field, such as account number, last name, date of purchase, or molecular weight. When you sort the records in a table, dBASE creates a totally new table with the records in the order that you specify. The original table isn't changed, as illustrated in Figure 15-1.

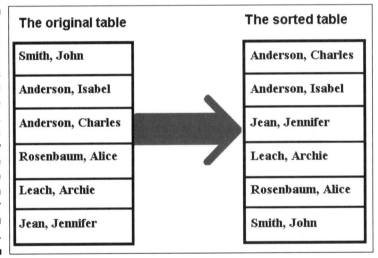

Figure 15-1: Sorting the records in a table leaves the original table undisturbed. It creates a completely new table with the records in the order that you want.

The original table	The sorted table
Smith, John	Anderson, Charles
Anderson, Isabel	Anderson, Isabel
Anderson, Charles	Jean, Jennifer
Rosenbaum, Alice	Leach, Archie
Leach, Archie	Rosenbaum, Alice
Jean, Jennifer	Smith, John

The only kind of field you can't use for sorting your records is a memo field because there's no way to compare memo fields to decide which should come first, which should come second, and so on.

You can sort records in two directions: ascending and descending.

- ✔ An *ascending* sort puts the records in order from lowest to highest, such as A to Z, 1 to 10, and January 1, 1995, to December 31, 1995.

- ✔ A *descending* sort puts the records in order from highest to lowest, such as Z to A, 10 to 1, and December 31, 1995, to January 1, 1995.

The inside scoop on how dBASE sorts your data

It's not usually something you need to worry about, but dBASE and other data managers sort character-type fields by *ASCII codes*. Every letter, digit, punctuation mark, and other key on your keyboard has an ASCII code, which is a whole number between 0 and 255, inclusive. The codes 0 to 31 are for special characters, such as the carriage return character (ASCII 13) that's generated when you press Enter. The codes 32 to 127 are letters (uppercase letter codes are 65-90; lowercase letters are 97-122), punctuation marks, digits (1, 5, 8, and so on), and some special characters.

When you're sorting (or indexing) a table that has upper- and lowercase letters, punctuation marks, digits, and so on, you occasionally need to know about the ASCII codes to predict what order the records will be sorted in. If you do an ascending sort, for instance, the name *John* is placed before the name *john* because uppercase letters have lower ASCII codes than lowercase letters.

For the most part, knowledge of ASCII codes won't matter to you because names and other text items are normally typed the same way in every record. Thus, you will probably never have customer records with the first names JOHN, joe, jiM, JOsiaH, and so on. Unless the person typing in the data is *seriously* weird, all names and other text items usually follow the same uppercase/lowercase format.

And if you really must know, *ASCII* stands for *American Standard Code for Information Interchange.* It's designed to let different computers use the same codes for letters and other characters so that you can send data from one type of computer to another. An older code that's an even bigger mouthful is *EBCDIC,* which stands for *Extended Binary Coded Decimal Interchange Code.* It was invented by IBM for the mainframe computers that large organizations still use for jobs too enormous to do on a PC.

The basic steps for sorting records

Sorting records in a dBASE table is very easy. In essence, you simply open the table that you want to sort and tell dBASE which field to use for ordering the records. To sort records, follow these steps:

1. **In the Catalog window, double-click on the icon for the table you want to sort.**

   The table appears in the Browse window.

2. **Open the Table menu and select Table Utilities.**

   A submenu appears, as shown in Figure 15-2.

3. **In the Table Utilities submenu, select Sort Records.**

   The Sort dialog box appears, as shown in Figure 15-3. (You'll use this dialog box again later in this chapter to sort the Sales table from this book's example database.)

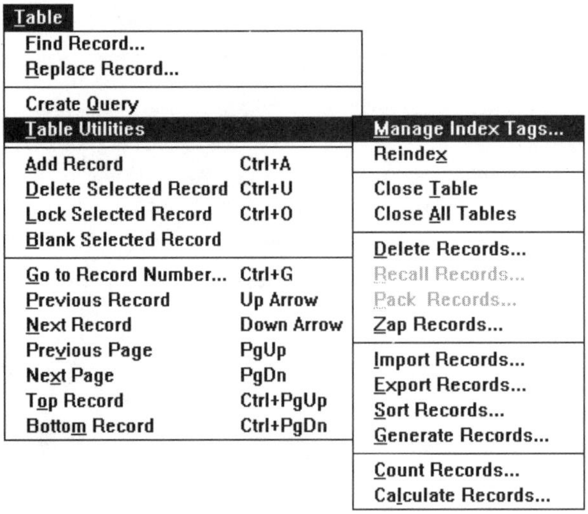

Table
Find Record...
Replace Record...

Create Query
Table Utilities   **Manage Index Tags...**
Add Record   Ctrl+A   Reindex
Delete Selected Record Ctrl+U   Close Table
Lock Selected Record   Ctrl+O   Close All Tables
Blank Selected Record
                                       Delete Records...
Go to Record Number... Ctrl+G   Recall Records...
Previous Record   Up Arrow   Pack Records...
Next Record   Down Arrow   Zap Records...
Previous Page   PgUp
Next Page   PgDn   Import Records...
Top Record   Ctrl+PgUp   Export Records...
Bottom Record   Ctrl+PgDn   Sort Records...
                                       Generate Records...

                                       Count Records...
                                       Calculate Records...

Figure 15-2:
The Table
Utilities
submenu.

4. **In the Target Table blank, type the name you want for the new, sorted table.**

   The Target Table blank is at the top left corner of the dialog box.

5. **In the Table Fields list, double-click on the field(s) you want to use in the sort.**

   The fields you select should appear in the Sort Fields list. If a field isn't in the list, it's not selected. If you have trouble double-clicking, you can select a field by single-clicking on it in the Table Fields list and then clicking on the Add button between the two lists.

6. **Finally, click on the OK button.**

   dBASE creates a new table with the records sorted on the field(s) you selected.

Sorting on more than one field

If you haven't done much of this sorting stuff, you probably have two questions at this point:

✔ What the heck is "sorting on more than one field"?

✔ Why the heck would any sane person do something like that, what with all the traffic jams and pollution and bad Top 40s music that's already in the world?

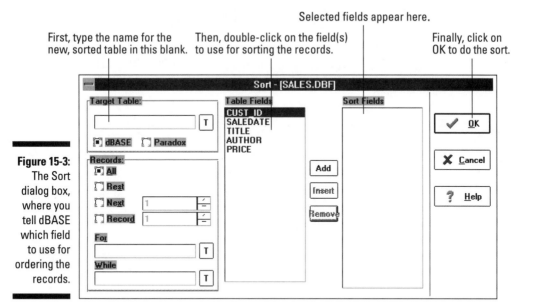

Selected fields appear here.

First, type the name for the new, sorted table in this blank.

Then, double-click on the field(s) to use for sorting the records.

Finally, click on OK to do the sort.

Figure 15-3: The Sort dialog box, where you tell dBASE which field to use for ordering the records.

The answer is simple. Suppose that you sorted the records in a customer table by the customers' last names. Does that mean that all's well with the world? No. For one thing, Pauly Shore makes a lot more money than you do. And if that isn't enough to convince you that something is seriously wrong in the universe, consider what may happen if you have several customers with the same last name. Although the records are in order by last name, they're almost certainly out of order by *first* name. Table 15-1 illustrates the potential problem.

Table 15-1   Why You Might Need to Sort on More Than One Field

How dBASE Might Sort Last Names	How You Want Them Sorted
Jones, Sarah	Jones, Andy
Jones, Ed	Jones, Ed
Jones, Tim	Jones, Sarah
Jones, Andy	Jones, Tim

That's why you very often want to sort on more than one field. All it means is using more than one field to put the records in order. In this example, you want the customer records in order by last name. But if two or more customers have the same last name, you want their records in order by last and first name. So when you do the sort, you need to tell dBASE to look at both the last and first name fields.

Basic steps for a multifield sort

You do a multifield sort in exactly the same way as you do a single field sort. Just follow the same steps outlined in the section titled "The basic steps for sorting records" — the only difference being Step 5, where you select more than one field.

It is *very, very important* that you select the sort fields in the correct order. The "big sort" field has to come first, while the "little sort" field comes second. This means that in the Sort dialog box (refer to Figure 15-3), the big sort field should be *above* the little sort field in the Sort Fields list.

For example, in sorting by first name and last name, you want the records in order by last name: that's the big sort. *Within* each group of records with the same last name, you want the records in order by first name: that's the little sort. If you mistakenly select the first name field before the last name field, records would be in order by first name. And within each group of customers with the same first name, records would be in order by last name, such as Andy Anderson, Andy Harris, Andy Robinson, and Andy Xenakis.

So be sure to select the big sort field first. If you're sorting with more than two fields, the same principle applies: bigger sort fields are selected before littler sort fields.

Sorting character fields that contain numbers

Sorting text-type fields that contain numbers, such as account numbers or Social Security numbers, is a special problem. If dBASE (or any other database manager) thinks it's dealing with text, then it sorts numbers incorrectly unless the numbers are padded with zeroes. Padding means that if you have a character field with a width of 5, and a number that's only one digit (such as 7), you should type enough zeroes to the left of the number to fill the field, such as *00007*.

Here's why. Suppose that your records have a text field containing the numbers 1, 2, 3, 4, 10, and 20. A sort begins with the first "letter" of a text field. In this case, the letter is a digit. The way dBASE sorts numbers and the way you actually want them sorted may not coincide, as Table 15-2 illustrates.

The problem in the preceding example is that dBASE doesn't know that the numbers are actually numbers. And if they're not numbers, then the first letter of *10* is *1*, while the first letter of *20* is *2*. So that's why dBASE sorts them the way it does.

Table 15-2	The Problem with Sorting Numbers
How You Want the Numbers Sorted	*How dBASE Actually Sorts Them*
1	1
2	10
3	2
4	20
10	3
20	4

This problem has two solutions. The first is to go back into the Table Design screen (see Chapters 4 and 7) and make the field a number field instead of a text field. The drawback is that number fields take up more disk space than text fields, although in a small database, it doesn't make much difference.

The second solution is to leave the field a character field but pad the numbers out to the left with zeroes. For example, *1* becomes *00001, 2* becomes *00002,* and so on. Then dBASE sorts the numbers correctly, and you get

✔ 00001

✔ 00002

✔ 00003

✔ 00004

✔ 00010

✔ 00020

Indexing: Usually Better Than Sorting

Sorting is mentioned first in this chapter because it's easier to understand than indexing. Moreover, indexing is a special, more efficient kind of sorting — so unless you understand sorting, you can't really understand indexing.

In real life, an index usually helps you find information (see Figure 15-4). The index of a book, for example, lists topics and has page numbers for each topic — a kind of pointer to the place where you can read about the topic.

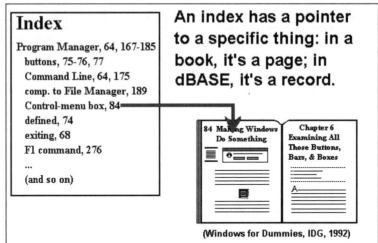

Figure 15-4:
How
indexes
work.

When you index a field, dBASE can find stuff in that field faster than it can in a nonindexed field. *However* — and it's a big however — in smaller databases, indexing makes very little difference. If you have only a few hundred records in a table, indexing *slightly* speeds up search operations and queries, but not enough so that you'll be able to notice the improvement.

An index in dBASE works almost exactly like a computerized book index. When you tell dBASE to index a table on a certain field, you can view the table records in order by that field. But unlike sorting, indexing doesn't physically rearrange the records in a new order, nor does it create a new, sorted version of the table. Instead, it simply *displays* the records in order by the indexed field.

If you ever need to search for data in a particular field — such as searching for a customer's last name or a particular account number — creating an indexed field speeds up the search. When dBASE searches for a value in an indexed field, it simply looks in the index to find the location of the records that have that value.

The biggest advantage of indexing is speed and convenience. Because indexing doesn't physically rearrange the table's records, you can quickly switch between different sorted views of your data. With sorting, you have to load a completely different file every time you want to see your data in a different order. Moreover, if you add new records to a sorted table, you must re-sort the table to get the new records in their properly sorted positions. With an indexed table, dBASE updates the order automatically: you don't need to worry about it.

The basic things you have to know

Here are the basic things that you have to know about how indexes work in dBASE:

- ✔ To index on a particular field, you have to go into the Table Designer window: that's where you design the table in the first place. On the row for the field you want to index, you should open the list box in the last column, the one with the label Indexed at the top. Then select either Ascend (A to Z order) or Descend (Z to A order). This tells dBASE to create an index for that field.

- ✔ When you index any field in a table, dBASE creates a *master index file* for that table. This file holds all the indexes for all the fields in that table. The master index file has the same name as the table, but ends with the extension .MDX. Thus, if you had a table called CUSTOMER.DBF (dBASE always adds the letters .DBF to the table name), the master index file would be named CUSTOMER.MDX.

- ✔ When you open a table, the master index file is automatically opened. This is a big advance over older versions of dBASE, in which you had to remember to open each index file yourself. If you ever forget to open an index file in the older versions of dBASE before changing the data in your table, then you've changed the table data without updating the index. The index file gets out of date, and you have to "re-index."

- ✔ Within the master index file, each individual field index is called an *index tag*. To display the records in order by a particular field, you need to tell dBASE to make that field's tag the *master tag*.

To index or not—the tradeoff with speed

If indexing helps dBASE find stuff more quickly, why not just index every field? The reason that you don't want to do this is that every index you create makes dBASE do more work to manage your records — and that takes extra time. If you are entering records in a table that has a great deal of indexed fields, it can take longer for dBASE to save new records because each time dBASE saves, it has to update all the index tags in the master index file.

If a table has one indexed field, dBASE must create a new entry in the index tag every time you enter a new record. If the table has ten indexed fields, dBASE has to create ten new entries in ten different index tags for each new record. Even with a fast program like dBASE and a fast PC, the slowdown can become significant. Therefore, you shouldn't automatically index every field. If you know that you'll be searching a particular field often or that you need to use it to link up with other tables, indexing is a good move. Otherwise, don't do it.

Making sure that the correct fields are indexed

Before you can display your data in an indexed order, the relevant fields have to be indexed. Any field that you want to use to sort your records needs to be indexed. For example, you may want to display the data in a customer table by the customer's account number, last name, or ZIP code. If so, then all these fields should be indexed. If you're not sure which of a table's fields are indexed, you can follow these steps:

1. **In the Catalog window, right-click on the icon for the table you want to index.**

   The table SpeedMenu appears.

2. **In the SpeedMenu, select Design Table Structure.**

   The Table Designer window appears. Note that the far right column is labeled Index.

3. **In the Index column, select Ascending or Descending for the fields you want to index.**

   dBASE creates an index for each field you select. Ascending and descending mean the same thing with indexing as they do with sorting. An ascending index puts things in order from low to high (A to Z, 1 to 10), while a descending index puts things in order from high to low (Z to A, 10 to 1).

4. **Open the File menu and select Save.**

   The table design is saved with the newly indexed fields. If none of the fields was indexed before, it also creates the master index file.

5. **Close the Table Designer window.**

   dBASE returns you to the Catalog window.

Displaying your records in indexed order

After you've indexed the fields you want, you can use their index tags to display the records in order by those fields. The basic steps are as follows:

1. **In the Catalog window, double-click on the icon for the table that you want.**

   dBASE displays the table in a Browse window.

2. **Open the Table menu and select Table Utilities.**

   The Table Utilities submenu appears, as shown earlier in Figure 15-2.

3. **In the submenu, select Manage Index Tags.**

   The Master Index Tag dialog box appears, as shown in Figure 15-5. The figure illustrates what the dialog box looks like with the book's example Customer table.

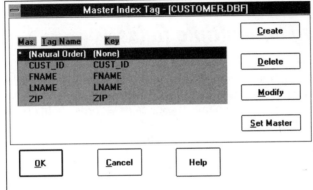

Figure 15-5:
The Master
Index Tag
dialog box.

4. **In the field list at the left, click on the field that you want to control the record order.**

   When you click on the field name, the horizontal highlight moves onto that field. For instance, if you want the records displayed in order by last name, click on the LNAME field.

5. **Click on the Set Master button at the lower right.**

   dBASE orders the records by the highlighted field. If you're a keyboard whiz, you can simply press Alt+S instead of clicking on the Set Master button.

6. **Click on OK.**

   dBASE returns you to the Browse window. Your table's records are now displayed in order by the fields you selected.

If it looks like some of the records are suddenly "missing" in the index-ordered table, press PgUp or PgDn. The records are not really missing: they just aren't visible on the screen.

It doesn't happen often, but if your master index file becomes damaged some-how — maybe your electric power jumps just as you're entering a record, or Windows crashes, or your spouse has been fooling around with your PC when you explicitly told him or her that it was "hands off" — then your records may not display in the correct indexed order.

If this problem occurs, don't despair. Instead, display the table in a Browse window. Then open the Table menu, select Table Utilities, and on the submenu, select Reindex. This procedure rebuilds the index file.

Indexing on multiple fields

You may want to index on multiple fields for the same reason that you may want to sort on multiple fields. If your customer records are in order by last name, for example, you may want each group of records with the same last name to be in order by first name. If your sales records are in order by date, as another example, you may want each day's records in order by the name of the item sold or by the dollar amount of the purchase.

Unfortunately, indexing on multiple fields isn't quite as easy as sorting on multiple fields. Oh yes, it's easier than getting a straight answer out of a politi-cian; it's easier than finding a good video on MTV; but it's still a little harder than it should be.

To index on multiple fields, you have to go to the dBASE Command window and create a new index that includes all of the fields that you want to use. If you want records in order by last name and first name, then these would be the fields you'd use. Notice that multiple field indexes are a lot different from the single field indexes that are so easy to create in the Table Designer window. Here, you gotta do some typing.

If you're adventurous, if you're pumped, if you're *ready*, here's how to do it. Just so these instructions don't become too abstract, assume that you want to index this book's example Customer table on last name and first name. If you're following these instructions with your own real-life table, just make the appro-priate substitutions.

1. **Open the Window menu and select 2 Command.**

   The Command window appears on your screen, ready for you to type some dBASE commands.

2. **In the Command window, type** use **and press Enter.**

   Any tables that may be open are now closed.

3. Type set exclusive on **and press Enter.**

dBASE is prepared to open the file in *exclusive* mode, a requirement if you want to create a multifield index.

4. Type use customer, **where *customer* is the table you want to index.**

The table you want to index opens. You can't index a table unless you open it first.

5. Type index on lname + fname tag fullname **and press Enter.**

This creates the multiple-field index tag, names it *fullname,* and automatically makes it the master index. Of course, you can still go back to the Master Index Tag dialog box and change the master index to another indexed field any time that you want. (Remember that in the customer table, the last name field is called *LNAME* and the first name field *FNAME.*) Even though you created it in the Command window, the *fullname* index tag will be listed in the dialog box.

6. Type browse **and press Enter.**

dBASE displays your table in a Browse window. You can see that the records are now in order by last name and first name.

After all that typing, you must be exhausted or, at the very least, having traumatic flashbacks to all those years of childhood piano lessons. If you want, put down the book, rest your eyes, dust off that exercise bicycle you've had in the closet for the last six months, or just kick back for a while. In the next chapter, you'll learn some easy ways to print reports about your data.

Chapter 16

Quick and Easy Ways to Print Database Stuff

• •

In This Chapter

▶ What are reports?

▶ Using Print Preview to see how something will look on paper

▶ Printing stuff from a Browse window

▶ Printing stuff from a form

• •

Did you ever notice that the word *report* always seems to mean something bad? There's the report *card,* which usually means no TV for a month; the *credit* report, which recounts in loving detail the $11.75 dry cleaning bill you forgot to pay six years ago; the *gunshot* report, which you usually hear a split second after you accidentally put a bullet through your foot; and, of course, the ever-popular *tax* report, by which you render unto Caesar everything you've earned since his last April 15 payday.

The good news is that in dBASE, report means something *good.* A report is just a printout of your database data. It can be plain or it can be fancy. It can have all your data or just some of it. It can be grouped and organized, include totals and summaries, and use boldface type and other printing effects. Everything is up to you. And the great news is that dBASE makes it easy to create all types of reports.

For example, here are some reports you can produce from the example Caveat Emptor bookstore database:

    ✔ A simple printout from a Browse window or form.

    ✔ A name, address, and phone number list for all bookstore customers.

    ✔ A list of all sales broken down by state for a given month.

    ✔ A customer list that includes the items each customer purchased and the total amount spent by each customer. This report would involve information from both the Customer Records and Sales tables.

    ✔ A summary of sales for the entire year, with revenues broken down by quarter.

To understand the ideas in this chapter, you should know the concepts of a table (Chapter 4), a Browse window (Chapter 5), and a form (Chapter 10). To create reports using the example database in this book, you need to have created the Customer Records table (Chapter 4), put data into it (Chapter 5), and created a form (Chapter 10).

If you're creating reports with your own real-life database, read this chapter to get the basic ideas. Then follow the steps with your own database instead of the one in this book.

Different Kinds of Reports

All the different variations of reports boil down to three categories. First, you can produce an *informal report,* which basically is just a printout of a Browse window or form in your database. The big advantage of an informal report is that it takes about 10 seconds to create. The big *dis*advantage is that it presents your data just as it appears in the Browse window or form; informal reports aren't very flexible.

Second, if you have something appropriate to wear, you can produce a *formal report.* A formal report is what you'd normally think of as a snazzy business report. It can present your database information in rows and columns, include page numbers, footers, totals, and so on. And the report doesn't have to use a row-and-column format: if you prefer, you can select a different layout, such as for a single-column or summary report. You can even include graphs and bar charts.

Third, you can create a *special-purpose report.* This type of report lets you create mailing labels and form letters.

In this chapter, you learn how to create informal reports. Formal reports are covered in the next chapter, with mailing labels and form letters described a bit later.

For most of the exercises in this chapter, you need to use your printer. Make sure that your printer is turned on, has plenty of paper, and is ready to print. If you see the word *online* (or *select*) somewhere on the front of the printer, the little light next to it should be turned on — the light means that the printer is ready to go.

If you're in a big hurry, you can create an informal report just by opening the Browse window or form you want to print, opening the File menu, and clicking on Print. But if you have at least two minutes, you can use a few tricks to make even your informal reports look great. The following exercises show you how to print a quick report.

Printing from a Browse Window

If you haven't done so already, start dBASE and open the Caveat database. Make sure that the Database window is displayed and the Table tab is selected. Double-click on the Customer Records table to open its Browse window and then follow these steps:

1. **Make sure that your printer is on and ready to print.**

2. **Open the File menu and select Print.**

   The Print Records dialog box appears, as shown in Figure 16-1.

3. **Click on OK.**

   Your printer prints the Browse window.

Another way to print in dBASE — whether you're printing a Browse window or anything else — is to click on the Print button in the SpeedBar.

Did it occur to you that when you run a query (Chapters 12 and 13), the result is a kind of table — and a table can be displayed in a Browse window? When you run a query, you can print the result just as you can any other data displayed in a Browse window.

But it doesn't all fit on one page!

The Browse window printout you just produced includes all the data in your table. Unless you have a very unusual printer, the printout looks pretty weird. What's weird is that on the first page of the report, dBASE prints only the first few columns of the Browse window. All the columns farther to the right are printed on the second page.

No, you didn't do anything wrong. That's just the way dBASE works when you print a Browse window. Any columns that don't fit on the first page are kicked over to the second page. If you want to blame someone, blame the people who invented computerized spreadsheets in the first place: That's how *they've* always printed data, and it's not for nothing that the dBASE Browse window is sometimes described as being "in spreadsheet format."

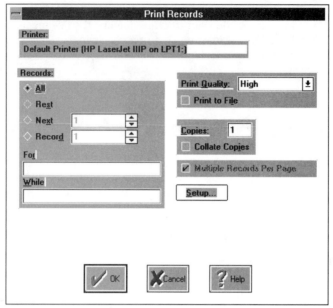

Figure 16-1:
The Print
Records
dialog box.
It may look
a little
different on
your screen,
depending
on what kind
of printer
you have.

You can do one of three things to resolve the problem:

✔ You can narrow some of the columns in the Browse window. In some tables — not the sample one you're working with, unfortunately — narrowing the columns is enough to fix the problem. You learned how to change column widths in Chapter 6.

✔ If you don't actually need to print all the columns in the Browse window, you can hide some of them so that dBASE prints only the ones you want. If those columns fit on a single page, the problem is solved.

✔ When you print the Browse window, you can switch from Portrait to Landscape mode. *Landscape mode* (illustrated by Figure 16-2) prints the Browse window sideways on the page. Because normal printer paper is longer than it is wide, choosing this option can often solve the problem. (It works for 8.5 × 11-inch paper used in the U.S. and the A4-size paper used in other countries.)

Because you already know how to change column widths (Chapter 6), try using the other two methods — hiding columns and printing in Landscape mode — with the sample printout. The following sections take you through each process.

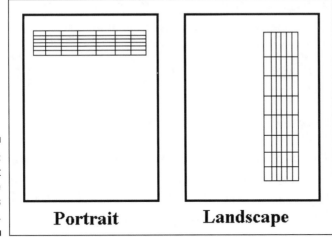

Figure 16-2:
Portrait
mode
versus
Landscape.

Portrait   **Landscape**

When you narrow columns in a Browse window, you need to be careful. Just because the column is wide enough on your screen doesn't mean it will be wide enough when printed: that depends on the printer font and type size you're using.

For example, you might narrow the CITY column in the Browse window in this book's example Customer table. On your screen, everything would look fine; even the fairly long city name *Santa Barbara* would fit in the column. When you print the Browse window, however, the city name may not fit in the printed column, meaning that the last few letters are lopped off — much as your head would be lopped off if the printed report goes to your boss.

The moral is that just because Browse window columns look wide enough on your screen, you shouldn't assume that they'll be wide enough when you print them. Do a test printout and make sure it's all right — *before* you do the official printout for the boss.

Hiding columns in the Browse window

Hiding columns is very simple. The basic steps are as follows:

1. **In the Catalog window, double-click on the icon for the table you want to print.**

   dBASE displays the table in a Browse window.

2. **Open the Properties menu and select Table Records Window.**

The Browse Inspector dialog box appears on your screen, as shown in Figure 16-3. The field list on the right side, labeled *Browse Fields,* shows all the fields that currently appear as columns in the Browse window for this table. If your Browse Inspector doesn't look like Figure 16-3, check the tabs at the bottom: the tab for Fields should look like it's in front. If it doesn't, click on the Fields tab.

3. **In the Browse Fields list, click on the field you want to hide in the Browse window.**

4. **Click on the Remove button (it's left of the Browse Fields list).**

The field that you highlighted disappears from the Browse Fields list. It appears in the Table Fields list (on the left side of the dialog box).

5. **For each additional field that you want to hide, repeat Steps 3 and 4.**

When you're finished, the Browse Fields list should contain only the fields you want included in the Browse window.

6. **Click on OK.**

The Browse window now includes columns only for the fields in the Browse Fields list.

7. **To print the Browse window, open the File menu and select Print.**

dBASE prints the Browse window.

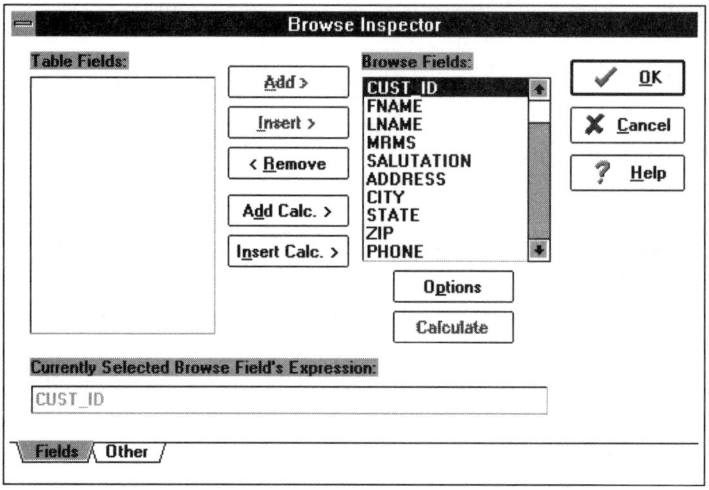

Figure 16-3:
Using the
Browse
Inspector
to hide
columns. In
the figure,
the fields
shown in the
Browse
Inspector
are from this
book's
example
Customer
table.

Browse Inspector		
Table Fields:	Add >	Browse Fields:
	Insert >	CUST_ID
	< Remove	FNAME
	Add Calc. >	LNAME
	Insert Calc. >	MRMS
		SALUTATION
		ADDRESS
		CITY
		STATE
		ZIP
		PHONE

Options
Calculate

OK
Cancel
Help

Currently Selected Browse Field's Expression:
CUST_ID

Fields / Other

Making hidden columns visible again

Earlier, when you used the Browse Inspector to hide some columns, you may have noticed that in addition to the Remove button, there's also an Add button. To make hidden columns visible again, follow these steps:

1. **Reopen the Browse Inspector.**

2. **In the Table Fields list, click on a field you want to unhide.**

   The field is highlighted in the list.

3. **Click on the Add button.**

   dBASE adds the hidden field back into the Browse Fields list.

4. **For each field you want to unhide, repeat Steps 2 and 3.**

5. **Click on OK.**

   The Browse window reappears. The fields you picked have been added back as columns in the Browse window.

Hands on: hiding columns in the Customer table

Now try hiding columns with the book's example database. Open the Customer table and display it in a Browse window. Suppose that you decide that you don't need the MRMS, SALUTATION, ADDRESS, PHONE, and NOTES fields in the quick Browse window printout. To hide them, follow these steps:

1. **Open the Properties menu and select Table Records Window.**

   The Browse Inspector appears on your screen.

2. **In the Browse Fields list, click on the MRMS field to select it.**

   The MRMS field is highlighted.

3. **Click on the Remove button.**

   The MRMS field disappears from the Browse Fields list and appears in the Table Fields list.

4. **Repeat Steps 2 and 3 for the SALUTATION, ADDRESS, PHONE, and NOTES fields.**

   When you're finished, all the fields you removed are in the Table Fields list and none of them is in the Browse Fields list.

5. **Click on OK.**

   The Browse window reappears. Now, however, the columns you removed aren't visible. You can see all the remaining columns on the screen at once.

6. **Print the Browse window.**

   Open the File menu, select Print, and click on OK in the dialog box. The printout looks fine.

Printing a Browse window in Landscape mode

If you want to print a Browse window in Landscape mode, you need to do only one thing differently from what you do when you print in Portrait mode. As you do when you print in Portrait mode, open the File menu and select Print. When the Print Records dialog box appears, click on the Setup button. Then follow these steps:

1. **When you see the Print Setup dialog box, as shown in Figure 16-4, click on the Landscape radio button.**

   Your click tells dBASE to print the Browse window in Landscape mode.

2. **Click on OK to return to the Print dialog box.**

3. **Click on OK to print the Browse window in Landscape mode.**

4. **When you finish printing, open the File menu and select Print Setup.**

5. **In the Print Setup dialog box, click on the Portrait radio button to switch back to normal printing.**

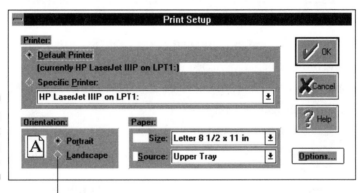

Figure 16-4:
The Print Setup dialog box.

Click here to print
in Landscape orientation.

Printing from a Form

Printing a form view of your data is almost exactly like printing from a Browse window. The main difference is that you don't have to worry about columns disappearing off the right side of the page. To see how the process works, try using a form to print out the customer records from this book's Caveat database or use your own database and form. Follow these steps:

1. **At the left side of the Catalog window, click on the Forms icon.**

   At the right side of the Catalog window, dBASE lists any forms you've created.

2. **Double-click on the icon for the form you want to use.**

   The form appears on your screen, filled with data from the table associated with the form.

3. **Open the File menu and select Print.**

   The Print Records dialog box appears. It's slightly different from the Print Records dialog box that appears when you print a Browse window, but the differences aren't important.

4. **Click on OK.**

   dBASE prints the table data, using the form you selected.

That's it for this chapter! You're now a master of printing informal reports. But don't throw away that tux: in the next chapter, you learn how to create snazzy-looking formal reports!

Chapter 17

Creating Simple Reports with dBASE

In This Chapter

▶ Creating a row-and-column report

▶ Changing the report layout

▶ Changing column labels and formatting

▶ Saving and printing a report

*P*rinting Browse windows and forms, as you did in Chapter 16, is fine when you need a quick-and-dirty list of the stuff in your database. But if you're printing the data for somebody else — for example, to impress everyone at an important meeting — the report needs to look better. Not only do you want it to *look* nicer, but you probably want it to *show* more, such as grouping your records or calculating totals. You need to create a *formal report*.

Don't worry too much about the word *formal*. It does not mean difficult, and it doesn't mean you have to put on a tie. All that it means is that your report is going to look good and do more than a simple printout from a table. Of course, if you love to play around on your PC, you can create a report that's as complicated as you want. But producing a formal report that includes the basic stuff — columns, totals, and so on — is simple, especially with the help of dBASE's amazing Crystal Reports feature. In fact, Crystal Reports is a very popular program that you can buy separately. But you don't need to worry about that: it's included with dBASE!

In this chapter, you learn how to create a simple row-and-column report. Fancier reports — and lots of special report tricks — are covered in Chapter 19.

Before you can create a formal report, you need to have

- ✔ Learned basic database concepts, such as catalog, table, and field (Chapters 1 and 2).
- ✔ Created a table (Chapter 4) and put data in the table (Chapter 5).

To do the steps in this chapter with this book's example database, you need to have created the Customer Records table (Chapter 4) and put data in it (Chapter 5).

If you're creating a report for your own database, follow along with the example and learn the ideas and techniques that can be applied to your own database.

Creating a Simple Report

You can use dBASE's amazing Crystal Reports feature to create a simple row-and-column report. To start up Crystal Reports, follow these steps:

1 If dBASE isn't already running, start it up and open the appropriate catalog.

If you're following with this book's example database, open the Caveat catalog. Or open your own real-life catalog.

2. Click the Reports icon.

dBASE displays all the reports that have previously been created for this catalog.

3. Double-click the Untitled icon.

dBASE displays a dialog box, asking which table you want to use.

4. Select the table that has the data for the report.

In the example database, select the Customer Records table. The Crystal Reports window appears, as shown in Figure 17-1.

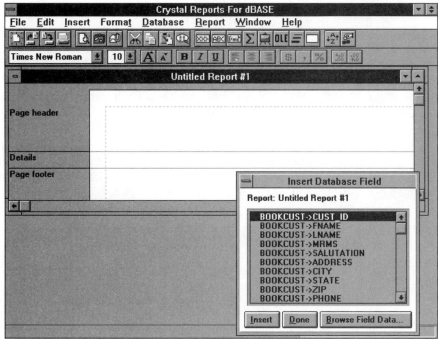

Figure 17-1:
The Crystal
Reports
window.

Parts of the Crystal Reports window

There's no denying it: the Crystal Reports window looks pretty scary. But it's really much simpler than it looks, so don't let it worry you too much. There are six main parts of the Crystal Reports window:

✔ The Menu Bar, located at the top of the window, is just a garden-variety menu bar similar to others that you've seen. The only difference is that its menu choices apply to creating reports.

✔ The SpeedBar, located below the Menu Bar, is another garden-variety dBASE feature. There are some really useful buttons on this SpeedBar — such as ones that let you insert pictures into reports or sort your records by various fields. When you know exactly what you want to do, the SpeedBar buttons let you bypass the menus to get things done more quickly.

✔ The Ribbon, located below the SpeedBar, lets you adjust the size, font, and style of text in your report.

✔ The Report Layout is the white, rectangular part of the Crystal Reports window. It's divided into various *bands* (such as Page header and Details), which are explained in the next section.

✔ The Insert Database Field window, at the lower right of the Crystal Reports window, is used to include a field in a report. Just use the mouse to drag the field from this window to the Details band of the Report Layout.

✔ The horizontal scroll bar, at the bottom of the window, lets you move horizontally in your report layout. Sometimes you can't see all the columns in a report on the screen at once. This scroll bar lets you move to the left or right in your report layout to see additional columns.

Understanding a report layout

A report layout is divided into horizontal sections, called *bands*. The name of each one appears just to the left of the band. The band itself is in the white rectangular part of the window. Here are descriptions of the three bands:

✔ *Page header* contains stuff that you want to print at the top of each page, such as the title of each column in the report.

✔ *Details* contains the actual data from your table, such as each customer's first name, last name, and street address.

✔ *Page footer* contains stuff that you want to print at the bottom of each page, such as page numbers.

Laying out the report

Creating a basic report layout is remarkably simple. Just follow these steps:

1. **Maximize the Report Layout window.**

2. **Drag each field that you want in the report from the Insert Database Field window to the Details band of the Report Layout.**

   Notice that each field name (with the table name) becomes a column label. With this book's example Bookcust table, drag the CUST_ID field from the Insert Database Field window to the left end of the Details band, as shown in Figure 17-2. In the same way, drag the FNAME, LNAME, CITY, and STATE fields into the Details band. You'll need to use the scroll bar at the bottom of the window to move to the right in the Report Layout.

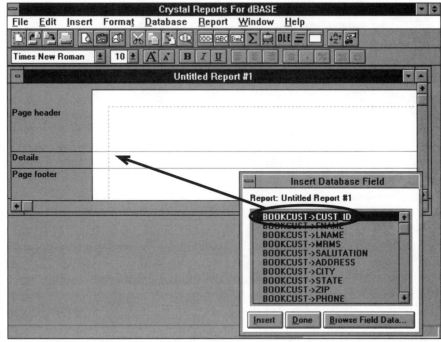

Figure 17-2:
Dragging a
field from
the Insert
Database
Field
window to
the Details
band of the
Report
Layout.

If you absolutely *hate* dragging stuff with the mouse, you can insert a field
in the Report Layout by clicking on it once in the Insert Database Field
window and then clicking Insert.

3. **When you're finished adding fields, click the Done button in the Insert
   Database Field window.**

   The Insert Database Field window disappears.

4. **In the Page header band at the top of each column, delete the field
   name.**

   Click on each field name in the Page header band and then press Delete.
   Field names make lousy column labels. Only a hard-core computer geek
   could understand something like BOOKCUST->CUST_ID.

   Be careful that you don't accidentally delete the field from the Details
   band! It's not the end of the world or even the breakup of the Beatles, but if
   you delete a field from the Details band, you have to insert it all over again
   from the Insert Database Field window. And that's a bother.

5. **Click the SpeedBar button marked ABC.**

   It's right under the Report menu. As soon as you click the button, the Edit
   Text Field dialog box appears, as shown in Figure 17-3.

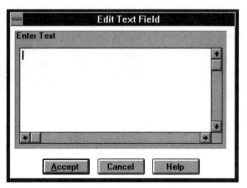

6. Type the new text for a column heading and then click Accept.

dBASE returns you to the Report Layout. The mouse pointer has turned into a box, which represents your new text. Move the box in the Page header bands to the top of the appropriate column and click the left mouse button. dBASE drops the new text in that location. With this book's example database, use this method to change the *CUST_ID* column heading to *Acct. Number* and then *FNAME* to *First Name*, *LNAME* to *Last Name*, *CITY* to *City*, and *STATE* to *State*.

7. Using the ABC button again, add a report title to the Page header band.

With this book's example database, call the report *Customers by City and State*.

8. If you wish, use the Ribbon to change the font, style, and size of any text in the layout.

First, click on the text you want to change, such as a column label. (It also works with a field in the Details band.) Then, in the Ribbon, select the font, size, and style that you want. The Ribbon is explained later in this chapter, under "Using the Ribbon to change text appearance."

Previewing the report

The Report Layout gives you only a very approximate idea of what the report will look like when it's printed. If you want to see an almost exact preview of the printed report, click the SpeedBar's Print Preview button. dBASE displays a print preview, as shown in Figure 17-4.

When you've had a good enough look, you can return to the Report Layout by clicking Close, at the bottom of the Print Preview window.

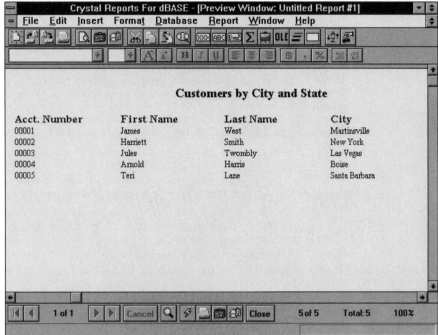

Figure 17-4:
A print
preview
of a report
layout.

Changing report column width

One thing you may have noticed about Figure 17-4 is that some of the report's columns aren't visible on the screen. If you wish, you can narrow or widen the report columns. Narrowing columns enables you to not only see more of the columns in Print Preview but also have more columns in the printed report itself.

You can tell if a column can be narrowed very much by comparing the width of the column label text (in the Page header band) and field size (in the Details band) with the rectangular borders that surround them. If a border is significantly wider than the text or the field (that's the Xs), you can narrow it. Take up the slack by dragging other labels and fields to the left.

To change the width of a report column, follow these steps:

1. Click on the field in the Details band.

The rectangular border around the field changes color. Two dots appear at the right and left sides of the border.

2. **Drag the right hand dot to the left (to narrow the column) or to the right (to widen the column).**

3. **If needed, repeat the process with the column label in the Page header band.**

4. **In the next column to the right, drag the column label and field to the left (if you're narrowing the columns) or to the right (if you're widening them).**

5. **Repeat Steps 1 to 4 until all the columns are the desired width and position.**

Using the Ribbon to change text appearance

Another way to fine-tune a report is to change the type font, size, and style used in the report title and column labels. Basically, you change the type font in the same way that you make other changes to a report: You select the item that you want to change and then use the menus or the toolbar to pick the new format.

To change the font in the example report, click on Customers by City and State in the Page header band. Then, in the toolbar, click the down arrow next to the font list, as shown in Figure 17-5. In the list, click the font that you want — Arial is always a good choice. dBASE automatically changes the font for you.

To the right of the type font list in the toolbar is a list of available type sizes. If you like, you can use this list to make the type bigger or smaller. You use it in the same way as any other list box: To select a different type size, open the list box by clicking the down-arrow button at the right end of the size blank. Then click the size that you want.

Finally, a little further to the right, are three buttons marked B, I, and U, for bold, italic, and underlined text.

You can use these same methods to change the type font, size, and style of any text that appears in the report, including field text in the Details band.

Figure 17-5:
Fine-tuning a report: changing the type font, size and style.

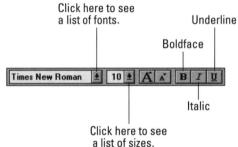

Click here to see a list of fonts.

Underline

Boldface

Italic

Click here to see a list of sizes.

Saving and Printing the Report

Now that you've done all the work, it's time for the fun part. First, save your report layout by opening the File menu and selecting Save. In the dialog box, enter a name for the report file. As usual, you need to use a DOS filename, so it can have up to eight letters, including underscores. If you're working with this book's example database, enter **by_city** as the report name and then click OK.

 Finally, click the Speedbar's Print Preview button to see what your report will look like. If you like what you see, click the SpeedBar's Print button to print the report.

You can use these same methods to create a layout of any type of formal report — whether it's a row-and-column report, a crosstab, a form letter, or mailing labels. Some other types of dBASE reports are discussed in Chapter 19.

Chapter 18

Divvy Up Your Database and Then Put It Back Together

. . . .

In This Chapter

▶ Using more than one table in your database

▶ Relating tables to combine their data

▶ Relating tables in different ways

▶ Using a common field to relate tables

. . . .

*T*ables are the building blocks of a database. When most people design a database for the first time, they try to cram everything into a single table: customer records, sales records, Bob Dylan records, and even bungee-jumping world records.

But that approach doesn't produce very useful results. One of the great strengths of dBASE is that it lets you divide your data into different tables. You have one table for customer records, another for sales records, and so on.

Dividing up your data would be pretty useless, however, unless you can put it back together when necessary. And that's just what you do when you link two or more tables together: by combining them in a query, you can tell dBASE to treat them temporarily as a single table.

Before you can combine data from two or more tables, you need to have

✔ Created two tables that have a common field, such as account number (Chapter 4).

✔ Put data in the tables (Chapter 5).

✔ Learned how to use the Query Designer (Chapter 12).

To do the exercises with this book's example database, you need to have

- ✔ Created the Customer Records table (Chapter 4) and the Sales table (Chapter 12).
- ✔ Put data in the two tables (all the data is in Appendix A).

If you're working with your own database, you can use this information to learn the basic concepts and techniques and then apply them to your own database.

The Basic Idea: Divide and Conquer

You *could* put all your data in one table, but remember that all the records in a table must be the same size. If you put all your data in a single table, some records would contain a lot of information and others would contain very little. Every record, however, takes up the same amount of disk space, so records with little information take as much disk space as ones that are packed to the gills.

This concept is pretty abstract, so consider this book's example Customer Records and Sales tables. Each customer record must have the customer's name, address, account number, and a few other pieces of information. Each sales record must have the buyer's account number, the date, a description of the item, and the amount of money received for the item.

Suppose that you put all the data from these two tables into a single table. Some customers may make 25 purchases a month, while others may make only one or two. That means that the records for customers who buy 25 times a month need 75 extra fields to hold their monthly sales data (25 purchases x 3 fields per purchase). But because all records in a table have to be the same size, the records for customers who buy once or twice a month *also* need 75 extra fields — even though most of those fields will always be empty. That's incredibly inefficient.

This approach presents another problem, too. What if a customer makes 26 purchases in a month? In that case, you're simply out of luck. There are no more fields to record the data for the 26th sale. You could add more fields, but that would require you to restructure the table (Chapter 8), and you probably don't want to waste your time doing that.

Dividing your data into different tables

As you learned earlier in this book, dBASE enables you to divide up your data into different tables. Instead of creating one big Customer Records/Sales table, you created a Customer Records table and a Sales table. Each customer record includes the same information (account number, name, address, and so on), and each sales record includes the same information (account number, sale date, book title, and so on). No disk space is wasted, and customers can make as many purchases as their over-the-limit credit cards allow.

But suppose that you want to print a report showing each customer's name and purchases for the month. The customer information is in one table, and the sales information is in another. You need a way to bring the two together, and that's what linking tables is all about.

Linking tables with a query

You bring tables together by combining them in a query. A query (Chapter 12) is just a question that you ask about your database. One of the questions you can ask is "What would happen if I combined the data from two or more tables? Would it be, like, totally bogus, or would it actually do some good?"

The answer is that most of the time, it would do you some good. Only rarely is combining tables in a query totally bogus, and even then, it won't hurt you unless your name is Bill or Ted. Or Chad. Or Skip.

Chapter 17 told you how to use a table as the data source for a printed report. If you want to create a report that combines data from two or more tables, you simply base it on a multi-table query instead of a single table. That way, because all the data in the tables is available in the query, the same data can also be used in the report.

Chapter 19 covers the actual mechanics of creating a multi-table report. Here, you learn how to combine data from different tables by using a query. It's called setting up a *relation* between the tables.

Different types of relations between tables

In dBASE, you can set up two different types of relations between tables: *one-to-one* and *one-to-many*. In a one-to-many relation, the *one* table (such as Customer Records) is sometimes called the *parent* table, and the *many* table (such as Sales) is called the *child* table.

An example of a one-to-one relation would be that of husband and wife. In Western countries (at least in theory), each husband has only one wife, and each wife has only one husband. An example of a one-to-many relation would be that of a customer record to sales records. Each customer may make many purchases, but each purchase can be made by only one customer. This type of relation is illustrated in Figure 18-1.

One-to-one relations between tables aren't used that often. Most of the time, you'll find yourself setting up one-to-many relations, as in the example of the Bookcust table: each customer record can have many sales records associated with it.

You should realize that for a one-to-many relation, each *one* record need not in fact have *many* records related to it. If you set up a one-to-many relation between a customer records table and a sales table, some customers may have only one sale, while others may have many or none at all!

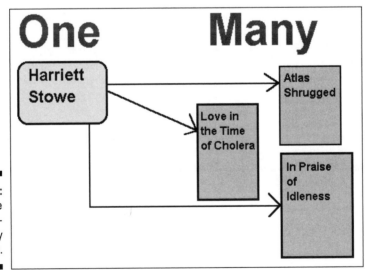

Figure 18-1:
An example of a one-to-many relation.

To be related, tables must share a field

For two tables to be joined or related, they must have a common field, such as an account number field. You need to know four main things about this shared field. Some of the things may seem a little technical, so don't sweat the details too much. Just take them on faith.

- ✔ The field does not need to have the same name in both tables, but it must contain the same data. In other words, it doesn't matter if the account number field is called *Cust_ID* in the Customer Records table and *Madonna* in the Sales table, as long as both fields contain account numbers.

- ✔ dBASE works faster if the common field is indexed in both tables. In a one-to-many relation, the common field *must* be indexed in the *many* table. (See Chapter 15 for an explanation of indexing.)

- ✔ The shared field must be the same data type in both tables.

- ✔ Usually, the common field is the *first* field in the table.

The Practical Part: Here's How You Do It

In the following exercise, you actually set up a relation between the Customer Records table and the Sales table. If you're working with your own database, just follow along, making the same moves with your own tables. If you're using this book's example database, make sure that the Caveat catalog is loaded and that the Catalog window is on-screen.

Checking the Sales table

Because the Sales table is going to be the *many* table, its CUST_ID field must be indexed. If you're at all unsure about whether you indexed that field when you set up the table (if you followed instructions in Chapter 12, you did), here's how to make sure that the field is indexed:

1. **In the right side of the Catalog window, click the Sales table.**

2. **Open the Catalog menu and select Design Table Structure.**

   The Table Structure window appears.

3. **In the first row (CUST_ID), look at the Index column.**

   The Index column should read `Ascend`.

4. **If the Index column for the row does *not* read** Ascend, **click in that column and pick Ascend from the list box. Then save the table design by opening the File menu and selecting Save.**

5. **Close the Table Structure window.**

Setting up the relation

To link the two tables, you need to set up a multi-table query that includes all the fields from both tables. This is the query you'll use if you create multi-table reports.

Now, if dBASE were an old-fashioned (1980s-style) database manager, you'd have to type something awful, like **set relation from "customer" into "sales" on "custID"** or a variation on that theme. But in dBASE for Windows, establishing the relationship is as easy as rolling the mouse:

1. **In the left side of the Catalog window, click on the Queries icon.**

2. **In the right side of the Catalog window, double-click on the Untitled icon.**

   In a dialog box, dBASE asks you which table to use for the query.

3. **Select the first table that you want to use.**

   In this book's example database, this is the Customer Records table. The Query Designer window appears, containing a skeleton of the first table.

4. **Maximize the Query Designer window so that it fills the entire screen.**

   Your screen should look something like Figure 18-2.

5. **Open the Query menu and select Add table.**

   dBASE again asks you which table to use.

6. **Select the second table you want in the query.**

   In this book's example database, this is the Sales table. As soon as you select the second table, its skeleton appears under the first table's skeleton in the Query Designer window.

7. **Click the leftmost field-selection square of both skeletons.**

   This field-selection square, shown in Figure 18-2, makes all the fields in both tables available for the query. Also, notice a little table icon at the far left end of each table skeleton.

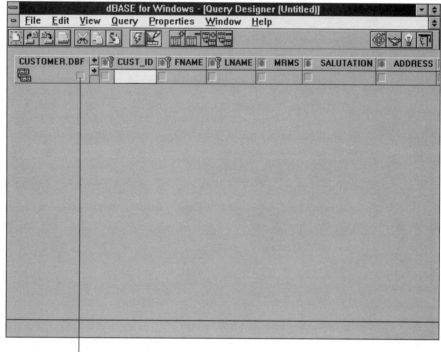

Figure 18-2:
The Query
Designer
window
with one
table added.

Click here to select all
fields in the table skeleton.

8. With the mouse, drag the icon from the Customer Records skeleton down onto the icon in the Sales skeleton.

The Define Relation dialog box appears. dBASE has picked CUST_ID as the probable common field in the example database. If you're using your own database, just select the common field. Then click OK.

The Query Designer window reappears. dBASE shows the link with a black line connecting the Customer Records and Sales tables (see Figure 18-3). You can now easily consolidate the information from the two tables in reports.

You're done! Save the multi-table query by opening the File menu and selecting Save. If you're saving the query for this book's example database, call it *Custsale*. Otherwise, call it whatever you want, remembering to follow the rules for naming DOS files: up to eight letters, digits, and underscores. Dirty, filthy query names will not be tolerated; you could get detention for a month!

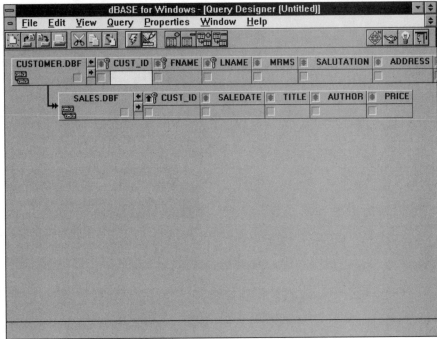

Figure 18-3:
dBASE
draws a line
to show that
the link is
established.

Deleting a relation

Deleting a relation is even easier than creating it. Simply click in the skeleton for the *many* (child) table. Then open the Query menu and select Remove relation. Zap! It's history! You're going to use the relation between the Customer Records and Sales tables in the next chapter, so don't delete that one. But if you ever do need to delete a relation, now you know how.

Part IV
Really Advanced Stuff to Impress Your Friends

The 5th Wave   By Rich Tennant

"FOR US, IT WAS TOTAL INTEGRATION OR NOTHING. FOR INSTANCE— AT THIS TERMINAL ALONE I CAN GET DEPARTMENTAL DATA, PRINTER AND STORAGE RESOURCES, ESPN, HOME SHOPPING NETWORK _AND_ THE MOVIE CHANNEL."

In this part . . .

*O*ften, the simple kinds of reports covered in Part III aren't enough. This part shows you how to create really sophisticated reports that group your data, do calculations, and draw information from more than one table. You also learn how to use dBASE to create form letters and mailing labels in case you want to do one of those annoying mass mailings.

Finally, this part shows how to include graphics, artwork, or even photographs in your printed reports — a way to make your data come alive.

Chapter 19

Hot Stuff! Creating Sophisticated Reports

● ●

In This Chapter

▶ Creating a grouped report

▶ Creating a really *jazzed-up* report

▶ Basing a report on a query instead of a table

▶ Creating a multitable report

● ●

*W*hen most people hear the term *sophisticated reports,* they naturally assume that it has something to do with tea and crumpets, watching *Masterpiece Theatre* on public television, or putting on a tie and jacket before sitting down at the computer.

Not true! It certainly helps if you wear a tie and jacket while using dBASE — at least, it helps the people who sell ties and jackets — but sophisticated reports are just another way for dBASE to print out your database information. Chapter 16 covers simple Browse window printouts, and Chapter 17 covers simple reports. This chapter shows you how to create and print fancier reports that organize your database information in a variety of different ways.

So make yourself a nice cup of tea (Earl Grey, hot), eat a crumpet (whatever the heck that is), and get ready to create some kick-it reports! Formal dress is optional.

Before you can create a super-sophisticated report, you need to have done the following:

　✔ Learned basic database concepts, such as catalog, table, and field (Chapters 1 and 2)

　✔ Created a table (Chapter 4) and put data in the table (Chapter 5)

　✔ Learned basic report concepts and parts of Crystal Reports (Chapter 17)

To do the steps in this chapter with this book's example database, you need to have done the following:

- ✔ Created the Bookcust table (Chapter 4) and Sales table (Chapter 12). Data for these tables is in Appendix A.

- ✔ Created the multitable query (Chapter 18). (This is for the multitable report only.)

If you're creating a report for your own database, follow the example to learn the basic ideas and techniques then use them to create and modify your own report.

The Basic Ideas

The basic ideas behind creating a report are the same no matter what kind of report you're talking about. A report is just a printout of the information in your database. You can print all the information or just some of it, put the information in alphabetical order, and include groups and totals.

Before you can print a report, you first have to create the *report layout*. The report layout shows where the parts of the report will appear on the printed page. When you create the layout, you also can *format* the parts of the report to control the type style, left or right text alignment, and so on.

dBASE makes it easy to create several different types of report layouts:

- ✔ *Row and column* arranges your data with records in rows and fields in columns, similar to how you see it in a Browse window. You created this kind of report in Chapter 17.

- ✔ *Grouped* enables you to group your records by any field you like. For example, you can use this layout to create a report that groups sales transactions by state and includes a subtotal of the revenues from each state and a grand total of all sales revenue at the end of the report.

- ✔ *Form letter* is a standard letter with each name and address inserted from a dBASE table.

- ✔ *Mailing label* enables you to design and print name and address labels to put on envelopes.

After you create the report layout, you can use Print Preview to see how it will look on paper. Then you can switch back to the Design window and change the layout. You can go back and forth from Print Preview to the Design window, adjusting the layout until it's exactly the way you want it. Then you save the report layout to disk. Any time you want to view or print the report, just double-click its icon in the Catalog window.

The Basic Steps

You work through a specific example in the next section. However, the basic steps in creating any report are the same, whether it's a simple row-and-column report, a grouped report, or any other kind of report.

To create a report, follow these steps:

1. **Start dBASE and open the catalog for which you want to do a report.**

2. **Click the Report icon in the left side of the Catalog window. Then click the Untitled icon in the right side of the Catalog window.**

   dBASE displays a dialog box asking you which table it should use as a data source for the report.

3. **Pick the table that will provide the data for your report.**

   The Crystal Reports window opens on your screen. Superimposed on the window is the Insert Database Field dialog box.

4. **Drag each field you want from the dialog box to the Details band of the report layout.**

5. **Tell Crystal Reports how records should be sorted and/or grouped.**

6. **Use Print Preview to see how the report will look on paper.**

   Switch from close-up view to full-page view by repeatedly clicking the mouse button.

7. **If needed, switch back to the Report Layout window and modify the report layout.**

   Switch back and forth between Design Mode and Print Preview until the report looks exactly the way you want it.

8. **From the Report Design window, save the report layout to disk by selecting Save from the File menu.**

Whenever you want to use the report layout, click the Reports icon in the left side of the Catalog window. Then double-click the icon for the report you want. To print the report, either click the Print button in the toolbar or open the File menu and select Print.

Creating a Grouped Report

A grouped report is similar to the row-and-column report you created in Chapter 17, except that in a grouped report, you can divide up the records. For example, if you want a report that lists customers by state and also includes totals of how many customers are in each state, you can use a grouped report.

Setting up the basic report

The following steps walk you through the process of creating just such a grouped report. First, open the Caveat Catalog window. Then click the Reports icon at the left and follow these steps:

1. **Double-click the Untitled icon.**

   dBASE asks what table to use for the report.

2. **Select the table you want to use.**

   If you're doing a grouped report with this book's example database, select the Bookcust table. The Crystal Reports window appears.

3. **Maximize the Crystal Reports window and the Report Layout window, as shown in Figure 19-1.**

4. **Drag the fields you want from the Insert Database Field dialog box to the Details band of the report layout.**

   As you drag each field into the Details band, its name appears above it as a column heading in the Page Header band. In this case, drag the STATE, CUST_ID, FNAME, and LNAME fields into the Details band.

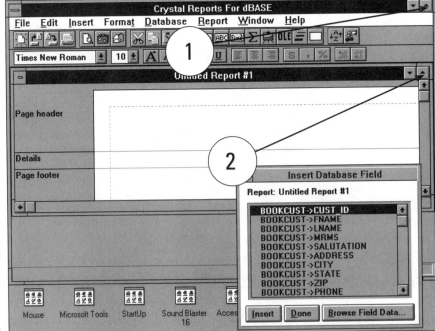

Figure 19-1:
Maximize
the windows
by clicking
on button 1
and then on
button 2.

5. Delete the column labels and replace them with more descriptive text.

One at a time, highlight each column label and press Delete. Then click the Text Field button in the SpeedBar. The Text Field box appears. Type the text you want for the column label and then click Accept or press Alt+A. Use the mouse to move the label to the top of the appropriate column. When it's in position, click the mouse.

At this point, you can also pretty up the report, using the Ribbon bar to make the type bigger, change the font, or use bold face. You can narrow the fields in the Details band and move the columns to the left so that more columns fit on the page. It's all up to you.

6. When you're finished adding fields, close the Insert Database Field dialog box by clicking Done.

7. Preview the report by clicking the Print Preview button in the SpeedBar.

dBASE may display a dialog box asking if you want to use the saved data. Just click the Use saved data button. If you're working with this book's example database, your screen should look something like Figure 19-2.

8. Close the Print Preview window by clicking Close.

The shortcut key for this command is the same as for closing any other window: Ctrl+F4. dBASE returns you to the Report Layout window.

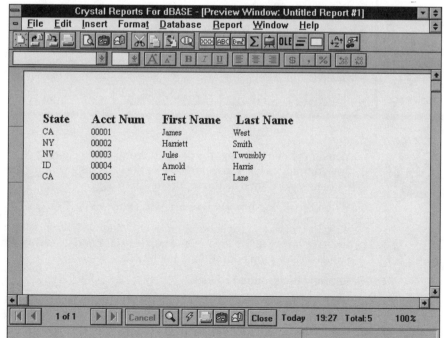

Figure 19-2: The Customers by State report without any grouping.

Adding the group sections

The report looks okay so far, but the states are all mixed up. It would help to have all the customers in each state grouped together, maybe even with a horizontal line between groups to help separate them on the page. *No problemo!*

To add grouped sections to a report, follow these steps:

1. Open the Insert menu and select Group section.

dBASE displays the Insert Group Section dialog box, as shown in Figure 19-3. As you can see, dBASE automatically picks the leftmost column as the one by which to group records. If you want to use a different field, click the list box button at the right end of the grouping blank and select a field from the list. Notice that there's also a list box blank for how dBASE should sort the records. Unless you say otherwise, the records appear in ascending (A to Z) order.

Click here if you need to change the grouping field. ———

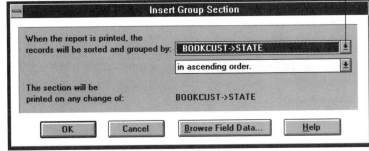

Figure 19-3:
The Insert Group Section dialog box.

You don't have to select *any* fields to group your report. If you don't select any grouping fields, the report will be the same as a simple row-and-column report, such as the report in Chapter 17.

2. When the dialog box choices are what you want, click OK.

dBASE returns you to the Report Layout window. Now, however, there are two new bands in the layout: a Group Header band just above the Details band, and a Group Footer band below it.

3. Preview the grouped report.

If you click Print Preview, you'll see that the records are now grouped by state. However, there are still two ways in which the report is not quite right. First, if there's more than one record in a particular group, the name of the grouping field repeats; the report would look better if it appeared only once per group. Second, a line between the groups would make the report easier to read. Close Print Preview when you are ready to make the two improvements.

4. Tell dBASE not to repeat the grouping field on multiple lines.

In the Details band, double-click the grouping field, the STATE field in this book's example database. The Format String dialog box appears. Click the check box next to Suppress if Duplicated to tell dBASE that if a field has the same value as on the previous line of the report, that value shouldn't be printed in the report. Then click OK.

5. Draw a horizontal line in the Group Header band.

To do this, open the Insert menu and select Line. The mouse pointer changes to a little picture of a pencil. Position the pencil point at the left end of your new line. Then hold down the left mouse button and drag the pencil to the right. When the line is long enough to separate the groups, release the mouse button. Your screen should look something like Figure 19-4.

If you again click the Print Preview button, you'll see that your records are nicely grouped by state, with a horizontal line separating each group from the one before it. In a table like this with only a few records, groups don't help very much, but you can probably imagine how much they'd help if you had a table with 1,000 records in 50 different groups.

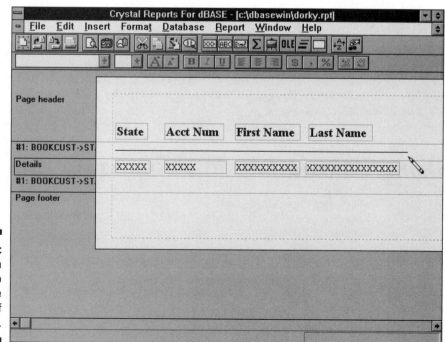

Figure 19-4: Drawing a line to separate groups of records.

Parts of the grouped report design

Take a look at the Report Layout window, shown in Figure 19-4. This report design, just like the simpler one in Chapter 17, consists of horizontal bands. Each band contains a different kind of information to print on the page:

- *Page Header band* contains stuff that prints at the top of each page, such as the titles of the columns in the report (State, First Name, and so on).

- *State Header band* contains stuff that prints at the top of each group in the report. In the figure, the report is grouped by state, so dBASE prints the name of the state for each group of records.

- *Details band* contains the actual data from the Bookcust table: names, account numbers, and so on.

- *State Footer band* contains stuff that prints at the bottom of each group. In the next section, you find out how to use the State Footer band to count the number of customer records for each state. You can also create totals and do other calculations that appear at the bottom of each group.

- *Page Footer band* contains stuff that prints at the bottom of each page, such as the page number.

- *New Trier High School Marching Band* contains immensely talented but sometimes out-of-step high school students. If it appears on your screen, you are in serious trouble and should call 911 immediately.

Saving the report

 To save the report, open the File menu and select Save. (If you prefer, you can click the Save button on the SpeedBar.) dBASE prompts you to name the report. If you're saving this book's example report, type **by_state** in the File Name blank and then click OK.

Doing Calculations in a Report

The grouped report you created in the preceding section looks pretty good. You can see that the records are grouped by state: you have two customers in California, one in Idaho, and so forth.

There's one other obvious way you can improve the report. It would be nice if, at the end of each state group, dBASE told you how many customers are in that state. That's surprisingly easy to do, and you'll learn a few other tricks along the way.

Changing the height of a report band

Before you can put a total of each group's records in the Group Footer band, you'll probably need to make the band a little taller. It's easy. Just move the mouse over the bottom border of the Group Footer band until the mouse pointer turns into a double up-and-down-pointing arrow. Then hold down the left mouse button and drag the border downward. As you do this, the band's height increases.

You can use the same technique to increase the height of any band in the report. And by reversing the process — dragging a band's bottom border *up* instead of *down* — you can decrease the band height.

With this book's example *by state* report, drag the bottom border of the State Footer band downward until it's about twice its original height.

Inserting a summary field

Counting records in a group is one way of summarizing information about the group. To summarize information you need to have dBASE put a *summary field* in the Group Footer band. In addition to counting records, a summary field can do other kinds of calculations. If you were creating a sales report with the records grouped by date, for example, a summary field could give you a total dollar amount for the books sold on each day.

To insert a summary field that counts the records in each group, follow these steps:

1. **Click one of the fields in the Details band.**

   It makes absolutely no difference which field you click. Obviously, if you were inserting a summary field to do something more than just count records — for instance, to calculate a total for a price field — then you'd need to click the specific field involved. But to count records, any field will do. If you're doing it with this book's example report, click the LNAME field.

2. **Open the Insert menu and select Summary Field.**

   The Summary Field submenu appears.

3. **In the submenu, select Summary.**

   The Insert Summary dialog box appears, as shown in Figure 19-5. In the top right is a list box that shows the type of summary field dBASE will use unless you say otherwise. Currently, it's set to calculate the maximum value in the LNAME field. That makes no sense at all (unless you believe in numerology) because LNAME is a Character field. To change the type of summary field, you need to pick something else from the list box.

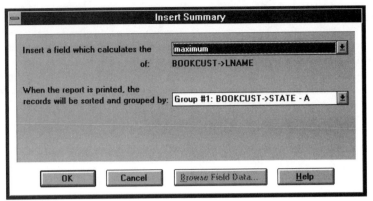

Figure 19-5:
The Insert
Summary
dialog box.

4. **Click the list box button in the Insert Summary dialog box.**

   The list of available summary field types drops down.

5. **Click count. Then click OK to close the dialog box.**

   dBASE returns you to the Report Layout window. The summary field is now visible in the Group Footer band.

Jazzing it up a little

Suppose that you printed the report as it is right now. At the location of the summary field, dBASE would print the number of records in each group. But it would be a bare number all by itself, with no caption to say what it's supposed to be. For counting records, again, that's not much of a problem. But if you were doing a more complicated arithmetic calculation, you'd want the report to explain the summary numbers.

Also, the summary field is too close to the Details band. If you go into Print Preview, you'll see that it looks confusing because the number is literally *right under* the LNAME field. The reason you increased the height of the Group Footer band was so that you could drag the summary field down a little.

To put the finishing touches on the report, follow these steps:

1. **With the mouse, drag the summary field down a little.**

   It should be just above the bottom border of the Group Footer band.

2. **Click the SpeedBar's Text Field button.**

   The Text Field box appears. In the blank, type **Number in this state:** and then click A̲ccept.

3. Move the text field so that it's just to the left of the summary field.

If you want, you can also shrink the two fields so that their borders aren't much wider than their contents.

4. Click the summary field and then click the Ribbon's Left-Align button.

Normally, a numeric field is right aligned: that means it's up against the right edge of the report column instead of the left edge, like ordinary text. But you want the record count to be close to the explanatory text, not ten miles off to the right.

You can drag the fields around a little more to suit your taste. If you now click the Print Preview button, your screen should look something like Figure 19-6.

If the report looks okay, switch back to the Report Layout window. Open the File menu and select Save to save the design to disk.

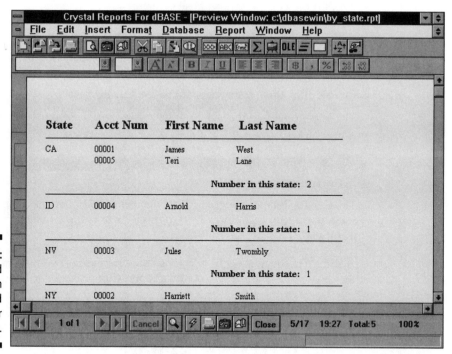

Figure 19-6:
The grouped
report with
a record
count for
each group.

Basing a Report on a Query

So far, all the reports you've created have used information from a table. But you can also base a report on a query. If you think about it, that's not too surprising, because the result of a query is a group of records and fields, very much like a table.

By using a query instead of a table, you can restrict the information that appears in a report. Suppose that you want a report that just includes information about customers who live in California. The easiest way to produce such a report is to create a query that asks, "Which customers live in California?" The answer to the query contains the records you want for the report. When you base the report on the query, dBASE automatically prints information about California customers only.

Basing a report on a query is only slightly different from basing it on a table. To base a report on a query, follow these steps:

1. **In the left side of the Catalog window, click the Queries icon.**

   In the right side of the Catalog window, dBASE displays all the queries that have been created for this database.

2. **Double-click the query you want to use for the report.**

   The query opens so that it can be used to create the report.

3. **Open the File menu and select New.**

   The New File submenu appears.

4. **In the submenu, select Report.**

   The Crystal Reports program starts up, using your query as the basis for the report. After this point, everything else works the same as if you were using a table instead of a query.

In the exercise in the next section, you use the query-report combination for another very special purpose: to create a report that draws information from more than one table.

Creating a Multitable Report

The multitable report you're about to create isn't fancy, but you can use the same process you learn in this example to create more interesting reports.

To create the sample multitable report, you'll use the Custsale query you created at the end of Chapter 18. Because this query *already* includes all the fields from this book's example Bookcust and Sales tables, all the data that the query draws from both tables can be printed in the report.

You're not limited to having only two tables in a report or query. You can include as many as you need.

To create a multitable report, follow these steps:

1. **In the Catalog window, double-click the multitable query that you want the report to use.**

   The query is opened so that it can be used by the report. If you're working with this book's example database, use the Custsale query from Chapter 18.

2. **Open the File menu and select New. In the submenu, select Report.**

   dBASE starts up Crystal Reports. Notice that the Insert Database Field dialog box includes fields from both tables.

3. **Maximize both the Crystal Reports window and the Report Layout window.**

   It's easier to do these steps if these windows take up the entire screen.

4. **Drag the fields you want into the Details band.**

   For the example report, use the LNAME, TITLE, and PRICE fields. You'll need to scroll down a little in the field list to get to the TITLE and PRICE fields. Notice that in front of each field is the name of the table it comes from.

5. **Click Done to close the Insert Database Field dialog box.**

6. **Change the column headings so that they're more readable.**

   In essence, you delete the original column headings and insert new ones. Complete instructions on how to do this are given in Chapter 17.

7. **If needed, tell dBASE not to repeat fields on successive lines.**

   In the example report, you don't want dBASE to print the same customer's name on several lines for each book purchased. To keep a field from repeating, double-click the field in the Details band. Then in the dialog box, click the check box next to Suppress if Duplicated.

8. **For a cosmetic touch, open the Insert menu and select Group section.**

   The Group Section dialog box appears. As usual, the leftmost field in the Details band is selected as the grouping field. If you're doing this book's example report, this is the LNAME field. Click OK.

9. **Again, open the Insert menu and then select Line. Draw a horizontal line in the Group Header band.**

   This line makes the report easier to read.

10. **Click Print Preview to see the report.**

    Your report should look something like Figure 19-7, except much bigger.

11. **Close the Print Preview window and save the report under the name *Custsale*.**

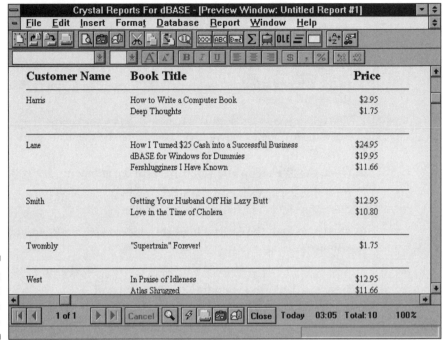

Figure 19-7:
Preview of a
multitable
report.

You can make a numeric field (such as the Sales table's PRICE field) display in dollar format by double-clicking the field in the Details band. In the dialog box, click the check box next to Currency symbol. Then click OK. Now, the numeric field will print (and display in Print Preview) with a dollar sign in front of it.

You can use other tricks you've learned to improve the report. In particular, in this book's example report, you could insert a summary field under the Price column to show the total amount spent by each customer. Use your imagination!

As usual, you can print the report by opening the File menu and selecting Print. When the dialog box appears, just click OK.

That's it for this chapter! In the next chapter, you learn how to use dBASE to create those annoying form letters that are always jamming your mailbox. But this time, you'll be able to send them to *other* people! (Plan on sending at least a thousand to Ed McMahon.)

Chapter 20

Creating and Printing Form Letters

● ●

In This Chapter

▶ What is a form letter?

▶ Designing a report as a form letter

▶ Using fonts and printing effects in a form letter

▶ Printing a form letter

● ●

ear [MRMS] [FNAME] [LNAME]:

You may already have won a valuable ballpoint pen in the *dBASE For Windows For Dummies* Miracle Sweepstakes! Yes, [FNAME], I personally selected you from *millions of suckers* to get this valuable prize! All you need to do to get your prize is to pay a one-time shipping fee of $29.95, and your pen (in an attractive gift box made of sturdy recycled cardboard) will be *rushed* directly to your home in beautiful [CITY] via fourth-class mail!

Sincerely,

Joe Jones

You get them all the time: personalized form letters. Your mailbox is stuffed with them. Even your dog gets them. And although some of them are just junk mail, others are really important.

Because you may need to send out the *important* kind of form letters — whether to customers, to patrons of charitable groups, or even to family members (if you have a very large family!) — dBASE enables you to create them from your table data. To do that, you use the Crystal Reports program included with dBASE.

Before you can create a form letter, you need to have

  ✔ Created a name and address table (Chapter 4) and put data in the table (Chapter 5).

✓ Learned basic database concepts (Chapters 1 and 2) and how to create a report (Chapter 17).

To do the steps with this book's example database, you need to have created the Bookcust table (Chapter 4) and put data in the table (Chapter 5).

If you're creating form letters with your own database, just read this chapter to get the basic ideas. Then follow the steps using your own table instead of the one in this book.

The Basic Ideas

The first thing you need to understand about creating a form letter is what the term *form letter* really means. A form letter is a document that combines standard, boilerplate text with information from a database table or a mail-merge file. If you've ever created a form letter in your word processor, you probably understand this concept, illustrated in Figure 20-1.

In dBASE, you use a table as the basis for a form letter. For example, if you want to send the form letter to customers in this book's example database, you'd use the Bookcust table as the data source for the form letter.

Figure 20-1:
Take a data source, such as a dBASE table. Add a document with slots for the data. Put the two together, stirring gently. Bake 20 minutes in a preheated oven. Cover with chocolate syrup and eat. Serves thousands.

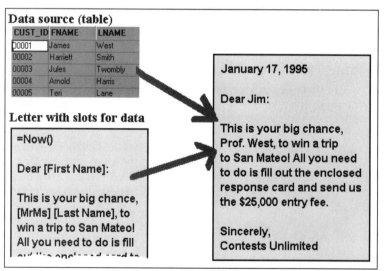

In dBASE, a form letter is a report ... sort of

The idea of taking data from a table and printing it on a page may sound a little familiar. If you guessed that a form letter in dBASE is a kind of report, you guessed right. You design a form letter exactly the same way that you design reports. The only difference is that a form letter is just a *teensy* bit more complicated than the reports you've created so far.

Figure 20-1 illustrates the source of the difficulty. In a normal report (for the most part), you just have captions and table fields. A form letter is different. It has table fields strung together on the same line and table fields intermixed with text

Suppose, for example, that you're creating form letters with a name-and-address table, like the example Bookcust table. When you first set up the table, you gave each field enough width to hold the largest piece of data that would probably be put into it. The MRMS field may have a width of five, while the FNAME field may have a width of 10, and so on. In a normal report, this causes no problems. You put the table's fields in the Details part of the report layout, and the data prints like this:

```
Mr.    James      West
Ms.    Harriett   Stowe
Mr.    Jules      Twombly
```

But what if you're printing a form letter (or a label, as you'll see in Chapter 21)? Then the field widths can cause problems, as you can see in the following form letter excerpt:

```
Mr.    James      West
Mythic University
Martinsville,    CA      98035

Dear Mr.    West,

It's your lucky day, Jim      ! You and one other person from
          Martinsville              have been
chosen as delegates to the Model U.N. ...
```

The field widths cause big gaps to appear in the printed text. Because the FNAME field has a width of 10, the field takes up 10 spaces in the first address line of the letter, even though there are only five letters in James. Obviously, that's not how you want the letter to look. It *should* look like this:

```
Mr. James West
Mythic University
Martinsville, CA 98035

Dear Mr. West,

It's your lucky day, Jim! You and one other person
from Martinsville have been chosen as delegates to
the Model U.N. ...
```

Using formulas to fix things

To get the field data to display the way you want it, you need to create a formula and insert it in the report layout. Formulas (which are also sometimes called *expressions*) are special instructions — *not* in English, unfortunately — that tell Crystal Reports how to handle certain things in the letter.

Formulas are not hard to use. You just need to make sure that you don't let them intimidate you. The form letter you create in this chapter requires only a few simple formulas, so it'll be as easy as finding overpriced tickets for a Broadway show.

Formula trick number one: use the RTrim function

The first formula trick you need is provided by the Crystal Reports RTrim function. The big problem you just saw was that Crystal Reports puts extra spaces to the right of what's in a report field. The RTrim function, as you can guess from the name, trims off those extra spaces. When you set up a formula with the function, it looks like this:

```
RTrim( {bookcust.fname} )
```

You'll set up this function in the Crystal Reports formula builder, which you'll learn about in a moment.

Formula trick number two: glom stuff together with the plus sign

The second formula trick lets you put more than one field on the same line. You don't *have* to use the plus sign for this, but if you don't, even the RTrim(x) function won't keep your form letter from looking weird. Here's how you'll set it up in the Crystal Reports formula builder:

```
RTrim( {bookcust.mrms} ) + RTrim( {bookcust.fname} ) +
        bookcust.lname
```

How to Do It: Setting Up a Form Letter

Particularly with form letters, an abstract discussion of the basic steps won't tell you very much. You really have to do it to see how it works. The following steps use this book's example database. If you're creating a form letter for your own database, just follow along, making the appropriate changes to your own table and fields.

If your screens don't exactly match the screens in the book, *don't panic.* Like all good software products, dBASE for Windows is constantly being improved. If a dialog box looks or works differently from the way it does here, that just means you have a later — and probably even *better* — version of dBASE than the one I used to write the book. Nothing big is likely to change, so you can handle any minor discrepancies with no trouble.

1. **Start Crystal Reports.**

   Click on the Reports icon in the left side of the Catalog window. Then double-click on the Untitled icon. dBASE asks you what table to use. As soon as you select a table, the Crystal Reports registration dialog box appears. Click on the button marked Proceed to Crystal Reports. The Crystal Reports window appears on your screen, along with the Insert Database Field dialog box.

2. **Maximize the Crystal Reports window, maximize the Report Layout window, and close the Insert Database Field dialog box.**

   You're going to insert fields in the form letter, but you'll do it by using the Crystal Reports formula builder. You won't need this dialog box.

3. **Expand the Page header band.**

   Everything in the form letter goes into the Page header band, so position the cursor inside it and press Enter to add more lines. If you don't add enough lines, you can add more later. When you lay out the form letter, do *not* put anything in the Details band.

4. **If the form letter needs a return address, type it at the top of the Page header band.**

   You can type the return address just as if you were in a word processor. Press the spacebar if you want to center a line; select your desired type font, style, and size from the ribbon; and start new lines by pressing Enter. Most of the time, you'll probably print form letters on letterhead paper that already has the return address printed on it. In that case, you can skip this step.

In the case of this book's example database, you do need to type the return address. At the top of the Page header band, type **Caveat Emptor Bookstore**. On the next two lines, type **123 Lane Street** and **Bloomington, Indiana 47401**. Use the spacebar to center the text on the page. If you want, click on the ribbon to change the type font, size, and style.

5. At the desired location, type the letter's date.

You'll probably want to press Enter a couple of times after that to separate the date from the first line of the recipient's address. In the example form letter, type **January 17, 1995**.

If you prefer to use a "live" date, so that the date changes to the current day whenever form letters are printed, open the Insert menu and select Special Field. Then select Date and position the date field wherever you want it to go on your form letter.

Inserting the recipient's name

Here's where it gets just a little bit sticky. Remember that you want the recipient's address to look this:

```
Mr. James West
Mythic University
Martinsville, CA 98035
```

To create the first line, you're going to use the Edit Formula dialog box. You'll use RTrim to trim the extra spaces out of the MRMS and FNAME fields. Then you'll use the plus sign to combine the MRMS, FNAME, and LNAME fields on the same line. LNAME is at the end, so extra spaces don't matter.

1. To insert the MRMS field, open the Insert menu and select Formula Field.

The Insert Formula dialog box appears, as shown in Figure 20-2.

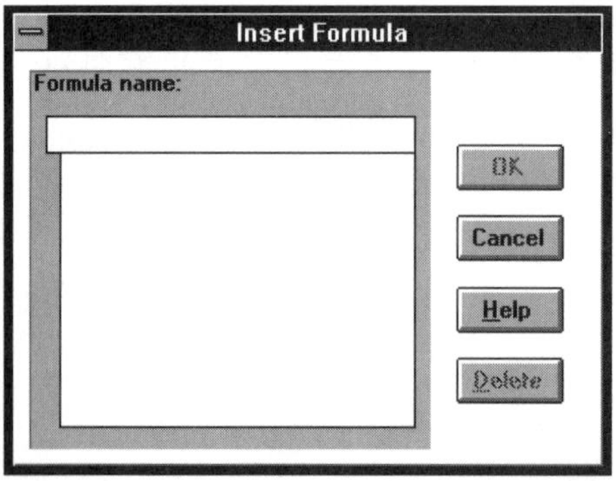

Figure 20-2:
The Insert Formula dialog box, where you name the formula you're inserting.

Insert Formula

Formula name:

OK

Cancel

Help

Delete

2. In the blank, type a name for the formula and then click on OK.

In the example form letter, type **NameLine** and click on OK. The Expression Builder dialog box appears, as shown in Figure 20-3. There's an awful lot of exciting stuff in this dialog box: much more, in fact, than you either need to worry about or *should* worry about at this stage of your dBASE education. Here, your goal is to learn how to create form letters, so just follow the steps and ignore everything else. Later, if you want to experiment on your own, you'll find you can do some incredible things with this dialog box.

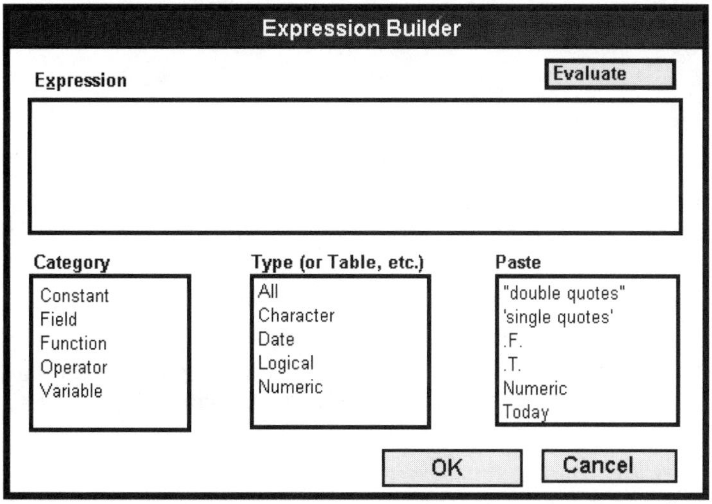

Figure 20-3:
The
Expression
Builder
dialog box.

3. In the Category list, click on Functions. In the Type list, scroll down and double-click on String data. In the Paste list, scroll down and double-click on RTrim.

The RTrim function appears in the Formula Text blank at the bottom of the dialog box. The cursor should be between the parentheses. If it isn't, you can move it there by clicking between them. If there's any text between the parentheses, delete it before going on to the next step.

4. In the Category list, click on Field. In the Type list, Bookcust is already selected because that's the only table in the report. In the Paste list, double-click on the MRMS field.

The MRMS field should appear between the parentheses of the RTrim function. Notice that it has the table name in front of it.

5. Click just to the right of the closing parenthesis.

6. Type + " " + after the closing parenthesis.

That's a space, a plus sign, a double-quote mark, a space, another double-quote mark, and another space, and another plus sign. Yeah, it's kinda boring, but it's not all that hard. And your form letter will look great!

7. **Again go into the Category list and click on Functions. In the Type list, double-click on String data. In the Paste list, double-click on RTrim.**

   RTrim( ) should appear to the right of the second plus sign. Again, delete any text between the parentheses. Then click between the parentheses to make sure that the cursor is there.

8. **Go into the Category list and click on Field. In the Type list, Bookcust is already selected. In the Paste list, double-click on FNAME.**

   As before, the FNAME field should appear between the parentheses.

9. **Just as before, type + " " + after the closing parenthesis.**

10. **Go into the Paste list and double-click on LNAME.**

    The LNAME field appears at the right end of the formula text. This time, you don't need to use RTrim to trim off extra spaces to the right. Nothing else is on this line of the form letter. Your screen should now look like Figure 20-4.

11. **Check the formula.**

    Click on the Evaluate button in the Expression Builder dialog box. If you constructed the formula correctly, Crystal Reports displays a little message saying that everything is okay. If you didn't, it displays a message saying what's wrong.

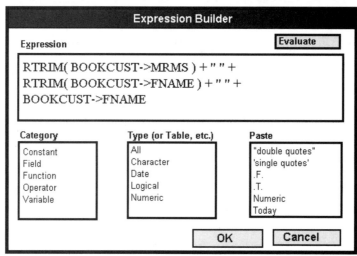

Figure 20-4: The Expression Builder dialog box with the completed name line.

12. **When you've made sure that the formula is right, click O̲K at the bottom of the dialog box.**

13. **Use the mouse to move the name under the date line. Then click the left mouse button.**

    Clicking the mouse button *anchors* the name in position on the form letter.

Adding the address lines

After all that fuss just to create the name line, you'll be relieved to learn that adding the street address is much simpler. After that, it's back to RTrim(x) and the Expression Builder dialog box to add the city, state, and ZIP code. But enjoy the moment: here comes your street address line.

1. **Open the I̲nsert menu and select D̲atabase Field.**

    The Insert Database Field dialog box appears, as shown in Figure 20-5.

2. **Click on the ADDRESS field and drag it just below the name line, as shown in Figure 20-5.**

    When the field is in position, release the left-mouse button. Next, it's back to the old Grind (with apologies to MTV's dance show of the same name) to add the city, state, and ZIP code line.

3. **Click on D̲one to close the Insert Database Field dialog box.**

4. **Using the Expression Builder dialog box, add the city, state, and ZIP code line.**

    You can use the previous steps describing how to enter the recipient's name as your guide. In the Insert Field dialog box, enter **CityStateZip**. When you're finished, the formula in the Edit Formula dialog box should look something like this:

    ```
    RTrim (bookcust->CITY) + "," + RTrim (bookcust->
          STATE) + " " + (bookcust->ZIP)
    ```

5. **Click on Evaluate to make sure the formula is okay. If it is, click on Ok.**

6. **Move the formula just below the address line and then click the left mouse button.**

    The city, state, and ZIP code line is anchored just below the address line.

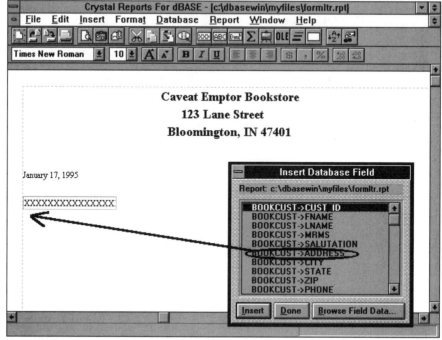

Figure 20-5:
Preparing to insert the ADDRESS field from the dialog box.

Entering the letter's text

Are you ready for some good news? First, your taxes are going down, your salary is going up, and your significant other is planning a surprise party for you tonight! Not. Okay, are you ready now for the *actual* good news? The actual good news is that after all that hassle to add the recipient's name and address, doing the body of the letter is very simple. Just remember that in the body of the letter, lines of text come in two different flavors:

✔ Lines that have one or more table fields in them, and

✔ Lines that don't

As an example of the first, you may write something like

*It's been our policy, **Joe,** to serve our customers with pride, and with our clothes on.*

You're embedding the first name field in a line of text. As an example of the second, you may write something like

If you don't pay your bill, my mother will come over and break your legs.

When you have a line containing one or more table fields, it's back to the Expression Builder dialog box. But when you have a line without any fields in it, you can simply type it on the report layout, just as you did with the return address. Ready for some more steps? You're now going to enter the Dear so-and-so line. Don't get stressed — you're in the home stretch!

1. **Open the Insert menu and select Formula Field.**

   When the Insert Field dialog box opens, name the formula **Dear**. The Expression Builder dialog box appears.

2. **Use the same method as before to construct the following formula.**

   ```
   "Dear " + RTrim (bookcust->SALUTATION) + ","
   ```

   You have to type "Dear," the plus signs, and the ",".

3. **Click on Evaluate to make sure that the formula is all right. If so, click on Accept.**

4. **Move the formula two lines below the city, state, and ZIP code line and then click the left mouse button.**

   Crystal Reports anchors the Dear so-and-so line in the correct position.

5. **Click two lines below the Dear so-and-so line. For the body of the letter, type the following. (You need to press Enter at the end of each line.)**

   ```
   It's been a pleasure serving you with fine books all these
   years. If you come into the store, I'll give you some
   passes to the movies.

   Your friend,


   Janis
   ```

Believe it or not, you're done! Now, all you need to do is preview the letter to make sure it looks the way you want, save the form letter as a report, load some paper in the printer, turn on the printer, go out for an extended (but nonalcoholic) lunch, and then come back, get a cup of coffee, and print your form letters!

Previewing and saving the form letter

Finally, click on the Print Preview button in the toolbar. Your form letter should look like the one in Figure 20-6.

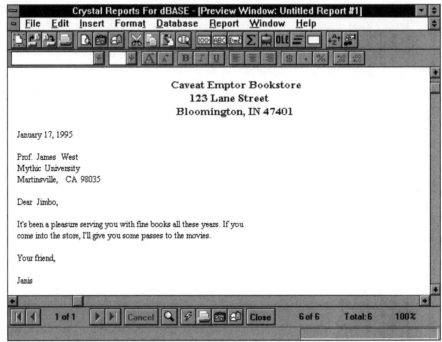

Figure 20-6:
The finished
form letter.
The name is
from the first
record in the
Bookcust
table.

Click on Close at the bottom of the window. Crystal Reports takes you back to
the Report Layout window. Open the File menu and save the form letter under
the name *CustLtr*.

Printing the form letter

If you wish, you can now print the letter just like any other report. To do so,
make sure that your printer is turned on and ready to print. Then simply open
the File menu and select Print. dBASE does the rest.

Chapter 21

Designing and Printing Mailing Labels

• •

In This Chapter

▶ Selecting the label format

▶ Laying out the label

▶ Printing the labels

• •

*M*ailing labels are another kind of report you can create with dBASE. And because Crystal Reports helps you every step of the way, it's super easy unless you want something *really* weird. You can create any normal mailing label in a minute or two.

Before you can create mailing labels, you need to have

> ✔ Created a name and address table (Chapter 4) and put data in the table (Chapter 5).
>
> ✔ Learned basic database concepts (Chapters 1 and 2) and how to create a report (Chapter 17).

To do the steps with this book's example database, you need to have created the Bookcust table (Chapter 4) and put data in the table (Chapter 5).

If you're creating labels with your own database, just read this chapter to get the basic ideas. Then follow the steps using your own table instead of the one in this book.

The Basic Ideas

The basic concept of a mailing label is probably familiar to you. It's about 2 inches by 3 inches, has someone's name and address on the front, and has glue on the back so you can stick it on an envelope.

You may not have considered, however, that when you design and print mailing labels in dBASE, you're really just creating a very simple kind of report. Normally, you'd print mailing labels on special mailing label paper, but there's no law (except in Indiana) that you *must* do so. You can print out a mailing label report on plain paper to create a simple, quick-and-dirty customer list, for example. (Believe it or not, with some older database managers, that was the *only* way to produce simple reports!)

In addition, you don't have to put names and addresses on your labels. You can create videotape labels, inventory labels, and so on. Just as you can use a mailing label report for just about anything, you can use the labels themselves for just about anything, depending on the data source of your mailing label report.

The Basic Steps

The basic steps in creating and printing mailing labels are very similar to those for producing any other kind of report. Here's a brief look at the process:

1. **Start Crystal Reports.**

   To do that, click on the Labels icon in the left side of the Catalog window. Then double-click on the Untitled icon. dBASE asks you what table to use. As soon as you select a table, and click on the Proceed button, the Crystal Reports window appears on your screen, along with the Mailing Labels dialog box, shown in Figure 21-1. This is where you select a mailing label format and, optionally, give Crystal Reports special instructions on how to print the labels.

   If you've already used Crystal Reports and haven't quit dBASE since then, Crystal Reports may simply assume that you want to use the same table you used before. In that case, it won't ask you what table to use.

2. **Select a label format.**

   Crystal Reports comes with a large number of predefined mailing label formats. To pick one, click on the list box button at the top right of the Choose Mailing Label Type area (see Figure 21-1). As soon as you click on the button, a list of available formats drops down.

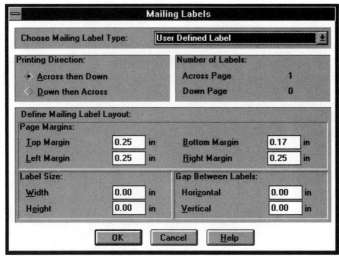

Figure 21-1:
The Mailing
Labels
dialog box.

Somewhere on your mailing label box or packaging, you should find an *Avery number.* In the dialog box, select the label size that has the same Avery number as your mailing labels. Notice that there's a scroll bar on the right side of the Avery number list: This means that you can scroll down to see more of the list. Crystal Reports offers a large number of different label types.

Select the choice that matches the type of label you're using. Based on your choice, Crystal Reports sets page margins and how many labels to print across the page. You can change them if you wish. When you're satisfied with the label format, click on OK. The Label Layout window appears, as shown in Figure 21-2.

3. Close the Insert Database Field dialog box.

Most of the time, you're going to be inserting table fields by using the Expression Builder dialog box, so just get the Insert Database Field dialog box out of the way.

You can format text or fields on a label in any way you like. Just use the mouse to highlight text or select a field. Then use the Crystal Reports Ribbon to bold or italicize text, use larger type size or a different type font, or center field text.

4. Put table fields on the label format.

For the lines that have more than one field on them, open the Insert menu and select Formula Field. Then *concatenate* (glue together, as if with cat spit) the fields together in the Expression Builder dialog box, as you'll see

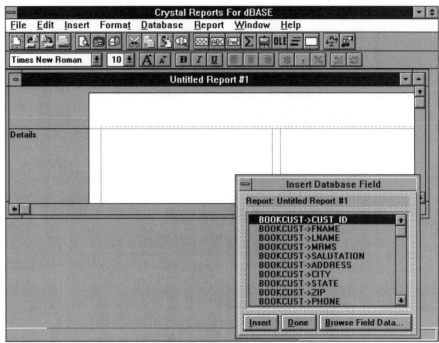

Figure 21-2:
The Label
Layout
window.

in the upcoming hands-on example. Even though it's easier just to use the Insert Database Fields dialog box, this results in big gaps appearing between words on the label.

5. Preview the label format.

Click on the Print Preview button in the SpeedBar to make sure that your label looks the way you want.

6. Save the label format.

Open the File menu and select Save. Give the label format a DOS-compatible file name (up to eight letters, with no spaces or punctuation marks).

7. If you're ready, print the labels.

Make sure that your printer is turned on and that labels are loaded and ready to print.

In dBASE, a label is a report ... sort of

As you already know, a mailing label printout in dBASE is a kind of report. You design a mailing label in exactly the same way you design reports. The only difference is that a mailing label is just a *teensy* bit more complicated than the reports you've created so far.

The difficulty is this. In a normal report (for the most part), you have only captions and table fields. A mailing label has several table fields strung together on the same line.

Suppose, for example, that you're creating labels with a name-and-address table, like the example Bookcust table. When you first set up the table, you make each field wide enough to hold the largest piece of data that would probably be put into it. The MRMS field might have a width of 5, while the FNAME field might have a width of 10, and so on. In a normal report, this causes no problems. You put the table's fields in the Details part of the report layout, and the data prints like this:

```
Mr.    James      West
Ms.    Harriett   Stowe
Mr.    Jules      Twombly
```

But what if you're printing a mailing label? Then the field widths can cause problems, as you can see in the following example:

```
Mr.    James      West
Mythic University
Martinsville,   CA      98035
```

The field widths are causing big gaps to appear in the printed text. Because the FNAME field has a width of 10, the field takes up 10 spaces in the first address line of the letter, even though there are only 5 letters in James. Obviously, that's not how you want the label to look. It *should* look like this:

```
Mr. James West
Mythic University
Martinsville, CA 98035
```

Using formulas to fix things

To get the field data to display the way you want it, you need to create a formula and insert it in the label format. Formulas (which are also sometimes called *expressions*) are special instructions — *not* in English, unfortunately — that tell Crystal Reports how to handle certain things in the label.

Formulas are not hard to use; you just need to make sure that you don't let them intimidate you. The mailing label you create in this chapter requires only a few simple formulas (or *formulae,* if you went to a private school), so it'll be a walk in the park. Hopefully, not a walk in New York's Central Park at night.

Formula trick number one: use the RTrim function

The first formula trick you need is provided by the Crystal Reports RTrim function. The big problem you just saw was that Crystal Reports puts extra spaces to the right of text in a label field. The RTrim function, as you can guess from the name, trims off those extra spaces. When you set up a formula with the function, it looks like this:

```
RTrim( {bookcust.fname} )
```

You'll set up this function in the Crystal Reports formula builder, which you'll learn about in a moment.

Formula trick number two: glom stuff together with the plus sign

The second formula trick lets you put more than one field on the same line. You don't have to use the plus sign for this, but if you don't, even the RTrim function won't keep your mailing label from looking weird. Here's how you'll set it up in the Crystal Reports formula builder:

```
RTrim (bookcust->mrms) + RTrim (bookcust->fname) + bookcust-
          >lname
```

Hands on: Labels for a Bookstore Mailing

The following exercises, in which you create labels for a mass mailing to customers of the Caveat Emptor bookstore, show you the specific steps involved in producing labels.

From every mailing label you've ever seen on an envelope, you know that you want the label to look something like this:

```
Mr. James West
Mythic University
Martinsville, CA 98035
```

The following sets of steps use this book's example database. If you're creating a form letter for your own database, just follow along and make the appropriate changes to use your own table and fields.

Adding the name line

To create the first line, you're going to use the Expression Builder dialog box. You use RTrim to trim the extra spaces out of the MRMS and FNAME fields. Then you use the plus sign to combine the MRMS, FNAME, and LNAME fields on the same line. LNAME is at the end, so extra spaces don't matter.

1. **To insert the MRMS field, open the Insert menu and select Formula Field.**

    The Insert Formula dialog box appears, as shown in Figure 21-3.

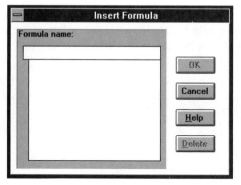

Figure 21-3: The Insert Formula dialog box, where you name the formula you're inserting.

2. **In the blank, type a name for the formula and then click on OK.**

    In the example form letter, type **NameLine** and click on OK. The Expression Builder dialog box appears. There's an awful lot of exciting stuff in this dialog box — much more, in fact, than you need to worry about or *should* worry about at this stage of your dBASE education. Here, your goal is to learn how to create form letters, so just follow the steps and ignore everything else. Later, if you want to experiment on your own, you'll find that you can do some incredible things with this dialog box.

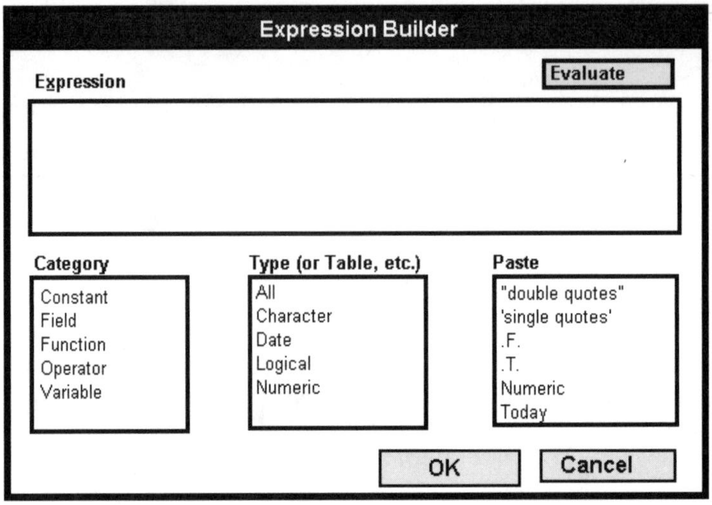

```
╔══════════════════════════════════════════════════════════╗
║                    Expression Builder                      ║
╟──────────────────────────────────────────────────────────╢
║  Expression                              ┌─────────────┐   ║
║                                          │  Evaluate   │   ║
║  ┌────────────────────────────────────────────────────┐   ║
║  │                                          ,         │   ║
║  │                                                    │   ║
║  │                                                    │   ║
║  │                                                    │   ║
║  └────────────────────────────────────────────────────┘   ║
║                                                            ║
║  Category        Type (or Table, etc.)      Paste          ║
║  ┌──────────┐    ┌──────────────────┐    ┌──────────────┐  ║
║  │ Constant │    │ All              │    │ "double quotes"│ ║
║  │ Field    │    │ Character        │    │ 'single quotes'│ ║
║  │ Function │    │ Date             │    │ .F.           │  ║
║  │ Operator │    │ Logical          │    │ .T.           │  ║
║  │ Variable │    │ Numeric          │    │ Numeric       │  ║
║  │          │    │                  │    │ Today         │  ║
║  └──────────┘    └──────────────────┘    └──────────────┘  ║
║                              ┌─────────┐  ┌─────────┐      ║
║                              │   OK    │  │ Cancel  │      ║
║                              └─────────┘  └─────────┘      ║
╚══════════════════════════════════════════════════════════╝
```

Figure 21-4:
The
Expression
Builder
dialog box.

3. **In the Category list, click on Functions. In the Type list, scroll down and double-click on String data. In the Paste list, scroll down and double-click on RTrim.**

   The RTrim function appears in the Formula Text blank at the bottom of the dialog box. The cursor should be between the parentheses. If it isn't, you can move it there by clicking between them. If there is any text between the parentheses, delete it before going on to the next step.

4. **In the Category list, click on Field. In the Type list, Bookcust is already selected because that is the only table in the report. In the Paste list, double-click on the MRMS field.**

   The MRMS field should appear between the parentheses of the RTrim function. Notice that it has the table name in front of it.

5. **Click just to the right of the closing parenthesis.**

6. **Type + " " + after the closing parenthesis.**

   That's a space, a plus sign, a double-quote mark, a space, another double-quote mark, another space, and another plus sign.

7. **Again, go into the Category list and click on Functions. In the Type list, double-click on String data. In the Paste list, double-click on RTrim.**

   RTrim() should appear to the right of the second plus sign. Again, delete any text between the parentheses. Then click between the parentheses to make sure that the cursor is there.

8. **Go into the Category list and click on Field. In the Type list, Bookcust is already selected. In the Paste list, double-click on FNAME.**

   As before, the FNAME field should appear between the parentheses.

9. **Just as before, type** + " " + **after the closing parenthesis.**

10. **Go into the Paste list and double-click on LNAME.**

    The LNAME field appears at the right end of the formula text. This time, you don't need to use RTrim to trim off extra spaces to the right. Nothing else is on this line of the form letter. Your screen should now look like Figure 21-5.

11. **Check the formula.**

    Click on the Evaluate button in the Expression Builder dialog box. If you constructed the formula correctly, Crystal Reports displays a little message saying that everything is okay. If you didn't, it displays a message saying what is wrong.

12. **When you've made sure that the formula is right, click OK at the bottom of the dialog box.**

13. **Use the mouse to move the name to the top line of the left-hand label in the Label Layout window. Then click the left mouse button.**

    Clicking the mouse button *anchors* the name in position on the mailing label. The field will probably be too long to fit on the label format. If it is, you need to drag the field's right border over to the left so that the field doesn't go over the edge of the label format. If you don't, the label will print all shook up and gnarly, and no one except burned-out headbangers will be able to read it.

    Notice that the field has a little square dot at each end. To drag the field border and make it narrower, use the mouse to grab onto the right-hand dot.

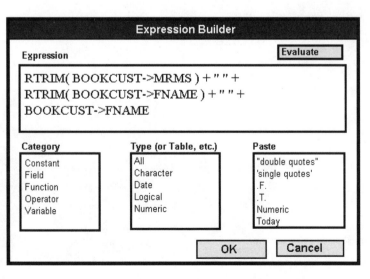

Figure 21-5: The Expression Builder dialog box with the completed name line.

14. **Position the mouse pointer on the right-hand dot.**

15. **Hold down the left mouse button.**

16. **Drag the dot to the left until the field border fits inside the label format.**

These steps take care of the name line. Now you're ready to add the other lines in the label.

You can also type text directly onto a label format, which you may want to do if your mailing label contains text that is not in your table, such as *SPECIAL OFFER FOR* followed by the person's name and address.

Adding the address lines

After all that fuss just to create the name line, you'll be relieved to learn that adding the street address is much simpler. After that, it's back to RTrim(x) and the Expression Builder dialog box to add the city, state, and ZIP code. But enjoy the moment: Here comes the street address line:

1. **Open the Insert menu and select Database Field.**

The Insert Database Field dialog box appears, as shown in Figure 21-6.

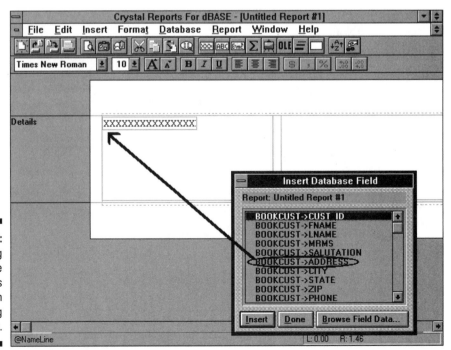

Figure 21-6: Preparing to insert the Address field from the dialog box.

2. **Click on the ADDRESS field and drag it just below the name line, as shown in Figure 21-6.**

   When the field is in position, release the left mouse button.

3. **Click on Done to close the Insert Database Field dialog box.**

4. **Using the Expression Builder dialog box, add the city, state, and ZIP code line.**

   You can use the previous steps describing how to enter the recipient's name as your guide. In the Insert Field dialog box, enter **CityStateZip**. When you're finished, the formula in the Expression Builder dialog box should look something like this:

   ```
   RTrim (bookcust->CITY) + ", " + RTrim (bookcust->STATE}) +
        " " + bookcust->ZIP
   ```

5. **Click on Evaluate to make sure the formula is okay. If it is, click on OK.**

6. **Move the formula just below the address line and then click the left mouse button.**

   The city, state, and ZIP code line is anchored just below the address line. As you did with the name line, shrink the address line so that it fits onto the label.

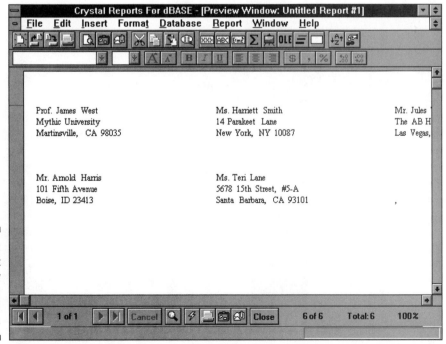

Figure 21-7:
Print Preview of the completed label format.

You can now preview your labels by clicking on the Print Preview button in the SpeedBar, as shown in Figure 21-7. If you're satisfied, then click on Close to get out of Print Preview. Open the File menu and select Save. If you're saving the label format for this book's example database, save the format as **cust_lbl**.

Using these same techniques, you can design any kind of labels you need, using any data source you want.

Chapter 22

Secret Power Tricks with dBASE

. . . .

In This Chapter

▶ Selecting which records to print

▶ Printing stuff sideways

▶ Putting a picture in a report

. . . .

*E*very area of life has its little secrets. dBASE for Windows is no different. There are literally hundreds or even thousands of things you can learn about using dBASE. In this chapter, you get a glimpse of some of the lesser known tricks to make your database purr like a Ferrari, or at least, like a well-maintained Ford Pinto. Because there are so many possibilities, this chapter gives you just a taste of what's possible. If you want more than a taste — who can eat just one? — the rest is up to you.

To learn the skills in this chapter, you need to have learned about

✔ Basic database concepts (Chapters 1 and 2).

✔ Tables and fields (Chapter 4).

✔ Creating and modifying forms (Chapters 10 and 14).

✔ Printing data and creating reports (Chapters 16, 17, and 19).

Selecting Which Records to Print

Sometimes, you want to print all the records in a table. Other times, you don't. There are a couple of different ways to print only the records you want. The first method is easy, using some special features of the Print dialog box. It lets you create simple lists of records. The second method uses formal reports to give you more flexibility about how the information is presented. However, it requires more work because you have to create a query first.

Quick-and-dirty with the Print dialog box

When you want a quick-and-dirty printout of a Browse window, the Print dialog box offers several ways to choose the records you want to print. To get to the Print dialog box, shown in Figure 22-1, you simply display the Browse window you want to print and then open the File menu and select Print. (The Print option isn't available unless a table is open on your screen.)

As you can see, the left side of the Print dialog box offers several options for choosing which records to print. You can pick any of the first four options by clicking in the little circle just to its left, called a *radio button*. The options with black dots in their radio buttons are the selected options. The For and While options are a little different and don't have radio buttons. Instead, you select them by clicking on the wrench button at the right end of the blank.

Here's a description of the available options:

- **All** prints . . . guess what? *All* the records. dBASE automatically selects this option unless you select a different one.

- **Rest** prints the rest of the records in the table, from the current record to the end. For example, suppose that in the Browse window, you have the cursor on record 5 in a 10-record table. If you select this option, dBASE prints only records 5 through 10.

- **Next** is similar to Rest, except that it doesn't go all the way to the end of the table. It lets you print a certain number of records from the current record. For example, if you're at record 5 when you select this option and enter **3** in the blank next to it, dBASE prints records 5, 6, and 7.

- **Record** allows you to print only one record. To print a record, you simply enter the number of the record that you want to print in the blank next to this option. Entering **9** would print record number 9, and so on.

- **For** is the most sophisticated option. It lets you do a miniquery and print only records that satisfy a certain condition. For example, in a Sales table, you may want to print only those sales records in which the dollar amount is greater than $15. Because this is the only option that requires more than one step, you'll see how to use it in a minute.

- **While** lets you print records from the current record forward, but only *while* a certain condition is true. It's most useful with indexed tables when the records are in order by a particular field. For example, if you have a sales table in order by a price field, and many of the records have the same price in them, you can tell dBASE to print out the records *while* the price stays the same. Only those records with the same price as the starting record would be printed. You probably won't use this too often.

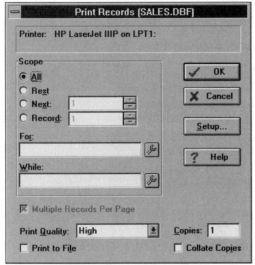

Figure 22-1:
The Print
Records
dialog box.

The For and While options have one other interesting feature. When you've selected a group of records by using a radio button, the For and While options apply to that group of records. If you select All and use For to look for sales records in which the price is over $10, then you'll see *all* the records with prices over $10. If you select Rest and use For to search for prices over $10, you'll see records from the current record to the end of the table with prices of more than $10. The same principle applies to other combinations of For and While.

Using the For option

The For option isn't hard to use, but it does involve several steps. The best way to see how it works is to go through an example. The following steps use this book's example Sales table and print out all the sales records for which the price is greater than $15. If you're using the For option to print data from your own table, just follow these instructions with your own table and its fields instead of the one in this book.

1. In the Catalog window, double-click on the table's icon.

If you're doing the steps with the book's example database, double-click on the Sales table's icon. The table appears in a Browse window.

2. Open the File menu and select Print.

The Print dialog box appears. At the left side of the dialog box, the printing options are listed next to radio buttons

3. Click on the wrench button next to the For text box. Be sure that the radio button for All is selected.

The Build Expression dialog box appears, as shown in Figure 22-2.

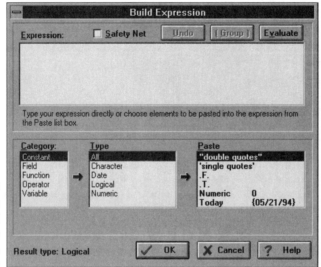

Figure 22-2:
The Build Expression dialog box.

At the top of the dialog box is the Expression blank, where you tell dBASE which records you want to print. In the bottom part of the dialog box are three list boxes. The Category list box shows you the kinds of things you can use to build expressions. The Type list box shows you what data types you can use for that category. Finally, the Paste list box provides a list of items you can put in the Expression blank.

That's pretty abstract, so to get a better idea of what it's all about, continue with the example.

4. Click in the Category list box for the type of category you want.

In this case, you want to tell dBASE to print all the records with a value in the price field greater than $12, so click on Field. When you do this, the name of the Sales table appears in the Type list box because it's the table you have displayed in the Browse window.

5. In the Type list box, click on the data source you want to use.

For this example, click on SALES (the Sales table). In the Paste list box, a list of Sales table fields appears.

6. **In the P̲aste list box, double-click on the item you want to put in the expression.**

   For this example, double-click on PRICE. The Price field appears in the E̲xpression blank.

7. **In the C̲ategory list box, click on Operator.**

8. **In the T̲ype list box, click on Relational.**

9. **In the P̲aste list box, double-click on ">   greater than."**

   The greater-than sign appears in the E̲xpression blank, just to the right of the Price field name.

10. **Click in the E̲xpression blank, just to the right of the greater-than sign.**

11. **Type 12.00. (Don't type the period after the two zeroes.)**

12. **Click on OK.**

    dBASE closes the Build Expression dialog box and takes you back to the Print dialog box. Notice that the expression you created is now listed in the Fo̲r blank.

13. **To print, just click on the OK button in the Print dialog box.**

    Make sure that your printer is turned on, has paper, and is online. dBASE prints the records you specified. If you wish, you can also use the Scope option to further limit the records that will be printed.

The 5th Wave   By Rich Tennant

PORTRAIT OF A CYBERHOLIC

HEY, MISTER! WHEN I SAY PUT YOUR HANDS UP, I MEAN BOTH OF THEM!

Being more sophisticated with a formal report

Sometimes, the Print dialog box isn't enough. If you want to print a formal report, you may need to print only certain records, but you can't do it with the simple method outlined so far.

Fortunately, there's an equally simple method you can use with formal reports. Instead of basing the report on a table, as in Chapter 17, you can base the report on a query, as in Chapters 12 and 13. When you create the query, just enter conditions to select the records that you want to print. To create the report, follow the same steps as you do in creating a report with a table, except that you must run the query *before* you create the report. That makes the query's results available to the report design.

Printing Stuff Sideways

Printing stuff sideways is a very easy but important skill in dBASE. Suppose that you want to print a Browse window or a report, but it's wider than the seven inches or so that will fit on a standard 8.5 x 11-inch page. Printing it "sideways" (formally known as *landscape printing*) can sometimes solve your problem.

To print anything sideways, follow these steps:

1. **Open the File menu and select Print.**

2. **In the Print dialog box, click on the Setup button.**

   The Print Setup dialog box appears. At the lower right of the dialog box are two radio buttons labeled Portrait and Landscape. Portrait is the normal way of printing; landscape is sideways printing.

3. **Click on the Landscape radio button.**

4. **Click on OK.**

   dBASE returns you to the Print dialog box.

5. **Click on OK.**

   dBASE prints your table or report sideways on the page.

Putting a Graphic in a Report

You can also put almost any kind of graphic image in a report. It can be a company logo, art work, or even a photograph. All you need is a graphic that's been put in computer format and copied to the appropriate dBASE directory.

dBASE lets you use graphics in the following formats (don't worry about what they mean):

- Windows bitmap (graphic files ending in BMP)
- Compuserve GIF files (graphic files ending in GIF)
- PCX Paintbrush files (graphic files ending in PCX)
- Tagged Image Format files (graphic files ending in TIF)
- Targa Graphics files (graphic files ending in TGA)

To incorporate a graphic into a report, create the report in Crystal Reports the same as if it weren't going to have a graphic in it. Then, using the Crystal Reports Insert menu, load the graphic file from your PC's hard disk and position it on the report. Here are the basic steps:

1. **Create the report just as you normally would.**

2. **Expand the Page Header band to make room for the graphic.**

3. **Open the Insert menu and select Graphic.**

   If you prefer, you can click on the Graphic button in the SpeedBar. The Choose Graphic File dialog box appears.

4. **Select the graphic file to insert.**

   The graphic appears in the Page Header band. In the process, it probably messed up the rest of the text in the band.

5. **Resize the graphic so it's the size you want.**

   When the graphic first appears, it should be selected. In other words, it should have a border around it with little rectangles, as shown in Figure 22-3. Grab the black rectangles in the border and drag them to resize the graphic.

6. **Move the graphic to where you want it.**

   With the graphic selected, you can move it around on the report layout by clicking in the center of the graphic, holding down the left mouse button, and dragging the mouse. When it's where you want it, release the left mouse button. Figure 22-4 shows an example of a graphic in a report.

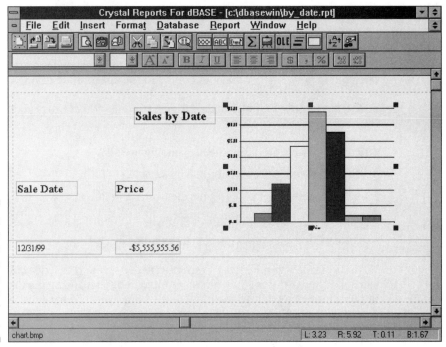

Figure 22-3:
Preparing to
resize the
graphic in
the report's
Page
Header
band.

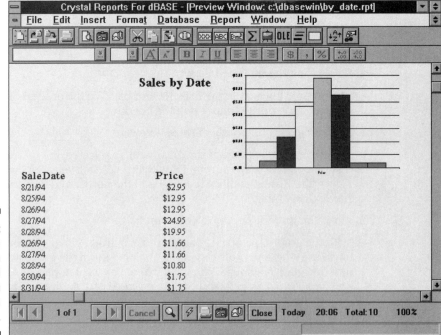

Figure 22-4:
Example of a
report with
an inserted
graphic: in
this case, a
bar chart.

Part V
The Part of Tens

In this part . . .

This part talks about things you probably would rather not think about. What if you get in trouble on your PC while using dBASE? What should you know if you've been using the DOS version of dBASE and have just switched to dBASE for Windows? What are the secrets of dBASE that those M.I.T. computer wizards are hiding from you? And what will you do if a computer wizard corners you at a party and starts to spout a lot of database jargon?

In this part, you'll learn how to handle *all* those situations. Except how to get invited to a party in the first place. You already know that. (Don't you?)

Chapter 23

Ten Things to Do When You're *Really* in Trouble

In This Chapter

▶ Preparing for the Big Database Disaster

▶ When dBASE locks up

▶ When dBASE is *really* slow

▶ When you make a terrible mistake

▶ When dBASE can't load a database

▶ When something won't print

▶ When something is supposed to be happening, but dBASE just sits there

*1*n California, people are blasé about what they call "The Big One." They know that a catastrophic earthquake is coming. It's not a matter of *if*, only *when* it hits.

Database disaster is the same kind of thing. It's out there waiting for you, just around a corner, down a dark street, at 3:00 in the morning when the big report is due to the boss at 8:00. That's when it falls on you like a truckload of bricks — or at least a minivan full of oil-drilling equipment. The main difference between your imminent database disaster and "The Big One" is that your house won't slide into the middle of the street — you hope. Thank goodness for small blessings.

To understand the ideas in this chapter, you should know the concepts of a database (Chapter 2), a table (Chapter 3), data entry (Chapter 5), and printing data (Chapters 16, 17, and 19). You also need to have experienced *suffering* — the hopeless feeling you get when the PC has just gone "Kapow!" while you're writing an important letter to your parole officer.

If you're in the middle of a database disaster, thumb through the chapter until you spot the section you need. Then follow the steps with your own database. And don't *worry*. It will be all right. Unless it isn't.

Before Disaster Hits: Back Up, Back Up, Back Up!

The most important thing you can do to prepare for a database disaster is to back up your database.

Backing up means copying your database to one or more floppy disks — or, if you have the equipment, to a tape cassette. After you've done a backup, you should store the backup disks or tapes in a place far removed from your PC. That way, even if your building burns down, you'll still have your data. Your data is more valuable than your computer. Replacing a PC may cost a few thousand dollars. If you run a business, losing your customer records could cost you your business.

You should back up all your databases every day. And remember that your database consists of more than just tables. For each database, there's a catalog file whose name ends in .CAT and one or more table files ending in .DBF. There may also be memo files ending in .DBT, index files ending in .MDX or .NDX, form files ending in .WFM, query files ending in .QBE, and report files ending in .RPT. There are other types of database files as well, but those listed here are the ones you're likely to have.

The most common way to back up your database (and anything else on your PC's hard disk) is to use the MS-DOS or Windows backup command. Here, it's assumed that you installed Windows Tools when you set up Microsoft Windows and that you're using MS-DOS version 6.0 or a later version.

If you prefer to back up from MS-DOS, exit from Windows and type **help msbackup** at the C: prompt. If you want to back up from Windows, open the Microsoft Tools window and double-click on the Backup icon, shown in Figure 23-1. The Windows Backup program window appears (see Figure 23-2).

If all your database files fit on a single floppy diskette, you can just copy the files to the diskette by using the Windows File Manager or the MS-DOS copy command. If you need more help with MS-DOS, check out *DOS For Dummies* by Dan Gookin (IDG Books); for help with Windows or Windows Backup, find a copy of *Windows For Dummies* by Andy Rathbone (IDG Books).

Backing up isn't the only way to protect your data. It's a good idea to save your work every few minutes.

Figure 23-1:
The Backup
icon in the
Microsoft
Tools
window.

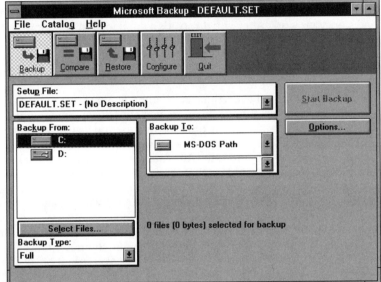

Figure 23-2:
The
Windows
Backup
program.

When dBASE Locks Up

Sometimes, dBASE locks up. No matter what you do, the program just sits there and refuses to work. A lockup can happen for several reasons: some of them minor, some of them a real pain to fix. But if you follow my advice from the preceding section — back up, back up, back up — you have very little to worry about. Except maybe that tooth that's been hurting since you crunched it on a macadamia nut.

It's worth mentioning that lockups do not mean that dBASE is a bad program. dBASE is a *great* program. But so many things can go on at once in Windows that any program can lock up once in a while.

The simplest solution: reboot

Unless your keyboard also locks up, the simplest solution is to *reboot*. In other words, you tell Windows that you need to shut it down because the program you're in has stopped working. To reboot, press Ctrl+Alt+Delete. After you tell Windows you want to reboot, your next step depends on whether Windows can detect that dBASE has locked up.

If Windows sees that there's a problem, you're in luck: Windows lets you shut down dBASE but leave everything else running. To do that, simply press Enter. If you're running other programs in Windows, you can then switch back to them and save your work. After you do so, it's a good idea to shut down and restart Windows. You don't have to, but restarting is an extra safety measure. Sometimes a lockup can destabilize Windows and cause problems with other programs. If you shut down and restart Windows, however, you avoid this risk.

If Windows thinks that everything is OK, though, you have to press Ctrl+Alt+Delete again. When you do so, you shut down Windows and reboot the entire PC. If you're running any other programs, you lose any unsaved work in those programs, as well as your unsaved work in dBASE. If you can switch to your other programs by pressing Alt+Tab, you can try to save your work from those programs. The trouble is that when a Windows program locks up, it often destabilizes the whole system, and that can sometimes prevent you from switching out of dBASE to other programs. But it's worth a shot.

If your keyboard locks up, you can't reboot in the normal way. Instead, press the little button marked Reset on your PC. If your computer doesn't have a reset button, you have to turn your PC off. Once you turn it off, wait at least 30 seconds before turning it on again so that the hard disk has a chance to stop spinning. After you turn your PC back on, you should check your hard disk for errors by running the MS-DOS CHKDSK command; if you have MS-DOS 6.2, use SCANDISK instead. See *DOS For Dummies* if you need help.

Common reasons for lockups

dBASE can lock up for a variety of reasons, including

✔ **No printer driver is installed.** A printer driver is a little piece of software that tells Windows how to format text for a particular type of printer. Although setting up a default printer driver is a normal part of installing Windows, you may have skipped this step if your PC isn't hooked up to a printer. dBASE, like most programs, needs a printer driver so that it can figure out how to display a Print Preview on-screen. If you haven't installed a default printer driver, dBASE can lock up when you try to use Print Preview.

The solution is to install a default printer driver in Windows. See _Windows For Dummies_ if you need help.

✔ **dBASE doesn't get along with your Windows video driver.** Just as a printer driver tells Windows how to work with a printer, a video driver tells Windows how to work with your PC's screen. If you have an out-of-date or slightly weird video driver installed in Windows, dBASE can lock up.

The solution is to get an up-to-date video driver or install a generic video driver that corresponds to your monitor type. Again, see _Windows For Dummies_ if you need help.

✔ **While trying to open a file (table, form, and so on), dBASE hits a snag.** The programmers of dBASE tried to anticipate most of the problems you might encounter in using the program. But if you try to open a file and there's some kind of unexpected problem — say, the file's been damaged in a way that dBASE doesn't detect — then the program can lock up.

The easiest and safest solution is to try rebooting out of dBASE by pressing Ctrl+Alt+Delete. After you do so, it's still a good idea to shut down and restart Windows.

✔ **dBASE just decides to lock up for no particular reason.** Anyone who tells you that computers are perfectly logical has never worked with one. Computers and programs are just like people: each has a personality, and sometimes they just feel ornery and want to give you a scare.

If this happens, just reboot and don't worry about it too much. dBASE may never lock up again. If it does, _then_ you can try to find the problem. Remember to back up once a day and save your work every few minutes.

When dBASE Is Really Slow

To work properly, dBASE requires that your PC have a great deal of electronic memory — called _RAM_ (random-access memory).

You don't need to know all the technical stuff, but dBASE needs an absolute _minimum_ of 6MB (megabytes, or million bytes) of RAM to work at all. (Eight megabytes is better, 16 is good, and more than 16 is ecstatic.) A byte is enough memory to store one letter, such as _A_. RAM is like an electronic desktop. Whatever your PC is working with at the moment goes on the desktop. If the desktop isn't big enough, then it either won't hold everything that the PC needs for it to hold, or it will do so only with difficulty.

If dBASE is running short of memory, it slows down and can even lock up. If you have other programs running in Windows, the easiest solution is to switch to those programs and close them. That way, the memory they were using becomes available to dBASE.

Another thing that eats up memory is Windows wallpaper, which you can turn off through the Windows Control Panel. Finally, if you're running a disk cache program, such as Microsoft's SmartDrive, you can reduce the amount of memory it uses. See *Windows For Dummies* if you need help with the Control Panel and *DOS For Dummies* for help with SmartDrive.

Unfortunately, the best solution costs money. The best solution is to take your PC back to the store and get more RAM. Eight megabytes is good; 16 is even better.

When You Make a Terrible Mistake in Data Entry

As usual, the best defense against data entry mistakes is to back up your database at least once a day.

But dBASE also provides a couple of ways for you to save yourself after you enter incorrect information, delete a record, or make some other horrific change in your database. If you make a data entry error and you're still in the record where you made the error, you can just open the Edit menu and select Undo (or Ctrl+Z). If you deleted a record (which actually just *marks* the record for deletion), you can undelete or *recall* it any time before you select Pack Records from the Table Utilities submenu. You marked it in the first place by positioning the cursor in the record and pressing Ctrl+U; to unmark it, you just position the cursor in the record and press Ctrl+U a second time.

When You Make a Terrible Mistake in Design

If you make a mistake when designing tables, forms, and reports, you can sometimes undo a change simply by opening the Edit menu and choosing Undo. If you've already saved the changes, however, you can do two things:

✔ Go back into the Table Designer window and change things back.

✔ Restore your database from the backup copy, which, of course, you made yesterday.

When You Accidentally Delete a Table

If you accidentally delete a table, you have only one way to get it back: retrieve it from your backup copy. *Don't* accidentally delete tables. But in any event, be sure that you back up your databases every day.

When dBASE Can't Load a Database File

There are two reasons why dBASE may not be able to load a database file, such as a catalog or table, that you've created:

- dBASE can't *find* the file.
- dBASE can't *read* the file.

Remember that your hard disk is divided into lots of little folders, called *directories*. If dBASE looks in the wrong directory, it won't find, and therefore can't load, the database. No big deal: the file is probably just in a different directory.

The name of the catalog should be the name you chose when you created it (such as Caveat, the example database in this book), plus a period and three letters, CAT. So when you're looking for the Caveat catalog, you look for the following file:

```
CAVEAT.CAT
```

If you look through all your dBASE directories and still can't find the database, have Windows scan your entire hard disk for it. The easiest way to do so is to go into the Windows File Manager (in the Main program group), open the File menu, and choose Search. When the Search dialog box appears, type ***.CAT** in the blank (see Figure 23-3). Make sure that the little box next to Search All Subdirectories has an X in it.

Figure 23-3:
The Search
dialog box
from the
Windows
File
Manager.

Search
Search For: `*.CAT`
Start From: `C:\`
☒ Search All Subdirectories
OK
Cancel
Help

By typing ***.CAT**, you ask Windows File Manager (in the Main program group) to list all the dBASE database files on your disk, no matter what they're called. (You want dBASE to do so because you may have saved the database with a different name than you thought.) If you see a database whose name you don't remember or one that's in the wrong directory, that file's probably the one you want.

When Something Won't Print at All

When a report, form letter, or Browse window won't print at all, the problem usually isn't with dBASE. More likely, there's a problem with the printer. Here are the things to check:

- ✔ Is the printer plugged in and turned on? Strange but true, this is the most common reason why things won't print. (If your printer is plugged in but won't turn on, make sure that you paid your electric bill this month. If you didn't, pay it. Or send the money to me.)

- ✔ Is the printer online? Most printers have a little button labeled Online. Next to this button is a little light. If the printer is online, this light should be on. If it's off, press the button and see if the light comes on. If it does, you're all set.

- ✔ Is the printer out of paper? If the printer's out of paper, put some in. We're not talking rocket science, here.

- ✔ Is the printer cable tightly connected at both ends? Shut down dBASE, shut down Windows, and turn off both your PC and printer. And just to be extra safe, unplug both your PC and printer. Look at the back of your PC and locate the cable that goes to your printer. Then make sure that the cable is tightly connected to the port at the back of your PC and the similar port on the back of your printer.

When Something Won't Print Right

By "not printing right," I mean anything ranging from crummy printing to incomprehensible garbage. Here are several things to check:

- ✔ If a report or other document is printing sideways, dBASE is printing in Landscape mode. Stop printing and try again. This time, when the Print dialog box appears, click on the Setup button to open a dialog box that lets you change from Landscape to Portrait orientation. The Landscape-Portrait stuff is at the lower left corner of the dialog box.

✔ If you're getting garbage on the printed page, go into the Windows Control Panel and make sure that Windows is using the right printer driver for your printer.

✔ If you're printing some kind of report, did you make some minor error in the report design? Double-check.

✔ Turn off the printer, wait a moment, and then turn it back on. Sometimes, this is all that's needed. You may never know what went wrong. But as long as it's fixed, who cares?

A few words of wisdom: It's usually not the really hard stuff that trips you up: you're _careful_ with that stuff. It's usually something so simple that when you find it, you want to kick yourself. (But don't kick yourself. At your age, you could sprain your knee.)

When You Finish Your Work and There's Nothing Good on TV

When you finish your work, it's time to kick back and relax for a little while. But what to do? All that's on CNN is a bunch of talking heads jabbering about the latest international crisis. All that's on the local channels are infomercials for a fake baldness cure and the Psychic Friends Network.

Don't despair! Here are some things you can do to occupy your time away from dBASE:

✔ Read your dBASE manuals. Naah.

✔ Play Windows' neat games, Solitaire and Minesweeper.

✔ If you have a CompuServe account, you can type GO WINFUN to get to the Windows Fun Forum, where you can download both shareware and free-ware games that run under Windows. (Remember: if the game is shareware and you keep it, you should send some money to the shareware author!)

✔ Learn a foreign language. Spanish is a good choice. It's becoming more and more common in the United States, particularly in the Southwest.

✔ As a last resort, try talking to your spouse or significant other. He or she will probably be glad to see you.

Chapter 24

Ten Awful Database Terms (And Suggested Penalties for Using Them)

● ●

In This Chapter

▶ Ten of the *awfulest, dumbest* database terms in the world, and that means the *entire universe,* not just the planet Earth, although Earth people do seem to be awfully good at coming up with awful words to confuse everyone, and Earth people are especially good at writing long run-on sentences that seem to keep going forever, like did you ever try to read Hegel in the original German or make your way through a *New Yorker* magazine article about just about anything, geez what a bore, and when you think about how much money those people make it's really incredible, well, it's time for me to take a breath now so I have to stop.

▶ Why are you reading this part anyway? Get on with the chapter!

● ●

✔ **Application:** The only defensible meaning of this term is *program,* in which case it's redundant because there's already a word for program, which is — guess what?! — program. Sometimes it's used to describe a program that is written in a database language such as dBASE BASIC and works only inside a database program, in which case it's called a *database application.* But it's just more clutter in the language. *Penalty:* Application of three coats of wax to the offender's tongue, using the celebrated "wax on, wax off" method.

✔ **Field:** By this point in the book, you know what it means. But this has to be one of the most obscure words ever to be swiped by computer science from agriculture. The official story is that the term originates with old-style punched computer cards. In reality, database fields are named after Syd Field, a legendary screenwriting instructor in Los Angeles, who is rumored to have started his career as a computer repairman for IBM. Not. *Penalty:* Rewrite the script for the movie *Field of Dreams,* making the characters say the word "database" at least once every five minutes.

✔ **Easy:** Means nothing. Every database program ever created is supposed to be easy, and if you got a perfect score of 800 on your math SATs, the programs probably *are* easy to you. *Penalty:* Keep retaking the math SAT test every day until a perfect score of 800 is achieved.

✔ **Fourth-generation language (4GL):** A computer programming language that is *easy* (see the preceding term) and *powerful* (see the following term). Because *easy* and *powerful* don't mean anything, *fourth-generation language* doesn't either. dBASE's own programming language, a little of which you used in this book, is a fourth-generation language, or maybe not — who knows? *Penalty:* Learn *machine language* for the PC, which is said to be a *first-generation language* that is neither *easy* nor *powerful*.

✔ **Powerful:** Means nothing. Every database program ever created is supposed to be powerful, but all it means is that the program does what it's supposed to do. Arnold Schwarzenegger is *powerful,* but database programs either work or they don't. In that sense, dBASE really *is* powerful, but because the word is abused so much, powerful doesn't tell you anything useful. *Penalty:* Go to a discount store and buy a really *powerful* cologne. Then wear it to the office all week.

✔ **Key:** Can mean either the main field by which a table is sorted or the thing you're looking for when you search a database. More often, it means what you're looking for when you can't get into your house. *Penalty:* Watch all of the next *Green Acres* marathon on Nick at Nite. Even if it lasts a week.

✔ **Normalize:** Get rid of redundant data, although what that has to do with a word like normalize is a complete mystery. The idea is that you shouldn't store the same data in several different places because it wastes disk space and increases the chance of error. Each piece of data should be in a database only once, which is a very simple idea. People who use the word *normalize* just want to be sure you know they graduated from M.I.T. or Stanford. *Penalty:* Attend a monster truck show and make friends with three people who are definitely not normal.

✔ **Post:** When you have one table to hold data about sales transactions and two other tables to hold inventory and customer balance data, you update the latter two tables by *posting* the data from the transaction table. This term seems to be derived from accounting, which explains a lot. *Penalty:* Think of at least one anagram of post that begins with the letters *s* and *t*. Then do it.

✔ **Relational:** Has three meanings. First, it can mean that a database "conforms to the relational model," one of those heavy-duty computer science things that is long on theory but doesn't make much difference in practice. Second, it can mean that a database has linked tables, in which case the word is being used incorrectly, because nonrelational databases can have linked tables, too. Third, it can mean simply "Good! Buy this!" — which is the most common meaning. *Penalty:* Attend this year's family reunion and reacquaint yourself with all of those relations that you've tried so hard to forget.

✔ **SQL:** *Structured Query Language,* a database language that's used to find and manipulate data. More often, SQL simply means *good*. People tend to look for database managers that "support SQL" even though they have no idea at all what SQL is or what they'd do with it if they knew. *Penalty:* Learn what SQL is and figure out what you'd do with it if you knew.

Chapter 25

Ten Things to Know if You've Used dBASE II, III, or IV

In This Chapter

▶ dBASE for Windows is compatible ... *but*

▶ Moving from the Control Center and the dot prompt

▶ Using the mouse

▶ Using your old database files from dBASE for DOS

▶ The fundamental things apply ...

*I*f you've used previous versions of dBASE — after all, it's been around since the late 1970s, and so have you, give or take 50 years — you probably wonder how much you'll have to learn when you move up to dBASE for Windows. The good news is *not much*. Although there are important differences between dBASE for Windows and earlier versions of dBASE, Borland worked very hard to make the Windows version compatible with earlier versions.

What this means is that you can use most of your existing dBASE files and skills from the minute you fire up dBASE for Windows. However, there are a few things to remember — in fact, *ten* of them, which is very convenient, because this chapter is in the "Part of Tens."

Unlike Tom and Roseanne, dBASE for Windows Is Very Compatible

You can use all your old dBASE III and dBASE IV tables (formerly called *database files*), indexes, forms, queries, reports, and even dBASE program files. No modification is necessary. Of course, if you're just running stuff you designed to work in earlier versions of dBASE, then you're not really taking advantage of the power of dBASE for Windows. But you can run them, nonetheless, and they'll work fine.

You *will* need to learn a few new menus. But apart from that, you can take things one step at a time. If you just want to learn one new dBASE for Windows feature a month, you can do that and nobody will say you're any less of an American.

But There's No Control Center

On the other hand, if you're a real Control Center fanatic, prepare for a shock: *it ain't there no more.* In its place, you'll see the Navigator and Catalog windows. Instead of opening files by highlighting them in a panel and pressing Enter, you do it by double-clicking on screen pictures.

The Dot Prompt Is Now the Command Window

Likewise, if you get all misty eyed and sentimental about the dot prompt, you'd better wear black for the next week or so: the dot prompt, which terrified millions of dBASE users throughout the 1980s and early 1990s, *is no more.* Now, dBASE sports an up-to-date, ergonomic, vitamin-enriched Command window.

The big advantage of the Command window is that it has two panels, one on top of the other. You enter your commands in the top panel and see the results in the bottom panel. This makes your screen a lot easier to read than the old dot prompt method, which mixed commands and results together on the dBASE screen.

You Pretty Much Have to Use the Mouse

And if you like using a mouse, you'll be glad to hear that almost everything in dBASE for Windows relies on the mouse. Even simple tasks like, opening menus or switching from one window to another, are done with the mouse. You can still use the keyboard if you want — there are keyboard equivalents for most mouse commands — but your friends will giggle behind your back, and people in the street will mock you as being incurably passé.

Some Files You Need, Some Files You Don't

Most of the files in your old dBASE databases and programs can be used without any change at all. Database files (tables), catalogs, memo (DBT) files, screen formats, multiple index (MDX) files, old-style index (NDX) files, view (VUE) files, query (QBE) files, and several other less-common files will work "as-is."

If you have any encrypted tables, memo files, or indexes from dBASE IV, you need to decrypt them before you can use them with dBASE for Windows. To do this, start up dBASE IV and, at the dot prompt, enter **set encryption off**. Then enter the following at the dot prompt for each encrypted file:

1. **Use <encrypted filename>**
2. **Copy to <new, unencrypted filename>**

Then you can use the new, unencrypted files in dBASE for Windows.

You May Need to Update Catalog Paths

If you have dBASE for Windows installed in a different directory than a previous version of dBASE, you'll probably need to update the disk directories in your database catalogs. Otherwise, they'll be looking for their files in the *old* directories and won't be able to find them.

On-Screen Help Is Much Better

On-screen help in older versions of dBASE is pretty good — by the standards of DOS programs. But dBASE for Windows has far more extensive on-screen help than you've ever seen in dBASE before. Instead of a sparse index and some basic Help screens, you have the ability to search for help on what you want, Interactive Tutors to walk you through most common database tasks, and Experts to do the tasks for you if you're in a real hurry (the big game starts on cable in five minutes!).

The SpeedBar Is a Big Improvement

Using the mouse is often a pain in the PC. But when it comes to dBASE for Windows, the mouse is a big plus — especially if you learn to use the SpeedBar buttons. Instead of going through several steps to do most tasks, you can just click on a button.

To see what a SpeedBar button does, just put the mouse pointer on it and leave it there for a moment. The status bar at the bottom of the screen will display a brief explanation of what the button does. The buttons are explained in more detail wherever they're used in the chapters of this book.

It's Easier to Customize Than It Used to Be

There used to be two ways to customize dBASE. The first old way was to use a text editor to change the CONFIG.DB file on your PC's hard disk. Sometimes, that was confusing even for dBASE experts. Setting screen colors, for example, required you to remember all kinds of obscure color codes. The second old way was a little better: by using the DBSetup program, which you had to run outside of dBASE, you could make some — but not all — of the changes you needed in the CONFIG.DB file.

dBASE for Windows makes it much easier to customize dBASE. Instead of editing a configuration file, or using an external utility program like DBSetup, you just open the Properties menu and select Desktop. Then use tabbed help windows, as shown in Figure 25-1, to make the changes you want.

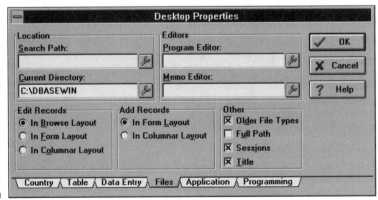

Figure 25-1: Configuring dBASE with a tabbed Help window.

Basic Tasks Remain the Same

There's one important thing to remember: just because dBASE has changed, it doesn't mean that your database needs have changed. One of the important lessons in this book is that the fundamentals of using a database manager — designing a table, dividing up your data, printing easy-to-understand reports, and so on — are the same now as they were ten years ago.

The fact that you now have an easier, more advanced tool to perform database tasks means that you can work more efficiently and productively than before. It *doesn't* mean that you should use new dBASE for Windows features "just because they're there." Analyze *what you need to accomplish* and plan your database on that basis. dBASE gives you incredible power to get things done — if you keep your eyes on the fundamentals.

Chapter 26

Ten Fun Facts About dBASE

● ●

✔ dBASE originated in the 1960s with Retriev, a database manager developed at the Jet Propulsion Laboratories (JPL) in Palo Alto, California.

✔ In the 1970s, Wayne Ratliff at JPL built on the ideas in Retriev to create Vulcan, which brought things one step closer to dBASE.

✔ dBASE spelled backward is ESABd, which makes no sense at all.

✔ In 1979, the rights to Vulcan were bought by Ashton-Tate, a small software company in Southern California. Ashton-Tate renamed the program dBASE II.

✔ In 1981, Microrim, Inc. released MicroRIM, the first major competitor to dBASE. RIM stood for Relational Information Management, and the product was eventually renamed R:BASE.

✔ In 1983, *Data Based Advisor,* featuring dBASE II, became the first database magazine for PCs.

✔ In 1984, Ashton-Tate competitor Micro Data Base Systems renamed its flagship database package several times, from KnowledgeMan to Knowledge Manager to The Knowledge Manager, then finally back to KnowledgeMan. And everyone got really, *really* confused.

✔ In the late 1980s, a controversy raged over "who owned the dBASE language." Eventually, an industry committee was formed to standardize the dBASE language, called Xbase.

✔ In 1991, Ashton-Tate and dBASE were acquired by Borland International, which had also acquired the Paradox database manager with its purchase of Ansa Software and the Reflex database manager with its purchase of Analytica, Inc.

✔ In 1994, Borland updated the venerable dBASE program with dBASE 5 for DOS and the very first version of dBASE for Windows — a program that Ashton-Tate had started developing in the late 1980s but was unable to finish.

Part VI
Appendixes

The 5th Wave   By Rich Tennant

"I STARTED DESIGNING DATABASE SOFTWARE SYSTEMS AFTER SEEING HOW EASY IT WAS TO DESIGN OFFICE FURNITURE."

In this part . . .

You can't do much with a database until you've put some data in it. In this part, Appendix A gives you sample data for use in the book's example database.

Likewise, you can't do much with dBASE until you have installed it on your PC. Appendix B shows you how to set up the program on your PC's hard disk so that you can use dBASE for Windows.

Appendix A
Database Data for This Book

●●

*T*o work through the example database that I set up in this book, you'll have to enter some data into the dBASE tables. You could hire a high school kid to do it, of course, but then you'd take the risk that something really great could come on MTV, and *then where would you be?* Out of data and out of luck, thank you, so you should probably do it yourself.

On the bright side, you can enter as many or as few of these data records as you like. And if something really great comes on MTV, you'll just have to restrain yourself and keep at it.

The Customer Records Table

1

Prof. James West
Jimbo
Mythic University
Martinsville, CA 98035
(415) 555-4678

2

Ms. Harriet Stowe
Ms. Stowe
14 Parakeet Lane
New York, NY 10087
(212) 555-2345

3

Mr. Jules Twombly
Jules
The ABC Hotel
Las Vegas, NV 34567
(201) 555-6213

4

Mr. Arnold Harris
Arnie
101 Fifth Avenue
Boise, ID 23413
(321) 555-9876

5

Ms. Teri Lane
Ms. Lane
5678 15th St., #5-A
Santa Barbara, CA 93101
(805) 555-1234

6

Ms. Susan Brown
Ms. Brown
World-Wide Import
5541 LaBrea
Los Angeles, CA 90069
(310) 555-8617

7

Dr. Thomas Baker
Tom
342 Gallifrey St.
Shreveport, LA 14325
(205) 555-7681

8

Ms. Janet White
Janet
Gates Office Supply
745 Microsoft Way
Redmond, WA 98052
(206) 555-3111

9

Mr. Harris Harrison
Mr. Harrison
21 El Embarcadero
Goleta, CA 93105
(805) 555-9026

10

Ms. Tracy Dancer
Tracy
11 Waterside Place
Zuma Beach, CA 90078
(213) 555-7741

11

Ms. Diane Walker
Ms. Walker
Walker-Townsend PR
551 Second St.
San Francisco, CA 94107
(415) 555-1079

12

Ms. Shirley Edison
Ms. Edison
Dept. of Electricity
Bloomington University
Bloomington, IN 47401
(812) 555-5873

13

Mr. Don Wilds
Don
Vintage Phoenix
114 E. 6th St.
Bloomington, IN 47408
(812) 555-9770

14

Mr. Jack Stein
Jack
Majorland Oil & Gas Corp.
113 E. 6th St.
Bloomington, IN 47408
(812) 555-1299

15

Prof. Irwin Jones
Shirley
Dept. of Prognostication
Bloomington University
Bloomington, IN 40401
(812) 555-1191

The Sales Table

Although there are 15 customers in the Customer Records table, the sales are only for account numbers 1 to 5 in case you didn't enter all 15 customer records. The fields are listed in order: CUST ID, SALEDATE, TITLE, AUTHOR, and PRICE.

4

8/21/94
How to Write a Computer Book
Obscurantis, Jargun
2.95

1

8/25/94
In Praise of Idleness
Russell, Bertrand
12.95

2

8/26/94
Getting Your Husband
Off His Lazy Butt
Russell, Mrs. Bertrand
12.95

5

8/27/94
How I Turned $25 Cash into a
Successful Business
Fleiss, Heidi
24.95

5

8/28/94
Access 2 For Dummies
Palmer, Scott
19.95

5

8/26/94
Fershlugginers I Have Known
Smith, Joe
11.66

1

8/27/94
Atlas Shrugged
Rand, Ayn
12.95

4

8/30/94
Deep Thoughts
Clinton & Quayle
1.95

2

8/28/94
Love in the Time of Cholera
Garcia Marquez, Gabriel
12.00

3

8/31/94
"Supertrain" Forever!
Silverman, Fred
1.95

Appendix B
Installing dBASE

Installing dBASE is really easy. But before you install dBASE on your PC— in fact, before you even *buy* dBASE — it's essential to make sure that your PC is capable of running it.

What You Need to Install and Run dBASE

Like most Windows applications, dBASE requires a lot of PC horsepower and disk space to work properly. You don't need to understand what all these things are, but you should make sure that your PC has *at least*

✔ An 80386 processor. An 80486 or Pentium (80586) processor is better. Processor speeds are rated in *megahertz* (MHz), so a 33 MHz 80386 processor is faster than a 20 MHz 80386 processor. However, higher-numbered processors are faster, so a 33 MHz 80486 processor is faster than a 33 MHz 80386 processor.

✔ A hard disk with at least 21 megabytes of free disk space — that's for a *minimum* installation, with just the essential stuff. More free space is better, and for a full installation of dBASE, you need 32 megabytes of free disk space. You can get by with less than 30 megabytes, but trust me, you don't want to.

✔ At least six megabytes of RAM (electronic memory). Eight is better, and 16 is terrific, and more than that is *spectacular.* The more RAM you have, the faster dBASE is likely to run.

✔ A mouse or other pointing device, such as a trackball.

✔ MS-DOS version 3.1 or later, and Windows 3.1 or later.

✔ If you're installing dBASE on a network, you need one of the following: Novell Netware, any version from 2.x to 4.x; Novell Netware Lite; Microsoft Windows for Workgroups; AT&T Stargroup 2.1a; Banyan Vines 5.0; DecNet Pathworks 4.1; IBM LAN Server 3.0; Microsoft LAN MAN 2.1; or Lantastic 5.0.

Installing dBASE on Your PC

To install dBASE on your PC, you should follow these steps:

1. **Put the first dBASE disk into the appropriate floppy disk drive. Usually, this is drive A, but it can also be drive B.**

2. **If Windows isn't already running, start it up.**

3. **From the Windows Program Manager, open the File menu.**

4. **Select Run from the File menu.**

5. **In the dialog box that appears, type** a:install **if the disk is in drive A or** b:install **if the disk is in drive B (and so on).**

6. **Click on the OK button. The dBASE Setup program will start.**

7. **Follow the instructions that appear on your screen. That's it!**

You can choose between three types of installation: *Default,* which installs the entire dBASE for Windows package; *Customized,* which lets you choose the parts of dBASE you want to install; and *Minimum,* which installs only the absolutely essential things you need to run dBASE.

In early versions of dBASE, one or more of the disks took a while to install, so don't worry if you insert one of the disks and nothing seems to happen for a while.

Index

• A •

About dBASE command (Help menu), 86

addition with plus sign (+), 162

addresses
  on form letters, 243, 247–248
  on mailing labels, 226, 260–262

aligning
  form items to grids, 168
  See also columns

Alt+key combinations

Alt+Backspace for undoing last editing change, 71

Alt+Enter for Table Properties command, 59

Alt+F4 for exiting dBASE, 20

for selecting menus or menu options, 36, 91

ampersands (&) in form captions, 174

AND operator, 154–159

annotating
  help screens, 89–90
  See also memo fields

applications (definition), 283

arithmetic operators, 162

arrow buttons (on help screens), 88

arrow keys for advancing cursor in tables, 63, 68

ascending sorts, 182

ASCII code sorts, 183

asterisk (*)
  for multiplication, 162
  as wildcard, 129, 144–145

• B •

Back button (on help screens), 87

background color, 175

backups, 101, 273–275

bands on reports, 208, 232

~.BMP extensions, 269

boilerplate. *See* form letters; templates

bookmarks (marking a place and returning to it), 88–89

Boolean operators, 153

Browse Inspector dialog box, 78, 200–201

Browse window
  changing look of window, 73–81
  described, 60–62
  disadvantages, 116
  how to move cursor/highlight in, 68–69

saving changes to, 81
switching to/from, 61
buttons
for help, 87–88
list-box, 52
print, 197
push, 29
radio, 175
See also SpeedBar

• C •

calculations
with Numeric data type, 50, 53
performing in queries, 160–162
performing in reports, 232–235
captions on forms, 166
case sensitivity
lacking for field names, 49
turning on/off for searches, 128
Catalog menu function overview, 39
catalogs
adding items to, 47–48
closing, 47
creating, 29–32, 46
deleting items from, 48
described, 22–23
naming, 22, 29
opening, 47
Catalog window, 35
~.CAT extensions, 47

cells (intersections of rows and
columns), 69
Character data type, 50
Clipboard, 38
closing
catalogs, 47
files, 37
menus, 19
submenus, 38
tables, 71
Columnar Layout, 60–61
columns
described, 24–25
headings for, 75–77, 104
hiding/unhiding in Browse
window, 199–202
moving, 79–80
width adjustments, 77–79
width settings as field property,
104
Command windows, 35
conditional operators, 154–160
contains operator ($), 143–144
Contents button (on help screens),
87
context sensitive help, 20
Control Center, 288
controls in forms, 168, 170–175
copying with Cut/Copy/Paste
operations, 38
correcting mistakes. *See* editing

Crystal Reports
  described, 205
  for form letters, 242–243
  for importing graphics into reports, 269–270
  for mailing labels, 251–254
  for simple reports, 206–208
  for sophisticated reports, 227–228
Ctrl+key combinations
  Ctrl+A for adding items to catalogs, 48, 59
  Ctrl+Alt+Delete to reboot, 276
  Ctrl+arrow keys, for moving cursor one word left/right, 71
  Ctrl+D for deleting, 101
  Ctrl+End for last column, 68
  Ctrl+F4 for closing files or catalogs, 37, 47
  Ctrl+G for going to *n* record number, 123
  Ctrl+Home for first column, 68
  Ctrl+Insert for copying to Clipboard, 71
  Ctrl+O for opening files, 37
  Ctrl+PgUp/PgDn keys for first/last record, 68
  Ctrl+S for saving, 55
  Ctrl+U for marking/unmarking records for deletion, 278
currency symbols in reports, 238
cursor
  as "focus" point, 64
  See also navigating

customizing dBASE, 290
Cut/Copy/Paste operations, 38

● *D* ●

database fields. *See* fields in tables
database files, 12
  See also tables
database management systems (DBMSs), 9–10
databases
  defined, 10
  importance of backups, 101
  parts of, 22–25
  planning, 21, 27–28
  troubleshooting unloadable, 279–280
  See also tables
data entry
  advantages of dBASE for, 12
  controlling with field properties, 102–106
  example for Caveat database, 58–67
  templates for simplifying, 104–106
  troubleshooting mistakes, 278
  See also editing; forms; tables
data types
  described, 25, 50–51
  for fields in related tables, 219

lists in list boxes, 52
selecting, 52–53, 98–99
Date data type, 50
dBASE for Windows
  advantages, 11–16
  compatibility considerations for
    previous versions, 287–289
  customizing, 290
  as database management system
    (DBMS), 9–10
  exiting, 20
  finding in Windows group, 16
  installing, 301–302
  memory requirements for, 277–278
  opening screen, 17–18
  origins and development of, 11,
    293
  starting, 16
  what to do when it can't load
    databases, 279–280
  what to do when it locks up,
    275–277
  what to do when it's slow, 277–278
  what to do when it won't print,
    280–281
  what to do when you've deleted
    tables by mistake, 278–279
  what to do when you've goofed
    data entry or table/report
    design, 278
~.DBF extensions, 47
DBMS (database management
  system), 9–10

~.DBT extensions, 110, 274, 289
decimal points. *See* Float data type
defaults for directories, 41
Delete key for deleting, 59
Delete Selected item command, 59
deleting
  fields in tables, 101–102
  help screen annotations, 90
  items from catalogs, 48
  and retrieving tables from back-
    ups, 279
  table relationships, 222
descending sorts, 182
Design Table Structure command,
  59, 97–98
Desktop Properties dialog box, 41
  for customizing dBASE, 290
  Exact and Near options, 129–130
detail band on reports, 208
dialog boxes, 29
directories
  changing, 29–31
  changing default, 41–42
  for holding disk files, 23
disk files, 23
disk space requirements for dBASE
  for Windows, 301
displaying. *See* viewing
division with slash (/), 162
dot prompt, 11, 288

• E •

editing
automatically with field properties, 102–106
data in tables with queries, 162–163
formatting with templates, 104–106
memo fields, 113–114
query answers, 142
text in tables, 69–71
with Undo command, 38
See also data entry
Edit menu
Annotate command, 89–90
overview of functions, 38
Edit Text Fields dialog box, 210
encrypted files, 289
Enter key for advancing cursor, 68
equal to operator, =, 143–144
error correction. *See* editing
Escape key for closing menus, 38
"Exact" option of searches, 129–130
exiting dBASE, 20
Experts command (Help menu), 85
Expression Builder dialog box, 245–246
expressions in form letter formulas, 242, 245
extensions
on dBASE disk files, 23
~.BMP, 269
~.CAT, 47

~.DBF, 47
~.DBT, 110, 274, 289
~.GIF, 269
~.MDX, 189, 289
~.NDX, 274, 289
~.PCX, 269
~.QBE, 274, 289
~.RPT, 274
~.TGA, 269
~.TIF, 269
~.VUE, 289
~.WFM, 274

• F •

F1 key for help, 20
F2 key
for Edit Records command, 59
for toggling between Form Layout and Browse Layout, 61
Field Properties dialog box, 76–77
fields in queries, calculated, 160–162
fields in tables
adding/inserting, 96–99
defined, 283
deleting, 101–102
described, 25
indexed, 49, 53
for memos about tables, 109–114
moving, 99–101
naming, 49–50, 52

numeric, 105

properties of, 102–106

read-only, 104

size limitations, 51

sorting, 49, 53, 182–187

fields on form letters, doubling two on one line, 242

fields on forms, arranging, 122, 166–170

File menu function overview, 38

files

closing, 37

encrypted, 289

list of, 18, 35

naming, 47

opening, 40

See also databases

finding

caution for downward search direction, 132

dBASE icon in Windows group, 16

embedded text, 133

hands-on example, 131–133

records in databases with Find Records command, 127–130

See also queries

Find Records command, 126–130

First Record button, 68, 123

Float data type, 50

focus (highlight/cursor spot), 64

fonts for text on forms, 172–174

footers. *See* headers/footers on reports

foreground color, 175

formatting

with templates, 104–106

See also editing

Form Designer, 169

Form Layout, 60–61

form letters

advantages of dBASE for, 14–15, 226

creating, 243–249

described, 239–241

formulas in, 242

previewing, 249

printing, 250

saving, 250

forms

adding text, 176–177

advantages, 115–116

changing controls' properties, 170–175

changing controls' size, 174–175

colors for, 175–176

creating from scratch, 117, 121–122

creating with Form Expert, 116–121

described, 25–27

entering data with, 124

moving fields and captions, 166–170

navigating in tables with, 122

printing from, 203

saving, 178

fourth-generation languages (4GL), 284

• *G* •

~.GIF extensions, 269

Go to (*record number*) command, 123

graphical user interface (GUI), 11

graphics in reports, 269–270

greater than, >, operator, 143–144

grouped reports. *See* reports

GUI (graphical user interface), 11

• *H* •

hand cursor, 80

hardware requirements for dBASE for Windows, 301

headers/footers on reports, 208–210, 231

headings for columns, 75–77, 104

Help menu, 19, 289

About dBASE command, 86

annotating screens, 89–90

displaying on-screen at all times, 90

Experts command, 85

help buttons, 87–88

How to Use Help command, 86, 90

hypertext links, 84, 86–87

Interactive Tutors command, 85, 92–93

Keyboard command, 85

Language command, 85

overview of functions, 39, 84–86

printing help screens, 90

Search command, 84, 91–92

Views and Tools command, 84–87

High Range field property, 105

History button (on help screens), 87

How to Use Help command (Help menu), 86, 90

hypertext help system, 84, 86–87

• *I* •

icons, 35, 40

used in this book, 4–5

importing/exporting

data, 16

graphics, 269–270

indexed fields

advantages for related tables, 219

advantages for searching, 49, 53

how they work, 187–193

when not to use, 135, 188

index tags, 189

Insert Formula dialog box, 244

Insert Group Section dialog box, 230

Insert Summary dialog box, 234

installing dBASE for Windows, 301–302

Interactive Tutors command (Help menu), 85, 92–93

• K •

keyboard

troubleshooting lockups, 276

See also shortcut keys

Keyboard command (Help menu), 85

keys for sorting or searching, 284

• L •

landscape orientation of printing, 198–199, 202, 268

Language command (Help menu), 85

Last Record button, 68, 123

less than, operator, <, 143–144

Like (pattern match) operator, 143–144

list-box buttons, 52

locating records. *See* finding

Logical data type, 50

logical operators, 153–163

Low Range field property, 105

• M •

mailing labels

advantages of dBASE for, 226

creating, 252–254, 256–262

putting multiple fields on one line, 255–256

trimming excess spaces, 256

marking a place and returning to it (bookmarks), 88–89

marking/unmarking records for deletion, 278

master index files, 189

master tags, 189

mathematical operations. *See* calculations

maximizing or minimizing windows, 34

~.MDX extensions, 189, 289

Memo data type, 50–51

memo fields, 109–114

memory requirements for dBASE for Windows, 277–278, 301

Menu Bar, 34, 207

menus

Alt+key combination for selecting options, 36, 91

closing, 19

how to use, 36–38

opening, 18–19

overview of functions, 38–39

SpeedMenus, 40

See also shortcut keys

minus sign (–) for subtraction, 162

mouse

advantages, 17, 288, 301

dragging, 34

for selecting icons, 40

for selecting menus, 36

moving

columns, 79–80

fields in tables, 99–101

fields on forms, 122, 166–170

windows, 34

See also Cut/Copy/Paste operations

MS-DOS version required for dBASE for Windows, 301

multiple conditions, 154

• *N* •

naming

catalogs, 22, 29

database fields, 49–50

fields in tables, 49–50, 52

files, 47

navigating

advancing along columns or rows, 63

in Browse window, 68–69

Navigator menu function overview, 39

Navigator window, 18, 35

~.NDX extensions, 274, 289

Near option of searches, 129–130

network software requirements for dBASE for Windows, 301

Next Record button, 123

not equal to operator, <>, 143–144

Numeric data type, 50, 53

numeric fields

with currency symbols on reports, 238

setting high-low ranges for, 105

• *O* •

opening

catalogs, 47

dBASE for Windows, 16

files, 40

menus, 18–19

opening screen, 17–18

operators

arithmetic, 162

Boolean, 153

conditional, 154–160

logical, 153–163

relational, 143–144

orientation of printing, 198–199

OR operator, 154–155, 159–160

• P •

padding numbers with zeroes for sorting, 64–65, 186–187

page headers on reports, 208

parent and child tables, 218

pasting with Cut/Copy/Paste operations, 38

~.PCX extensions, 269

PgUp/PgDn keys for advancing cursor in tables, 68

phone number formatting example, 106

placeholders (bookmarks), 88–89

plus sign (+) for addition, 162

pointers to memo fields, 110

portrait orientation of printing, 198–199

posting data, 284

previewing
  form letters, 249
  reports, 210–211

Previous Record button, 123

printer drivers, 276

printer preparation for printing, 196

printing
  form letters, 250
  help screens, 90
  orientation (portrait or landscape), 198–199, 268
  overview, 14
  selected records, 263–268
  troubleshooting problems with, 280–281
  See also reports

Print Records dialog box, 197–198, 264–267

Print Setup dialog box, 202, 268

processor requirements for dBASE for Windows, 301

prompt (infamous dot), 11

Properties menu
  for changing default directory, 41–42
  Desktop command for customizing, 290
  overview of functions, 39
  Replace Records command, 134–135
  Table Records Window option, 75

properties of controls, 170–175

push buttons, 29

• Q •

~.QBE extensions, 274, 289

queries
  advantages, 25–26, 126
  changing order of fields in answers, 142–143
  editing data in answers, 142
  how to use, 138–141, 145–146

linking tables with, 217

multiple condition (and/or), 154–160

performing calculations in, 160–162

rerunning, 151–152

sample, 146–151

saving, 151, 159

searches with, 143–145

See also finding; form letters; reports

query-by-example (QBE) approach, 154

Query Designer, 139–143

question mark as wildcard, 129, 144–145

quitting. *See* closing; exiting

• R •

radio buttons, 175

RAM requirements for dBASE, 277–278

Ratliff, Wayne, 11, 293

Read-only field property, 104

rebooting, 276

records

defined, 10, 25

finding with Find Records command, 127–130

marking/unmarking for deletion, 278

selecting for printing, 263–268

sorting, 49, 53, 182–187

See also databases; queries; reports; tables

related tables, 217–222

relational database management systems (RDBMSs), 9–10

relational operators, 143–144

removing. *See* deleting

Replace Records command, 134–135, 162–163

reports

column width adjustments, 211–212

creating from queries and multiple tables, 236–238, 268

creating grouped, 226–232

creating mailing labels, 196, 226

creating simple row-column format, 206–212

formatting text on, 212, 226

with graphics, 269–270

headers/footers/detail on, 208–210, 231–232

layouts for, 208–210, 226

performing calculations in, 232–235

planning for, 27, 195–196, 226

previewing, 210–211

printing from Browse window, 197–202

printing from forms, 203

saving, 213, 232

types of, 196–197, 226–227

See also form letters; printing; queries

resizing windows, 34

reverse video, 53

Ribbon, for text formatting on reports, 208

row and column reports. *See* reports

rows, 24–25

~.RPT extensions, 274

RTrim(x) function, 242, 256

• S •

saving

changes to Browse windows, 81

changes to tables, 98

form letters, 250

forms, 178

importance of frequent, 274

queries, 151, 159

records automatically, 64

reports, 213, 232

tables, 54–55

screens

dBASE's opening screen, 17–18

parts of, 34–36

switching between, 39

scroll bars, 36

scrolling on automatic for windows, 65

Search button (on help screens), 87

searching

for help topics, 84, 87, 91–92

See also finding; queries

sections of group reports, 230–232

selecting

icons, 40

menus, 36

Shift+key combinations

Shift+F2 for Design Table Structure command, 59

Shift+Tab for next column to left, 68

shortcut keys

how to use, 36–37

for SpeedMenus, 59

See also Alt+key combinations; Ctrl+key combinations; Shift+key combinations

sideways orientation of printing, 198–199, 202, 268

slash (/) for division, 162

snapping form items to grid, 168

sorting

described, 141

need for padding with zeroes for, 64–65, 186–187

records in tables, 49, 53, 182–187

See also indexed fields

Soundex option for searches, 129

spaces trimmed from printed fields, 242

special characters allowed/disallowed in field names, 49

SpeedBar
  for adding features to reports, 207–208
  described, 13, 35, 39–40, 61–62, 290
  print button, 197

SpeedMenus, 40, 58–59

SQL (Structured Query Language), 285

starting
  dBASE for Windows, 16
  See also opening

status line, 18, 36, 40

strings as text, 126

structure of tables, 44

submenus, 37–38

subtraction with minus sign (-), 162

summary fields in reports, 233–235

symbols. *See* icons

• T •

Tab key
  for advancing cursor, 63, 68
  for signaling automatic save of record, 64

Table menu, Find/Replace Records commands, 126–130

Table Properties command, 59

Table Records Properties dialog box, 103

tables
  closing, 71
  commands on SpeedMenus for handling, 59
  compatibility considerations for previous versions, 287–289
  creating, 43, 48–54
  defined, 12, 23–24
  how to use multiple related, 217–222
  importance of backups, 101
  moving cursor with SpeedBar, 61–62
  navigating in, 63, 68–69
  navigating with forms, 123
  one-to-one and one-to-many, 218
  parent and child, 218
  planning, 44–46, 215–216, 219
  redesigning fields, 95–106
  related, 217–222
  samples for customer records and sales, 298–300
  saving, 54–55
  See also databases; data entry; fields in tables; queries; reports

templates, 104–106

text. *See* Character data type

~.TGA extensions, 269

~.TIF extensions, 269

time. *See* Date data type

totals. *See* calculations

troubleshooting problems with dBASE, 273–281

tutors (Help menu), 85, 92–93

• U •

underlined letters in form captions, 174

underlined words as hypertext help links, 86

Undo command, 38, 278

uppercase on automatic, 103–104

• V •

Valid field property, 104

video drivers, 277

viewing

forms, 122

memo fields, 113–114

records in indexed order, 190–192

View menu functions overview, 39

Views and Tools command (Help menu), 84–87

~.VUE extensions, 289

• W •

~.WFM extensions, 274

When field property, 104

width adjustments

for database columns, 77–79

for report columns, 211–212

Width field property, 104

wildcards

in queries, 144–145

in searches, 129

window controls, 36

Window menu function overview, 39

windows

automatic scrolling of, 65

Columnar Layout, 60–61

Form Layout, 60–61

maximizing or minimizing, 34

moving, 34

See also Browse window; screens

Notes

Notes

Notes

Notes

Notes

Notes

Notes

Notes

Notes

Notes

Notes

Notes

PC WORLD MICROSOFT ACCESS BIBLE
by Cary N. Prague & Michael R. Irwin

Easy-to-understand reference that covers the ins and outs of Access features and provides hundreds of tips, secrets and shortcuts for fast database development. Complete with disk of Access templates. Covers versions 1.0 & 1.1

ISBN: 1-878058-81-9
$39.95 USA/$52.95 Canada
£35.99 incl. VAT UK & Eire

PC WORLD WORD FOR WINDOWS 6 HANDBOOK
by Brent Heslop & David Angell

Details all the features of Word for Windows 6, from formatting to desktop publishing and graphics. A 3-in-1 value (tutorial, reference, and software) for users of all levels.

ISBN: 1-56884-054-3
$34.95 USA/$44.95 Canada
£29.99 incl. VAT UK & Eire

PC WORLD DOS 6 COMMAND REFERENCE AND PROBLEM SOLVER
by John Socha & Devra Hall

The only book that combines a DOS 6 Command Reference with a comprehensive Problem Solving Guide. Shows when, why and how to use the key features of DOS 6/6.2

ISBN: 1-56884-055-1
$24.95 USA/$32.95 Canada
£22.99 UK & Eire

QUARKXPRESS FOR WINDOWS DESIGNER HANDBOOK
by Barbara Assadi & Galen Gruman

ISBN: 1-878058-45-2
$29.95 USA/$39.95 Canada/£26.99 UK & Eire

PC WORLD WORDPERFECT 6 HANDBOOK
by Greg Harvey, author of IDG's bestselling 1-2-3 For Dummies

Here's the ultimate WordPerfect 6 tutorial and reference. Complete with handy templates, macros, and tools.

ISBN: 1-878058-80-0
$34.95 USA/$44.95 Canada
£29.99 incl. VAT UK & Eire

PC WORLD EXCEL 5 FOR WINDOWS HANDBOOK, 2nd EDITION
by John Walkenbach & Dave Maguiness

Covers all the latest Excel features, plus contains disk with examples of the spreadsheets referenced in the book, custom ToolBars, hot macros, and demos.

ISBN: 1-56884-056-X
$34.95 USA/$44.95 Canada /£29.99 incl. VAT UK & Eire

PC WORLD DOS 6 HANDBOOK, 2nd EDITION
by John Socha, Clint Hicks & Devra Hall

Includes the exciting new features of DOS 6, a 300+ page DOS command reference, plus a bonus disk of the Norton Commander Special Edition, and over a dozen DOS utilities.

ISBN: 1-878058-79-7
$34.95 USA/$44.95 Canada/£29.99 incl. VAT UK & Eire

OFFICIAL XTREE COMPANION, 3RD EDITION
by Beth Slick

ISBN: 1-878058-57-6
$19.95 USA/$26.95 Canada/£17.99 UK & Eire

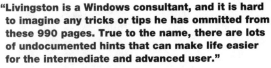

Order Form

Order Center: (800) 762-2974 (8 a.m.-5 p.m., PST, weekdays) or (415) 312-0650

For Fastest Service: Photocopy This Order Form and FAX it to: (415) 358-1260

Quantity	ISBN	Title	Price	Total

Shipping & Handling Charges

Subtotal	U.S.	Canada & International	International Air Mail
Up to $20.00	Add $3.00	Add $4.00	Add $10.00
$20.01-40.00	$4.00	$5.00	$20.00
$40.01-60.00	$5.00	$6.00	$25.00
$60.01-80.00	$6.00	$8.00	$35.00
Over $80.00	$7.00	$10.00	$50.00

In U.S. and Canada, shipping is UPS ground or equivalent.
For Rush shipping call (800) 762-2974.

Subtotal _____

CA residents add applicable sales tax _____

IN and MA residents add 5% sales tax _____

IL residents add 6.25% sales tax _____

RI residents add 7% sales tax _____

Shipping _____

Total _____

Ship to:

Name _____

Company _____

Address _____

City/State/Zip _____

Daytime Phone _____

Payment: ❑ Check to IDG Books (US Funds Only)   ❑ Visa   ❑ Mastercard   ❑ American Express

Card# _____ Exp. _____ Signature _____

Please send this order form to: IDG Books, 155 Bovet Road, Suite 310, San Mateo, CA 94402.

Allow up to 3 weeks for delivery. Thank you!

IDG BOOKS WORLDWIDE REGISTRATION CARD

RETURN THIS REGISTRATION CARD FOR FREE CATALOG

Title of this book: **dBASE 5 For Windows For Dummies**

My overall rating of this book: ❑ Very good [1] ❑ Good [2] ❑ Satisfactory [3] ❑ Fair [4] ❑ Poor [5]

How I first heard about this book:

❑ Found in bookstore; name: [6]

❑ Advertisement: [8]

❑ Word of mouth; heard about book from friend, co-worker, etc.: [10]

❑ Book review: [7]

❑ Catalog: [9]

❑ Other: [11]

What I liked most about this book:

What I would change, add, delete, etc., in future editions of this book:

Other comments:

Number of computer books I purchase in a year: ❑ 1 [12] ❑ 2-5 [13] ❑ 6-10 [14] ❑ More than 10 [15]

I would characterize my computer skills as: ❑ Beginner [16] ❑ Intermediate [17] ❑ Advanced [18] ❑ Professional [19]

I use ❑ DOS [20] ❑ Windows [21] ❑ OS/2 [22] ❑ Unix [23] ❑ Macintosh [24] ❑ Other: [25]_____
(please specify)

I would be interested in new books on the following subjects:
(please check all that apply, and use the spaces provided to identify specific software)

❑ Word processing: [26]

❑ Data bases: [28]

❑ File Utilities: [30]

❑ Networking: [32]

❑ Other: [34]

❑ Spreadsheets: [27]

❑ Desktop publishing: [29]

❑ Money management: [31]

❑ Programming languages: [33]

I use a PC at (please check all that apply): ❑ home [35] ❑ work [36] ❑ school [37] ❑ other: [38] _____

The disks I prefer to use are ❑ 5.25 [39] ❑ 3.5 [40] ❑ other: [41]_____

I have a CD ROM: ❑ yes [42] ❑ no [43]

I plan to buy or upgrade computer hardware this year: ❑ yes [44] ❑ no [45]

I plan to buy or upgrade computer software this year: ❑ yes [46] ❑ no [47]

Name: _____ Business title: [48] _____ Type of Business: [49] _____

Address (❑ home [50] ❑ work [51]/Company name: _____)

Street/Suite# _____

City [52]/State [53]/Zipcode [54]: _____ Country [55] _____

❑ **I liked this book!** You may quote me by name in future
IDG Books Worldwide promotional materials.

My daytime phone number is _____

IDG BOOKS

THE WORLD OF
COMPUTER
KNOWLEDGE

☐ **YES!**
Please keep me informed about IDG's World of Computer Knowledge.
Send me the latest IDG Books catalog.